THE ASSASSIN'S DOCTOR

A BIOGRAPHY OF DR. SAMUEL A. MUDD

ROBERT SUMMERS

For Mom
Marie Carmelite Mudd Summers

Dr. Samuel A. Mudd

CONTENTS

INTRODUCTION

Dr. Samuel A. Mudd is my maternal great grandfather. His son, Samuel A. Mudd II, was my mother's father. She was born and raised on the Mudd farm. Her room growing up there in the early 1900s was the same room John Wilkes Booth stayed in when he came to the Mudd farm after he assassinated president Lincoln in 1865.

My parents took me and my siblings to visit the Mudd farm quite often when we were growing up in Washington, D.C., but the only time I remember them mentioning Dr. Mudd was when they yelled at us to keep our feet off Dr. Mudd's sofa in the front room. We later learned that this was the sofa where Dr. Mudd examined Booth's broken leg.

I only became aware of Dr. Mudd's connection to the Lincoln assassination as an adult, and the more I learned, the more interested I became in finding out more. My interest in his work during the yellow fever epidemic at his prison led to my first book about Dr. Mudd at Fort Jefferson. This led to my second book about Dr. Mudd's slaves, and a third book about his wife, my great grandmother, Sarah Frances Dyer Mudd.

Finally, it made sense to bring everything in these early books, and more, together into this single comprehensive biography of Dr. Mudd - *The Assassin's Doctor*.

The Assassin's Doctor is the story of Dr. Samuel A. Mudd's involvement in the 1865 assassination of president Abraham Lincoln, his imprisonment at Fort Jefferson, his life-saving work during a horrific yellow fever epidemic there, and his life after being pardoned.

We all stand on the shoulders of those who came before us. In my case, Michael Kauffman, author of *American Brutus*, *In the Footsteps of an Assassin*, and *Memoirs of a Lincoln Conspirator*, always graciously answered my questions about the Lincoln assassination, and Michael Ryan, former National Park Service Chief Ranger at the Fort Jefferson National Park, Dry Tortugas, Florida, who showed me around the fort, answered my many questions about Dr. Mudd's time there, and provided me with historic National Park Service photos of the fort.

The staff members of the National Archives, Maryland State Archives, Library of Congress, Georgetown University Library, and other institutions also provided invaluable research assistance. And, of course, this includes the late and wonderful Danny Fluhart, who oversaw the operation and maintenance of the Dr. Samuel A. Mudd House Museum in Waldorf, Maryland for many years, and was always extremely helpful.

The Assassin's Doctor contains the text of several historical documents never published before. I believe you will find the book to be an interesting and informative addition to your bookshelf.

- Robert K. Summers

THE EARLY YEARS

Samuel Alexander Mudd was born on December 20, 1833 on his parent's large tobacco plantation known as Oak Hill, located near the small town of Bryantown, Maryland. He was the fourth of Henry and Sarah Mudd's 10 children.

In 1849, 15-year-old Sam left home to attend the all-boys St. John's College in Frederick, Maryland. At the time, there was not yet a clear-cut separation of high school and college as distinct academic entities. College was generally a six or seven-year high school-college course. The first two or three years were called the Preparatory Department or Junior Department, and the last four years the Senior Department. St. John's College offered a six-year program, while Georgetown College in Washington, D.C. (now Georgetown University) offered a seven-year program.

In Sam's second year at St. John's, Sarah Frances Dyer arrived in Frederick City to attend the all-girls Visitation Academy, located near St. John's. Sam and Sarah knew each other. They lived on neighboring farms back home, where both families grew tobacco with the help of slaves.

Sarah lived on the Dyer farm with her four older siblings, Jeremiah, Elizabeth Ann, Thomas, and Mary Ellen. She never knew her father, Tom Dyer, who died only ten days after she was born. When her mother Elizabeth died in 1849, Jeremiah assumed responsibility for running the farm and looking after the welfare of his siblings. This included enrolling Sarah at the Visitation school in Frederick, where he paid her tuition and other expenses for four years.

Sarah was probably very comfortable going to Visitation Academy. She knew other young girls in her community who had gone there, and her cousin Mary Rose Dyer was a nun who taught there.

Sam and Sarah were at Frederick City together for only one year. Sarah would continue at Visitation Academy until her graduation four years later, but Sam would transfer out of St. John's after his second year there.

St. John's College was a friendly rival to Georgetown College. Both were run by the Jesuits, known for their intellectual rigor and firm discipline. However, in the springtime at the end of his second year at St. John's, almost all the upper level collegiate students at St. John's withdrew from the school in protest over the school's strict discipline.

Many families, unhappy with the situation at St. John's, looked for another school for their child to attend. The Mudds settled on Georgetown College, which 17-year-old Sam entered on September 17, 1851.

There were 176 boys in Sam Mudd's 1852 sophomore Georgetown College class. Many were from Maryland, Virginia, and Washington, D.C., but the majority were from other states, including Georgia, Louisiana, Tennessee, Pennsylvania, New York, Mississippi, Alabama, North Carolina, Kentucky, South Carolina, and Texas, and also from other countries, including Canada, England, Germany, Ireland, Chili, Mexico, Venezuela, Cuba, and Poland.

Boarding students were not allowed to leave the college grounds for any reason, except to go home for summer vacation. All letters not from parents were opened and read by administrators. Pocket money was discouraged. Any money from parents had to be deposited with the college treasurer who dispensed it as he saw fit. Students were not allowed to have any books other than class textbooks, unless specifically permitted by the Prefect of Schools. It was a strict place.

But young Sam's career at Georgetown College would be cut short. Shortly after his 2nd year there began, he was expelled. Sam and a number of fellow students were protesting what they considered the unfair discipline of a fellow classmate, but they carried the protest a bit too far.

The Jesuits identified Sam and five other boys as protest leaders, and expelled them as a warning to the other students. The school wrote to the boys' parents, telling them to come pick up their sons. Sam's father drove to the school in his carriage, collected his son, and returned with him to the family farm. There is no record of what Sam's father said to him during the drive back home.

Sam's parents now had to consider what to do with their problem son. Someone suggested medicine, an honorable occupation, and in short order Sam was apprenticed to his cousin Dr. George Mudd, who ran a medical practice out of his home in nearby Bryantown. George was seven years older than Sam. He had graduated from the University of Maryland medical school in Baltimore four years earlier. It was common at the time for a young man who thought he might be interested in becoming a doctor to apprentice with a practicing physician before enrolling in medical school.

After two years of training with Dr. George Mudd, 21-year-old Sam Mudd entered the University of Maryland Medical Department in Baltimore on October 9, 1854. Dr. George Mudd was his Preceptor, or sponsor.

The physician training program lasted two years, from October to March each year. The school's Baltimore Infirmary provided students hands-on experience with patients. Only 10 of the best students were permitted to reside in the Baltimore Infirmary as clinical assistants. Sam Mudd was one of those students.

Sam completed the two-year course of instruction, wrote his 40-page graduation thesis on dysentery, and graduated on March 5, 1856. The young 23-year-old doctor then returned to his Charles County home to practice medicine.

In 1906, Sarah's daughter Nettie published a biography of her father entitled *The Life of Dr. Samuel A. Mudd*. In it, she quotes her mother as saying:

> *I was only seventeen and Sam eighteen years of age, so it was impossible to think of getting married just then. When Sam asked me, "Frank, are you going to marry me?" I answered "Yes, when you have graduated in medicine, established a practice for yourself, and I have had my fun out, then I'll marry you. You need not get jealous; I vow I will never marry anyone else."*

And so it happened... Sam married Sarah a year after he finished medical school, on November 26, 1857.

Everything was going Sam Mudd's way. He was smart, well-educated, and had married his childhood sweetheart. But there was even more to come. As a wedding present, Henry Mudd gave his son 218 acres of his best farmland, known as St. Catherine's, and built a new house for his son on the property.

While their house was being built, the young couple lived with Sarah's bachelor brother Jeremiah on the Dyer family farm where she had grown up. They moved into their new home in 1859, and like all their ancestors before them, began to acquire slaves to help them run the farm.

∼

SLAVERY AND THE MUDD FAMILY

Thomas Mudd (1647-1697)

The first Mudd in America was Thomas Mudd (1647-1697). He was born in England around 1647, and was Dr. Samuel Mudd's great-great-great-great-grandfather. Dr. Mudd's great-great-great-great-grandmother was the second of Thomas Mudd's three wives, Sarah Boarman Matthews Mudd.

Nothing is known of Thomas Mudd's parents, or exactly when he came to America. Maryland land records show that he was granted 450 acres of land in 1680 as compensation for paying for the cost of transporting himself and eight indentured servants to Maryland. The land grant refers to Thomas Mudd as a Gentleman, a term used at the time to describe a person of some social standing and means.

By the time he died in 1697, Thomas Mudd had tripled his land holdings from the original 450 acres to more than 1,500 acres. He had also acquired five slaves. In his will, Thomas Mudd gave four slaves to his third wife Ann, and one slave to his daughter, Barbara. The slaves' names are not mentioned.

The death of Thomas Mudd illustrates one of the great fears that slaves had all through the two centuries of American slavery. When an owner died, slaves were either divided among the surviving relatives, or sold. Either way, slave families were usually broken up on the death of the owner. Little regard was given to keeping husbands, wives, parents, or children together as a family.

Henry Mudd (1685-1736)

Dr. Samuel Mudd's great-great-great-grandfather was Henry Mudd (1685-1736), the second of Thomas Mudd's nine children. His great-great-great-grandmother was Elizabeth Lowe Mudd. In his will, Henry left his wife Elizabeth his *"three working negroes,"* his bedding, and his household items. He left his daughter Sarah *"a negro boy called Jack,"* two cows, a feather bed, and furniture. He left his daughter Henereter *"a negro boy called Tom,"* a feather bed, furniture, cows, and a horse.

If Henry Mudd's three adult slaves and two slave children were a family, the slave family was now broken up, scattered among three descendant families. Slaves were passed from one generation to the next like any other form of property. Next to land, slaves were a farmer's most valuable possession, and not passing one's slaves on to one's descendants would be quite unusual.

Slaves were often known only by a first name, and no last name. Frederick Douglass, a Maryland slave who rose to become a leader of the abolitionist movement, wrote *"It was seldom that a slave, however venerable, was honored with a surname in Maryland."*

Henry Mudd's wife, Elizabeth, acquired several more slaves after he died. When she herself died in 1761, she left her son, Bennett Mudd, *"one negro named Dick and all the tobacco that shall become due for the hire of said negro."* Elizabeth also left her daughter, Mary Bibben, *"one negro wench named Jane and her increase and one feather bed."*

The reference to *"her increase"* shows that slave owners not only owned their slaves, but also owned the children of their slaves. Slave children were little burden on slave owners, but as they grew, their value grew, both as field workers and in the slave market.

Elizabeth left her grandson, Ezekiah Mudd, "*one negro boy named Clem,*" and left Elizabeth Ann Salsbury "*one negro boy named Peter, and one negro named Mary.*"

Altogether, Elizabeth Mudd bequeathed seven slaves: one adult male named Dick, two adult women named Jane and Mary, and four boys named Jack, Tom, Clem, and Peter. It is unknown if they were related, but if so, any family relationship was broken up when they were sent off to different owners after Elizabeth's death.

Thomas Mudd (1707-1761)

Dr. Samuel Mudd's great-great-grandfather was another Thomas Mudd (1707-1761). Thomas was the first of Henry Mudd's nine children. His wife's maiden name was Gardiner, but her first name is unknown.

Thomas' will made his son Henry the executor of his estate and left him a large amount of land. The rest of his land and property, including three slaves, was divided among his three other children.

He left his son Richard "*one negro man called Anthony, also one cow and one heifer and one feather bed.*" He left his son Luke "*one negro man called George, and also one feather bed, one cow, and nine hundred and fifty pounds of crop tobacco.*" He left his daughter, Mary Johnson, "*one negro girl called Judith, also the best feather bed and one cow.*"

The Revolutionary War (1775-1783) was an opportunity for American colonists to be free from Britain, but it was also an opportunity for the 20 percent of Americans who were slaves to be free from the colonists. The British governor of Virginia, Lord Dunmore, offered immediate freedom to American slaves who could make their way to British lines. George Washington, who owned more than 300 slaves, said that Lord Dunmore was an "*arch traitor*" for promising to free American slaves. Several of General Washington's 300 plantation slaves, and his personal slave Henry Washington, ran away to the British lines and freedom.

The slave Ralph Henry, apparently inspired by his master Patrick

Henry's proclamation of *"Give me liberty, or give me death,"* also found his liberty behind British lines.

Maryland and Virginia allowed free blacks, but not slaves, to join Washington's army. Many slaves left their masters anyway, to join the British side. All together, between 80,000 and 100,000 slaves ran away from colonial plantations during the Revolutionary War.

By the end of the Revolutionary War in 1783, about 20,000 former slaves were living in the British enclaves of Savannah, Charleston, and New York. During peace negotiations with the British, General Washington agreed to let these slaves go. The former slaves, and the loyalists who had lost everything by siding with the British, filled ships leaving America.

Some of the former slaves were taken by unscrupulous ship owners to Caribbean islands where they were sold into slavery again. Others were taken to England, and others, after a failed attempt at settling inhospitable Nova Scotia, returned to Africa where they founded the African nation of Sierra Leone.

Henry Mudd (1730-1810)

Dr. Samuel Mudd's great-grandfather was another Henry Mudd (1730-1810). His life spanned the American Revolution. Harry, as he was called, was born a British subject in colonial Maryland, but died a citizen of the new United States of America. He was too old to serve the American cause in the Revolutionary War, but records indicate that up to 21 other Mudds did serve.

Harry was the first of Thomas Mudd's eight children. He and his wife, Blanche Spalding Mudd, had two sons and four daughters. When Harry died, he divided his slaves among his surviving children and grandchildren. His son Alexius had died before him.

Note that Harry mentions none of his slaves by name. This must have resulted in quite some confusion about who got which slave.

He left his son Henry Thomas Mudd *"three negroes."*

He left his grandson Henson Mudd *"two negroes, two tables, and one desk."*

He left his granddaughters Mary Ann Mudd, Harriot Mudd, Kitty Mudd, and Matilda Mudd "*two negro slaves.*"

He left to the three youngest sons of his daughter Mary Simms, viz. Aloysius, Joseph, and Alexius, "*two negroes to be divided among them.*"

He left his granddaughter Cecily Spalding "*one negro boy.*"

He left his daughter Mary Eleanor Elder "*two slaves.*"

He left his granddaughter Elizabeth Elder "*a negress, and if Elizabeth Elder should die without issue, the slave and her issue to be divided among the brothers of Elizabeth Elder.*"

Alexius Mudd (1765-1800)

Harry's son Alexius Mudd (1765-1800) was Dr. Mudd's grandfather. His wife was Jane Edelen Mudd.

Alexius' will bequeathed his land to his wife Jane "*during her widowhood,*" and thereafter to his two sons when they reached adulthood. As was the custom at the time, land passed from father to sons, not daughters. When Alexius died in 1800, his daughter Sarah Ann Mudd was 6, his son Thomas Alexander Mudd was 3, and his son Henry Lowe Mudd (Dr. Samuel Mudd's father) was 2. Alexius' bequeath of slaves to his minor sons is a bit complicated:

...the following negroes viz. Joe, Mary, and Hannah together with their increase to be equally divided between my two sons when my eldest son Thomas Alexander Mudd arrives at the age of twenty-one years then his equal part of the said negroes to be paid to him by my executor hereafter mentioned and my youngest son Henry Mudd to have his equal part of the said negroes paid to him by my executor when he arrives at the age of twenty-one years. But in case that either of my two sons Thomas Alexander or Henry Mudd dies before they arrive at the age of twenty-one years, my will is that the survivor of them shall have the said three negroes together with the increase of them, or in case that both of my said two sons Thomas Alexander Mudd and Henry Mudd should die before they arrive at the age of twenty-one years, in that case my will and desire is that the

said three negroes with their increase shall go to my daughter Sarah Mudd.

Alexius left his wife Jane *"the following negroes viz. Primus, Watt, Peggy, Cecily and her youngest child Nelly."* There is no mention of Cecily's older children. Presumably, Joe, Mary, and Hannah are her children. Once again, we see how slave families are torn apart at their owner's death.

Two years after Harry Mudd died, the United States and Britain were at war again. This time, the hard fighting didn't bypass Southern Maryland as it had in the Revolutionary War. British ships landed at Benedict, Maryland, just 10 miles from the Mudd farms. British soldiers destroyed property and crops as they marched up through Southern Maryland to Washington, where they burned the White House and other government buildings.

As they had in the Revolutionary War, many slaves fled their owners to seek freedom with the British forces. Whether any of the Mudd slaves were among them is unknown.

Twenty Mudd family members are known to have served during the War of 1812.

Southern Maryland planters suffered greatly during the War of 1812. As in the Revolutionary War, farm production dropped because men left their farms to fight the British. The crops that were raised couldn't get to market because the British Navy controlled the Chesapeake Bay and the rivers needed to ship farm products.

But the young new nation was about to experience an explosion of growth and prosperity, albeit at the expense of its slaves. In 1803, between the Revolutionary War and the War of 1812, President Thomas Jefferson purchased the Louisiana Territory from France. The new territory doubled the size of the country. It included all or parts of the states of Louisiana, Arkansas, Missouri, Iowa, North Dakota, South Dakota, Nebraska, Kansas, Wyoming, Minnesota, Oklahoma, Colorado and Montana.

The Louisiana Purchase came on the heels of the invention of the cotton gin, which freed slaves from the work of manually separating cotton seeds from the cotton. Slaves could now spend more time working in the cotton fields, resulting in much greater profits for the slave owners.

The cotton plantations that sprang up in the Lower South and in the new Louisiana territories needed thousands more slaves to plant and harvest the cotton. Luckily for the cotton farmers who needed laborers, a slave surplus had developed in the states of the Upper South, including Maryland. Upper South slave owners were glad to have a market for their surplus slaves, but they were unhappy that competition from lower-cost African slaves was keeping the price down.

The solution came from an unlikely alliance of abolitionists and politically powerful Upper South slave owners. Abolitionists wanted an end to the African trade as a step towards complete abolition. Upper South slave owners wanted an end to the African trade so they could get more money for their surplus slaves. The alliance resulted in passage of a law banning the import of African slaves, effective January 1, 1808. The African slave trade was ended, but a newly powerful domestic slave trade was born.

Lower South cotton growers' demand for slaves was a bonanza for Maryland slave owners. Between 1830 and 1860, more than 18,000 surplus Maryland slaves were sold to the Lower South. The price of slaves tracked the price of cotton. There were ups and downs in the price of both, but from the end of the African slave trade in 1808 until the beginning of the Civil War in 1861, the price for a prime male slave in the New Orleans slave market rose from about $500 to more than $1,800 (about $35,000 today). Wealthy cotton growers could easily afford the high prices.

The surplus of slaves in the Upper South had several causes. One was the natural increase in the number of slaves. Slave owners encouraged slave women to have as many children as possible since any child born to a slave woman was the property of the slave owner. Slave women were valued for their breeding ability, exactly the same as livestock. Slave children increased in value as they grew older.

They could be sold at any age for a good profit, or left to descendants as a valuable inheritance.

Another cause of surplus Upper South slaves was the switch from tobacco to wheat and other cereal crops. Cereal crops required workers at harvest, not year-round like tobacco. It was cheaper to hire harvest workers than to maintain a permanent slave work force. As a result, many farmers in the northern, western, and eastern parts of Maryland freed their surplus slaves, or sold them through slave traders to the southern cotton plantations.

There were also surplus slaves in Southern Maryland, but not because the farmers there switched to other crops. Rather, it was because many Southern Maryland tobacco farmers had abandoned farming and left the state. Tobacco leached nutrients from the soil, and after three or four crops was no longer productive. Traditionally, tobacco farmers had simply abandoned worn out fields and cleared new land for new tobacco crops. But undeveloped new land in Southern Maryland was becoming scarce, and farmers began to emigrate west to the untouched lands of the Louisiana Territory. Emigrating farmers took some of their slaves with them and sold the rest.

According to U.S. federal census figures, almost half the white population of Charles County departed between 1790 and 1860, declining from 10,124 to 5,795.

Several Mudd families emigrated to the slave states of Kentucky and Missouri, where many Mudd descendants may be found today. In 1885, 400 of the 600 citizens of Millwood, Missouri, were Mudds or Mudd relatives.

Henry Lowe Mudd (1798-1877)

While others abandoned their farms and left the state, Henry Lowe Mudd (1798-1877), the second of Alexius Mudd's three children, stayed put. He and his wife, Sarah, were Dr. Samuel A. Mudd's parents.

Henry was a shrewd businessman. Where others saw failure, he saw opportunity. As others abandoned their land, Henry bought it.

He bought St. Catharine's and Mudd's Double Trouble consisting of 308 acres, Hayes Secret consisting of 329 acres, parts of Reed's Swamp containing 75 acres, and Jordan, containing 145 acres.

Henry was also a good farmer. Tobacco remained his main crop, but he also began to grow wheat and other grain crops. He applied fertilizers, rotated crops, and used better plowing techniques. He introduced mechanization, using Linton's Iron Geared Threshing Machine to harvest his wheat crop. All of these techniques combined to renew soil that had previously been considered worn out.

Henry also continued to use slave labor. In 1820 he had nine slaves. In 1830 he had 14 slaves. The federal census for 1840 doesn't list any slaves for Henry Mudd, but this appears to be because the census tabulation for Henry and his immediate neighbors was incomplete.

Prosperity returned to Charles County during the 1840s and 1850s as a result of higher tobacco prices. Prices for tobacco fluctuated, of course, but the general trend was upward.

Those who benefited the most were those like Henry Lowe Mudd who adopted soil renewal practices and grew a wider variety of crops, including wheat. The growing cities of Washington and Baltimore, as well as the usual export markets, provided a steady demand and good prices for Southern Maryland farm products.

Times were good again, and Southern Maryland farmers needed more slaves to take advantage of the opportunity. Henry Mudd's inventory of slaves continued to increase. He had 41 slaves in 1850, and 61 in 1860. The number of slaves owned by all Mudd family members in Charles County increased to 82 in 1850, and to 145 in 1860.

The demand for slaves increased the cost of slaves, but the prosperous Southern Maryland slave owners could afford them. After all, regardless of the price paid, the resale value of a slave continued apace. The Port Tobacco Times of August 19, 1858, reported that a 17-year-old slave brought $1,115, a 15-year-old slave $1,010, and an 8 or 9-year-old slave $725. The total $2,840 for these three slaves would be equal to about $60,000 today.

In her 1906 book, *The Life of Dr. Samuel A. Mudd*, Nettie Mudd says there were more than 100 slaves on Henry Lowe Mudd's large tobacco plantation. The 1860 U.S. Slave Census lists 61 slaves. Since slave owners often rented out surplus slaves to other farmers, it is very possible that Henry Lowe Mudd owned more than the 61 slaves present when the census was taken at his farm. Whatever the exact number, Dr. Mudd's father was quite well off. The 1860 Federal Census valued his real estate at $8,000 and his personal estate at $40,000. In today's dollars, Henry Lowe Mudd was a millionaire.

Dr. Mudd's Slaves

Sam Mudd represented the seventh generation of Mudds in America. All six generations before him back to 1680 were slave owners.

Slavery permeated the society into which Sam was born and raised. His community, his state, his country, and his church had condoned slavery for more than two centuries. His wife's family had also owned slaves for several generations. Like Sam, she had grown up in a society that considered slavery to be perfectly normal and acceptable.

Sam and Sarah acquired at least nine slaves between 1859 and 1864. Their first five slaves were documented in the 1860 Federal Slave Census. They were a 26-year-old man, a 19-year-old girl, a 10-year-old boy, an 8-year-old girl, and a 6-year-old girl. The 26-year-old man was Elzee Eglent. The 19-year-old woman was his sister, Mary Simms. The 14-year-old boy was their brother, Milo Simms. The two little girls were called sisters, but their different last names suggest they were not. We do know they were orphans. The 8-year-old girl was Lettie Hall. The 6-year-old girl was Louisa Cristie.

Four additional slaves were acquired between 1860 and 1864. They were Rachel Spencer, Richard Washington, Melvina Washington, and Frank Washington. Rachel Spencer probably came from the plantation of Henry Lowe Mudd where her mother Lucy Spencer, her sister Maria Spencer, and her brothers Baptist Spencer and Joseph Spencer were slaves. Maria Spencer was married to William Hurbert, a slave on Susanna Mudd's plantation in nearby Prince

George's County. Richard Washington, Melvina Washington, and Frank Washington came from the Dyer plantation.

Jeremiah Dyer said at the assassination trial that "*I bought the woman Melvina for Dr. Mudd in 1859, 1860, or 1861, or about that time, just before the war.*"

Two of Dr. Mudd's nine slaves, Elzee Eglent and Dick Washington, had run away in 1863. Four of the remaining seven slaves, Melvina Washington, Mary Simms, Milo Simms, and Rachel Spencer, left the Mudd farm shortly after Maryland emancipation on November 1, 1864. The last three slaves, Lettie Hall, Louisa Cristie, and Frank Washington, remained on the Mudd farm for several years emancipation.

Mary Simms said she left about a month before Christmas 1864 because Dr. Mudd whipped her. But several former slaves testified at the assassination trial that Mary Simms was not trustworthy and could not be believed. Julia Ann Bloyce, a house servant, testified it was actually Mrs. Mudd who had struck Mary Simms:

> Mrs. Mudd told her not to go away on a Sunday evening walking, but she would go, and the next morning she (Mrs. Mudd) struck her about three licks with a little switch. The switch was small, and from the licks she gave her, I do not believe she could have hurt her.

New African-American workers began to appear at Dr. Mudd's farm after Maryland's emancipation, including Frank Washington's wife Betty Washington, Baptist Washington, and Julia Ann Bloyce. Betty Washington and Julia Ann Bloyce worked as house servants. Betty's husband, Frank, worked as a plow man. Baptist Washington was a carpenter. All testified on behalf of Dr. Mudd at the conspiracy trial.

Frank Washington said of Dr. Mudd: *He treated me first rate. I had no fault to find with him.*

Betty Washington said: *I have no fault at all to find with him myself. He treated me very well when I was there.*

Baptist Washington said Dr. Mudd always treated his workers

very well: *He treated me very well. I was always very well satisfied with the accommodations he gave me when I was there.*

We know a little about the later lives of some of Dr. Mudd's slaves.

Rachel Spencer worked for the family of a Mr. Day, who was a clerk in the office of Captain Erskine Camp, superintendent of Soldiers Rest, a Union Army rest camp in Alexandria, Virginia.

The name Milo Simms appears in the 1878, 1879, 1880, 1881, and 1888 Washington City Directories. The name is distinct enough that this is probably the same Milo Simms who was Dr. Mudd's slave. His occupation is listed variously as servant, laborer, oysters, and junk.

When emancipated in November 1864, slaves Frank Washington, Lettie Hall, and Louisa Cristie chose to remain with Dr. and Mrs. Mudd, living and working on the Mudd farm for many years.

Lettie Hall left the Mudd farm sometime after 1870 to live with Dr. Mudd's son Thomas Mudd in the Anacostia section of Washington, D.C.. She worked for him for 30 years as the nanny for his children. Lettie later moved to Alexandria, Virginia, and then to Butler, Pennsylvania.

In 1929, now married to Rev. David Dade, Lettie gave an interview to her local Butler Eagle newspaper:

Butler Woman Cooked Breakfast for Booth after He had Killed Lincoln at Close of Civil War.

From the days of Lincoln to the present is a far cry, but there dwells in Butler a colored woman whose life spans that long expanse of years, and she is Mrs. David Brown Dade, wife of a colored Baptist minister, living at 210 Mulberry Street, who claims the distinction of having cooked breakfast for that arch-conspirator, J. Wilkes Booth, the morning after he assassinated President Abraham Lincoln, in April 1865, almost before the thundering of the guns during the dark days of the Civil War had subsided. Cooking breakfast for Booth, however, was not by design on the part of the Butler woman, but rather a matter of duty. But let Mrs. Dade tell the story in her own words.

"I was born a slave in Maryland," she began. "When I was quite small, my mother and father were sold and I never knew where they went. So far

as I know, I never saw them again. Dr. Samuel Mudd was a son of Dr. Henry Mudd, who owned a lot of slaves in his day, but Dr. Samuel Mudd did not keep any slaves, as his wife did not believe in slavery. She took my younger sister and I to raise, and she was very good to us. My sister's name was Louisa, and mine was Lettie Hall.

"My master, Dr. Samuel Mudd, lived in Chester County, Md. One morning when I was about 15 or 16 years old (I never knew my age), my master called me about 2 or 3 o'clock in the morning, and said: 'Lettie, get up quick and get a fine breakfast, for we have some distinguished people here for breakfast, and get Louisa up to serve.' I never knew anything else but to obey. So I got up, killed a chicken, and had the finest biscuits I believe I ever baked. I put cream in for shortening, and they were so pretty and nice.

"A Mr. Harold, who had come horseback with Mr. Booth, came down with the family to breakfast, but Louisa was ordered to take Mr. Booth's breakfast upstairs where Dr. Mudd was setting his broken leg. I learned later that Mr. Booth gave my sister two 25-cent pieces, and told her to give me one.

"I shall never forget that first piece of money I ever had. I wanted to put a hole in it and a string to put around my neck, but my master said that would spoil it, so he put it away for me. I did not get to see Mr. Booth, as I was in the kitchen downstairs, but sister said he was a very handsome man.

"When breakfast was over, Mr. Booth was helped into his saddle, and both he and Mr. Harold galloped on down the road. In a short time the United States soldiers rode up and surrounded our house. My, but I was scared!

"They hurriedly searched the house, although my master told them those folk had gone on down the road. I heard one man, who seemed to be the leader, say 'He's not here. We are losing time.' And then they rushed out of the house, got on their horses and galloped on down the road. I heard later that they found Mr. Booth that day in a barn and shot him there."

Lettie Hall Dade died on Saturday, April 18, 1936 in Butler, Pennsylvania. Although she said that Dr. and Mrs. Mudd had no slaves, records show that she was indeed a slave of Dr. and Mrs. Mudd.

Slave Life in Charles County

Henry Lowe Mudd's farm was located near the small Charles County town of Bryantown, Maryland. Richard Macks was a slave who recalled Bryantown quite well:

> *I was born in Charles County in Southern Maryland in the year 1844 ... the county where James [sic] Wilkes Booth took refuge in after the assassination of President Lincoln in 1865.*
>
> *...In Bryantown there were several stores, two or three taverns or inns, which were well known in their days for their hospitality to their guests and arrangements to house slaves. There were two inns both of which had long sheds, strongly built, with cells downstairs for men and a large room above for women. At night the slave traders would bring their charges to the inns, [and] pay for their meals, which were served on a long table in the shed. Then afterwards they were locked up for the night.*
>
> *...When I was a boy, I saw slaves going through and to Bryantown. Some would be chained, some handcuffed, and others not. These slaves were brought up from time to time to be auctioned off or sold at Bryantown, to go to other farms in Maryland, or shipped south.*

To be shipped south was the worst thing that could happen to a slave. Slaves sold to other farms in Maryland retained some hope that they would see loved ones again, but to be sold south to the plantations of Georgia, Mississippi, or Louisiana meant the slave would most likely never see father, mother, brother, sister, or children again. One of the slave owners' most powerful means of control over slaves was to threaten to sell them south if they didn't completely submit to their master.

In Maryland, a slave always had hope he or she could escape to freedom in nearby Washington, Baltimore, or points north. In the deep south, there was no such hope. Some slaves sold south were taken to Baltimore and placed on ships to New Orleans. These were the lucky ones. Others were forced to walk the hundreds of miles to the deep south, chained together like animals in groups called coffles.

MARIA SPENCER, one of Henry Lowe Mudd's slaves, was a good example of how slaves were rented out to make money for the slave owner. She was a sister of one of Dr. Mudd's slaves, Rachel Spencer.

Maria was married to William Hurbert who had served with Company A, 23rd Regiment, U.S. Colored Troops during the Civil War. When he passed away in 1874, she applied for a widow's pension. The following excerpt from her pension application explains how she was rented out while a slave of Henry Lowe Mudd:

> *That she was born on the plantation of Henry L. Mudd between Beantown and Byrantown in Charles County, Maryland. That she made acquaintance of her husband during her early childhood. That she always belonged to Henry L. Mudd until she left his plantation during the year 1865 and came to Washington to live where she has lived ever since.*
>
> *That she never had any other change of residence except when she was hired out as a slave. First, when about 14 years old, she lived for three months as a hireling of Robert Smith of Beantown, Charles County, Maryland. Next, she lived for one year and nine months with Edward Smith near Beantown. Next, she was hired to Richard Harbin near Bryantown, Charles County, Maryland for two years.*
>
> *Having then stated her P.O. Address during the period of her childhood to have been Bryantown, and her places of residence as above stated, she states she was married to William Hurbert in the house of Henry L. Mudd, Charles County, Maryland by a Catholic priest named Courtenay during the year of 1854 or 1855. That the only owner she ever had was Henry L. Mudd.*

Slave Patrols

Charles County whites formed neighborhood patrols to keep a close watch on slaves' movements by day and night. Slaves couldn't leave their master's premises without a permit. Any slave caught by a patrol without a pass from the owner, particularly at night, was dealt with harshly. Former slave Richard Macks told about the Charles County slave patrols:

> In Charles County and in fact all of Southern Maryland tobacco was raised on a large scale. Men, women and children had to work hard to produce the required crops. The slaves did the work and they were driven at full speed sometimes by the owners and others by both owner and overseers. The slaves would run away from the farms whenever they had a chance, some were returned and others getting away. This made it very profitable to white men and constables to capture the runaways. This caused trouble between the colored people and whites, especially the free people, as some of them would be taken for slaves. I had heard of several killings resulting from fights at night.
>
> One time a slave ran away and was seen by a colored man, who was hunting, sitting on a log eating some food late in the night, He had a corn knife with him. When his master attempted to hit him with a whip, he retaliated with the knife, splitting the man's breast open, from which he died. The slave escaped and was never captured. The white cappers or patrollers in all of the counties of Southern Maryland scoured the swamps, rivers and fields without success.
>
> Former slave Page Harris told about his Charles County farm, where the owner trained bloodhounds for hunting runaway slaves:
>
> I was born in 1858 about 3 miles west of Chicamuxen near the Potomac River in Charles County on the farm of Burton Stafford, better known as Blood Hound Manor. This name was applied because Mr. Stafford raised and trained blood hounds to track runaway slaves and to sell to slaveholders of Maryland, Virginia and other southern states as far south as Mississippi and Louisiana.

In 1860, the year after Dr. and Mrs. Mudd began farming, the federal census recorded 603,000 people living in Maryland, including 87,000 slaves and 84,000 free blacks. Maryland had the highest number of free blacks of any state. In the six counties of Southern Maryland, more than half the total population was black.

Free blacks were not really free. In reality, they were tightly controlled by the white community. The August 6, 1857, issue of the Port Tobacco Times reported that 33 free blacks were rounded up and sold to the highest bidder for the balance of the year. One of those rounded up threatened to complain to the *"Port Tobacco authorities"* and received *"five stripes"* for his presumption.

Slavery and Religion

The Mudd family was a Catholic family. But how could Catholics like the Mudds own slaves when the Catholic Church we know today strongly condemns slavery as intrinsically evil? The answer is that in Dr. Mudd's time the Catholic church not only condoned slavery, but also allowed priests and nuns to own slaves. For example, the Catholic Jesuit scholar Thomas Murphy reports that the Jesuits owned 272 slaves on six Maryland plantations. Father Leonard Edelen, pastor of St. Francis Xavier Church, Newtown, Maryland, and his assistant pastor, Father Aloysius Mudd, had eleven slaves.

Even Catholic nuns had slaves. Matilda Mudd was a nun with the Sisters of Charity of Emmitsburg, Maryland. Her religious name was Sister Joseph. When she died in 1823, she bequeathed her four slaves, Adeline, Augustine, Hilary, and Alexius, to her cousin Thomas M. Mudd. She instructed Thomas to set them free –– the boys at age 25 and the girls at age 16 –– with new clothes and $12 each.

In *Carmel in America*, Father Charles Warren Currier writes about the Carmelite nuns of Port Tobacco, Maryland, located about 10 miles from where Dr. Mudd lived:

> *The first convent of religious women in the United States of America was founded in 1790, at a distance of about four miles from Port Tobacco, on the*

property formerly belonging to Mr. Baker Brooke. The place was hencefor-
ward called Mount Carmel... A portion of the property of the nuns, while
they were at Mount Carmel, consisted of slaves.

Many of the novices, on entering the community, brought their slaves
with them. These were comfortably lodged in quarters outside the convent-
enclosure and did the work of the farm. They were treated with great love
and charity by the sisters, and were considered as children of the family.
Their souls being regarded as a precious charge, for which the community
was responsible to God, they were carefully instructed in their religious
duties, and all their wants, both spiritual and temporal, faithfully attended
to.

On their part these poor creatures were devotedly attached to the
community. Their number was about thirty, and twice a year the sisters
would spin, weave and make up suits of clothing for them, besides spinning
and weaving their own clothing.

Families like the Mudds undoubtedly reasoned that if the Church
condoned slavery, and if it was all right for priests and nuns to own
slaves, then it was all right for devout Catholic farmers to do the
same. On the second floor of Henry Lowe Mudd's home, in addition
to the family bedrooms, was a chapel where the Mudd family prayed
together, where visiting priests celebrated Mass, and where Mudd
slaves were married.

Henry's son Samuel became a devout Catholic. He subscribed to a
Catholic journal called Brownson's Quarterly Review. When the
editor, Orestes A. Brownson, began to write during the Civil War that
slavery should be abolished in order to preserve the Union, Dr. Mudd
wrote to Brownson to cancel his subscription. Dr. Mudd's January 13,
1862 letter said in part:

...The present Civil War now raging was not brought about entirely by fear
on the part of the South, that their property in Slaves was endangered, but
more by an unwillingness to yield up rights guaranteed by the Constitution
of the United States.

...A majority of the people of the North believe Slavery to be Sinful,

thereby they attempt to force down our throats, their religious Conviction, which is Anti-Catholic and uncharitable.

...The people of the North are Puritanical, long faced or Methodistic and hypocritical—they deal in Sympathetic language to hide their deception— their actions are Pharisaical, covert, stealthy, and cowardly. They are law abiding so long as it bears them out in their selfish interest, and praisers and scatterers and followers of the Bible so long as it does not conflict with their passions. They make good cow drivers, pickpockets and gamblers.

...You know full well, that slavery being a State institution recognized by every administration and confirmed by many acts of Congress, can only be abrogated by State will.

...Christ, our Saviour found slavery at his coming and yet he made no command against its practice. Therefore I think it is a great presumption in man to supply the omissions which God in his infinity thought proper to make.

Why the Slaves Sang

Many slave owners believed their slaves were happy, and had a hard time understanding why their slaves took every opportunity to run away. Nettie Mudd wrote of the supposed happiness of the slaves at Henry Lowe Mudd's plantation:

Here on his father's estate may have been seen more than a hundred slaves, who made the evening merry with song, and with banjo, and with violin accompaniment. Scattered over various sections of the farm may also have been seen the quarters of these humble folk, who were always treated with the kindest consideration by their master and mistress, and who would say of these white friends, after they had passed from earth, "God bless my old Marse and Miss; I hope dey is in heaven."

Frederick Douglass, who had been a Maryland slave, explained why slaves sang:

I have often been utterly astonished, since I came to the north, to find persons who could speak of the singing among slaves as evidence of their contentment and happiness. It is impossible to conceive of a greater mistake. Slaves sing most when they are most unhappy. The songs of the slave represent the sorrows of his heart; and he is relieved by them, only as an aching heart is relieved by its tears. At least, such is my experience. I have often sung to drown my sorrow, but seldom to express my happiness. Crying for joy, and singing for joy, were alike uncommon to me while in the jaws of slavery. The singing of a man cast away upon a desolate island might be as appropriately considered as evidence of contentment and happiness, as the singing of a slave; the songs of the one and of the other are prompted by the same emotion.

How Slaves Grew Tobacco

Charles Ball, a Maryland slave, described how slaves grew tobacco:

The operation is to be commenced in the month of February, by clearing a piece of new land, and burning the timber cut from it, on the ground, so as to form a coat of ashes over the whole space, if possible. This ground is then dug up with a hoe, and the sticks and roots are to be carefully removed from it. In this bed the tobacco seeds are sown, about the beginning of March, not in hills or in rows, but by broadcast, as in sowing turnips.

The seeds do not spring soon, but generally the young plants appear early in April. If the weather, at the time the tobacco comes up, as it is called, is yet frosty, a covering of pine tops, or red cedar branches, is thickly spread over the whole patch...

... In the months of March and April the people are busily employed in plowing the fields in which the tobacco is to be planted in May. Immediately after the corn is planted, every one, man, woman and child, able to work with a hoe, or carry a tobacco plant, is engaged in working up the whole plantation, already ploughed a second time, into hills about four feet apart, laid out in regular rows across the field, by the course of the furrows. These hills are formed into squares or diamonds, at equal distances both

ways, and into these are transplanted the tobacco plants from the beds in which the seeds were sown.

This transplantation must be done when the earth is wet with rain, and it is best to do it, if possible, just before, or at the time the rain falls, as cabbages are transplanted in a kitchen garden; but as the planting of a field of one or two hundred acres with tobacco, is not the work of an hour, as soon as it is deemed certain that there will be a sufficient fall of rain to answer the purpose of planting out tobacco, all hands are called to the tobacco field.

And no matter how fast it may rain, or how violent the storm may be, the removal of the plants from the bed, and fixing them in the hills where they are to grow in the field, goes on until the crop is planted out, or the rain ceases, and the sun begins to shine.

Nothing but the darkness of night and the short respite required for the scanty meal of the slaves, produces any cessation in the labor of tobacco planting, until the work is done, or the rain ceases and the clouds disappear.

... Sometimes the tobacco worm appears among the plants ...every slave that is able to kill a tobacco worm is kept in the field from morning until night. Those who are able to work with hoes are engaged in weeding the tobacco, and at the same time destroying all the worms they find. The children do nothing but search for and destroy the worms.

... In the month of August, the tobacco crop is laid by, as it is termed; which means that they cease working in the fields, for the purpose of destroying the weeds and grass; the plants having now become so large, as not to be injured by the under vegetation. Still, however, the worms continue their ravages, and it is necessary to employ all hands in destroying them.

In this month also the tobacco is to be topped, if it has not been done before. When the plants have reached the height of two or three feet, according to the goodness of the soil, and the vigor of the growth, the top is to be cut off to prevent it from going to seed.

After the tobacco is fully grown, which in some plants happens early in August, it is to be carefully watched, to see when it is ripe, or fit for cutting. ...It does not all arrive at maturity at the same time; and although some plants ripen early in August, others are not ripe before the middle of

September. When the plants are cut down, they are laid on the ground for a short time, then taken up, and the stalks split open to facilitate the drying of the leaves. In this condition it is removed to the drying house, and there hung up under sheds, until it is fully dry. From thence, it is removed into the tobacco house, and laid up in bulk, ready for stripping and manufacturing.

SLAVES TO SOLDIERS

I n 1863, the Union Army began enlisting slaves and former slaves into its newly established U.S. Colored Troops regiments. One of the camps established to recruit and train them was Camp Stanton at Benedict, Maryland, just 10 miles east of Dr. Mudd's farm. Four regiments of 1,000 African-American soldiers each would train there.

Several slaves on the various Mudd family farms, including Dominick Eglin, James Macle, Baptist Spencer, William Hurbert, and John Henry Chase enlisted in U.S. Colored Troops regiments.

Dominick Eglin

22-year-old Dominick Eglin ran away from the plantation of Dr. Mudd's father, Henry L. Mudd, and enlisted in the 19th Regiment of the U.S. Colored Troops at Camp Stanton on January 4,1864. Dominick was probably related to Dr. Mudd's slave Elzee Eglent, who ran away from Dr. Mudd's farm in August 1863 after Dr. Mudd shot him in the leg for being "*obstreperous.*"

Eglin served with the regiment until becoming ill with chronic diarrhea in May 1865. He was sent to the U.S. General Hospital in Fort

Monroe, Virginia for treatment, and was discharged the next month for health reasons. Eglin died on August 30, 1874, survived by his wife Harriet and their five children, Charles, John, Benjamin, Richard, and James.

Baptist Spencer

23-year-old Baptist Spencer ran away from the plantation of Dr. Mudd's father and enlisted in the 19th Regiment on December 28, 1863. Baptist's sister Maria Spencer was also a slave of Dr. Mudd's father. Baptist was probably related to Rachel Spencer, one of Dr. Mudd's slaves.

The Baltimore Sun of June 2, 1864 reported that Baptist Spencer, slave of Henry Mudd, was among those just drafted in Maryland's Fourth Election District. Draft officials were apparently not aware that Spencer was already in the Union Army, having enlisted five months earlier, and was with the 19th Regiment at Petersburg, Virginia at the time of the draft.

Spencer spent most of his three years in the Union Army as a teamster assigned to the Quartermaster Corps. This may have saved him from being killed or injured since he did not have to serve as one of the 19th Regiment's front-line infantrymen at Petersburg and other battles. He was mustered out on January 15, 1867 at Brownsville, Texas.

Spencer's pension file contains a 1902 affidavit by his wife Frances Robinson Newman:

I do not know my age but I was a grown woman when the war broke out. My first husband was a slave belonging to Henry Mudd and he left and joined company H 19th USCT and served under name of Baptist Spencer in said company from January 1864 to January 1867. He never came back to me after he went away with the Army. He was a kind, loving and affectionate husband and after he went away he sent me money in letters but these letters I have lost. I was pregnant when he went away and he seemed to be very anxious about me and as he went away he kissed me and then as

*they marched away he kissed my likeness and hallowed back "take good
care of yourself and to meet him in heaven if he should be killed."*

*I never heard from him after his discharge from the Army nor have any
of his friends. I went to meet the Regiment on Federal Hill when it came
back to be discharged expecting to meet and greet my husband but I could
not find him and none of the men seemed to know of him.*

*I have not heard of his death but am confident if he had survived he
would have come back to me and the little child he was expecting when he
went away...*

Frances Spencer remarried after the Civil War, to former soldier
Moses Newman. But it seems that Baptist was not really dead. A
Freedman Bank record dated November 7, 1873 showed that Baptist
was then living and working as a laborer in Washington, D.C. In 1890,
a special Federal Veterans Census shows Baptist Spencer, his wife
Frances Newman, and Frances' second husband Moses Newman all
living together at the same address in Baltimore, Maryland.

James Macle

27-year-old James Macle was a slave of Dr. Mudd's father, and was
married to Catherine Edelen Macle. He enlisted in the 19th Regiment
at Camp Stanton on January 10, 1864. Macle suffered a gunshot
wound in the right thigh at the Battle of the Crater at Petersburg,
Virginia on July 30, 1864, and was sent to the L'Ouverture army
hospital in Alexandria, Virginia to recover. He returned to the regiment in March 1865, and went with the regiment to Texas after the
war. Macle was promoted to Corporal on November 30, 1866.

Macle mustered out with the rest of the regiment on January 15,
1867 at Brownsville, Texas. He then returned to live near Bryantown,
Maryland.

William Hurbert

William Hurbert (aka Herbert) ran away from the Maryland farm of Susanna Mudd to Washington, D.C., where he was drafted into the 23rd Regiment, U.S. Colored Troops on November 25, 1863.

Hurbert was seriously wounded at the Battle of the Crater at Petersburg, Virginia on July 30, 1864, and spent the next five months at the Satterlee and Summit House hospitals in Philadelphia before returning to the regiment in January 1865. Hurbert went with the 23rd Regiment to Texas after the war, and was mustered out there on November 30, 1865.

John Henry Chase

21-year-old John Henry Chase also ran away from the Maryland farm of Susanna Mudd to Washington, D.C., where he enlisted in the 23rd Regiment, U.S. Colored Troops on February 27, 1864. He was reported as killed in action at the Battle of the Crater at Petersburg, Virginia on July 30, 1864, but was later found to have been wounded and held by the Confederates as a prisoner of war from the day of the battle to the end of the Civil War.

~

PORT TOBACCO SLAVE ADS

The *Port Tobacco Times* was the local newspaper in Dr. Mudd's community. Almost every issue of the paper carried ads for buying and selling slaves, or capturing runaways. Slave owners often rented their slaves, just as they might rent a horse or cow. And, like a horse or cow, if the rental property was damaged, the renter was responsible for reimbursing the owner.

Following are examples of some of the slave ads that appeared regularly in the *Port Tobacco Times*.

COLLECTOR'S SALE.

I WILL offer for sale in Port Tobacco, on FRIDAY, the 19th of SEPTEMBER, negro Woman REBECCA, levied on and taken as the property of James L. Richards. She will be sold for Taxes due the State and county for the years 1843 and 1844.— Terms of sale, cash.

WM. NEVITT, Collector
sep. 4,   of Charles County.

☞ The sale is *postponed* till the 7th day of OCTOBER next.

VALUABLE FAMILY

OF

NEGROES FOR SALE.

THE subscriber is authorized, by the owner, to offer for sale a very valuable FAMILY OF NEGROES, slaves for terms of years, consisting of

1 NEGRO WOMAN, aged 36 years, to serve until January 1st, 1863, also her children—

1 Negro BOY, aged 15 years;

1 Negro GIRL, aged 12 years;

1 " " aged 10 years;

1 " " aged 4 years;

1 " BOY, aged 2 years.

The Children each to serve until the age of 30 years; the future issue of the woman. and the issue of the children. and the increase of said issue, in perpetuity, to serve until the age of 30 years.

The Woman is a very good Cook, and also a very useful field hand—the eldest Boy is a very good field hand—the eldest Girl is a very capable House Servant and is useful in various capacities—the second Girl is old enough to worm Tobacco and can do various other light jobs. These Servants have been very carefully brought up, and are believed to have as few faults as can be found in any family of negroes. They are all sound and healthy, and are sold for no fault, but because the owner has as many other slaves (servants for life) as he can advantageously employ

For further particulars apply to the subscriber.

D. R. MAGRUDER,

Attorney at Law,

Prince Frederick, Calvert Co., Md.,

sep 16—4t

NOTICE.

I WANT TO PURCHASE for some gentlemen in the South, for their own use, some FORTY or FIFTY NEGROES of both sexes, at ages varying from twelve to twenty-five years. Persons wishing to sell will please address—

JOHN L. JOHNSON,
Washington, D. C.

jy 1—ly.

PUBLIC SALE.

BY virtue of an order of the Orphans' Court of Prince George's County, the undersigned will sell at public sale, on

Thursday, 2d day of December, 1858,

(if fair, if not, the next fair day thereafter,) all the personal estate of the late John Brookes, deceased, (at Mt. Calvert, his late residence,) consisting of a large assortment of

Household and Kitchen Furniture.

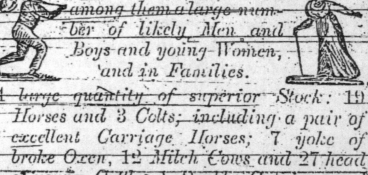

LIKELY NEGROES, *among them a large number of likely Men and Boys and young Women, and in Families.*

A large quantity of superior Stock: 19 Horses and 3 Colts; including a pair of excellent Carriage Horses; 7 yoke of broke Oxen, 12 Milch Cows and 27 head of young Cattle; 1 Double Carriage and Harness, 1 Rockaway Carriage and Harness, 1 Buggy and Harness and a large selection of Agricultural Implements; 11 Stacks of Timothy Hay, and 2 large Ricks of Clover and Timothy Hay mixed; also, the Crops of Corn and Corn Provender and Wheat Straw.

TERMS OF SALE.—Cash for all sums of and under $10—and bonds at four months with approved security, bearing interest from day of sale, for all sums above that amount, (except for the Negroes.) For the Negroes, cash or accepted drafts on Baltimore at six months, interest included.

RICHARD B. B. CHEW, Adm'r.
Nov. 11, 1858—ts   of John Brookes.

ONE HUNDRED AND FIFTY DOLLARS REWARD.

DURING my attendance in the Court, in Prince George's County, my

Negro Woman ROSE,

on the night of the 12th of November, without cause or provocation, absconded from my Farm in the lower part of Charles County. She took with her all her clothes, and also her bed and bed clothes. Rose is about 48 years of age, about 5 feet, 6 or 7 inches high, a light mulatto, with light eyes, and is very apt in telling stories. I have no doubt she was aided by some person in absconding from my plantation and she is now harbored by him, and is no doubt either on the Wicomico side of the Piccawaxen neighborhood, Charles County, or on the opposite side of the same river, in St. Mary's County, immediately above the village of Chaptico. I will give the above reward to any person who will deliver her to me, or to William T. Campbell, at St. Thomas' Manor, Charles County. Md.

PETER W. CRAIN,
Pottersville, Charles County, Md.

April 26, 1860.—tf

$100 REWARD.

Ranaway from the subscriber, living near Brandywine, Prince George's county, Maryland, about Whitsuntide, a negro man named NED MIDDLETON. He is about five feet, ten or eleven inches high, dark complexion, rather slenderly built, thin visage, and about twenty-five years of age, speaks quick when addressed, and has a pleasing countenance. Has a scar on one of his arms from a burn. He was raised in Charles county, and has a wife at Dr. Barber's farm, near Major John T. Stoddard's, and is no doubt lurking in that neighborhood.

I will give fifty dollars, if taken in the State of Maryland or District of Columbia; and the above reward if taken elsewhere;— in either case to be brought home or secured in jail so that I get him again.

ALEXANDER DENT.

aug 20—tf.

$50 REWARD.

RAN AWAY from the Subscriber, living near Port Tobacco, Charles county, Md., on Tuesday, the 19th of November, negro man BEN, who calls himself

BEN HAWKINS.

He is about 23 years old, about six feet high, and rather spare. His complexion is black. He was seen at camp Fenton, near Port Tobacco, on Thursday 21st inst.

I will give the above reward for his apprehension wherever taken, provided he be brought to me or secured in jail so that I get him again.

Any Communication in reference to him addressed to me at Port Tobacco, Charles county, Md., will be promptly responded to.

WILLIAM COX.

Nov. 26, 1861—tf

$50 REWARD.

RAN AWAY from Peter Wheeler, Esq., living near General Hooker's Headquarters, in Chickamuxen, on or about the 3d of December last, my Negro Boy,

MARTIN TOLSON.

He is 18 years old; low of stature—rather undersized for his age; complexion black; round and full face; eyes and mouth small; is slow of speech, and has rather a down-look when spoken to. He is thought to be lurking among the Regiments in that vicinity, or in the neighborhood of his parents, who live at the Rev. R. Prout's, in Nanjemoy.

I will give the above reward for him wherever taken, if delivered to me, or secured in jail, so that I get him again.

SAMUEL W. ADAMS,
Nanjemoy, Charles County, Md.

Jan. 9, 1862—tf.

Charles Co. May 8, 1850—tf.

CASH FOR NEGROES.

THE subscriber wishes to purchase any number of likely NEGROES for the New Orleans and Georgia markets. Persons having negroes for sale will find it to their advantage to call on me before disposing of them, as I am at all times in market, and will give the highest prices. Communications addressed to me at Piscataway, Md., or at Washington, D. C, will meet with prompt attention.   G. W. BRANDT,
          Agent for WM. H. WILLIAMS.
may 22—3m.

AN ADDITIONAL SUPPLY

PATROL NOTICE.

TO Elijah W. Day, Justice of the Peace for Charles County:—The undersigned think a Patrol necessary for the neighborhood lying between Zachia Swamp on the east, and Clarke Swamp on the west, and between the road leading from Port Tobacco to Piney Church on the north.
JOSIAS H. HAWKINS,
JOHN HAMILTON,
L. W. B. HAWKINS.

By virtue of the above application, I hereby appoint Josias H. Hawkins, John Hamilton, Luke W. B. Hawkins, John W. Hawkins, Peter W. Hawkins, Denham Horton, Oliver Horton, William Boswell, Warren Albrittain, Daniel W. Hawkins, Samuel Hawkins, James L. Padgett, William H. Berry and George W. Berry, a Patrol company; and I hereby appoint Josias H. Hawkins and John Hamilton Captains of the above Patrol. ELIJAH W. DAY, J. P.

☞ The Captains of the above Patrol wish it to be distinctly understood that any negro who may be caught from home after night without a pass from his owner will be severely dealt with.

dec 11—2t

CIVIL WAR

When Abraham Lincoln was seeking the Republican nomination for president in 1860, he said: *"Wrong as we think slavery is, we can yet afford to let it alone where it is..."* But most Southerners, including Southern Marylanders, didn't believe Lincoln would *"let it alone."* He failed to carry Maryland or a single southern state in the November 6, 1860 presidential election.

Whites in Charles County began military preparation in the event Maryland seceded from the Union. Various military units were formed, members acquired uniforms and weapons, and the units began to drill regularly. These included the Smallwood Rifles, the Nanjemoy Rifle Company, the Bryantown Minutemen, and the Mounted Volunteers of Charles County. We don't know if Dr. Mudd was an active member of any of these military units, but he was undoubtedly sympathetic to their purpose, which was to preserve slavery.

Jeremiah Dyer, Dr. Mudd's brother-in-law, and Jeremiah T. Mudd, a cousin of Dr. Mudd, were active in collecting money to arm and equip the Mounted Volunteers. When asked at the Lincoln assassination conspiracy trial about the purpose of the military unit he belonged to, Jeremiah Dyer said *"I do not know what the organization was particularly for."* He then added that *"our company broke up imme-diately on the breakout of the war ... some of them went to Virginia and joined the rebel army."*

The Civil War finally erupted on April 12, 1861 when Confederate forces in Charleston, South Carolina opened fire on the Union garrison at Fort Sumter in Charleston Harbor. Jeremiah Dyer testified that he fled to Richmond with members of his unit after the war began to avoid being arrested for disloyalty. However, after a month in Richmond, he decided not to join the Confederate Army after all, returned home, signed a loyalty oath, and settled back into the life of a tobacco farmer.

The Southern Maryland slave system and the economy it supported both began to disintegrate. In her 1906 book *The Life of Dr. Samuel A. Mudd*, Nettie Mudd wrote:

> *The Negroes, very soon after the war commenced, became imbued with the idea of freedom, and as this idea gained stronger hold in their minds their efficiency as servants diminished.*

Not only did their efficiency diminish, but they began to run away. In August 1861, Congress passed the First Confiscation Act, which authorized the president to seize any property, including slaves, employed in service to the Confederacy. While this Act allowed the army to provide refuge to fugitive slaves in the Confederacy, it did not technically apply to fugitive slaves from states not in rebellion, including Maryland. Nevertheless, as Union soldiers began to flood into Southern Maryland, slaves began to run away from their masters and seek refuge in the Army's camps.

More than 10,000 Union troops were stationed along the Charles County shore of the Potomac River opposite Virginia to prevent the Confederate Army from crossing into Maryland. General Joseph Hooker's corps was stationed at Chicamuxen Creek, about ten miles west of Dr. Mudd's farm. Its assignment was to protect the Union artillery batteries guarding the Potomac River. Runaway slaves sought refuge at General Hooker's camp, Camp Fenton, and other army camps around Charles County.

In November 1861, 400 Union soldiers of the 74th New York Volunteer Infantry, commanded by Colonel Charles K. Graham, fought skirmishes with rebel soldiers near Port Tobacco. Colonel Graham reported that when leaving the area:

A large number of negroes followed, some on board the gunboats, but a majority in a large launch, which by some means they had obtained.

For the Mudds, the runaways started in March 1862 when two little slave boys ran away from the farm of Dr. Mudd's father, Henry Lowe Mudd. The boys eluded the slave-catching patrols that operated between Bryantown and Washington, and found refuge at Fort Good Hope, a Union Army encampment located in what is now the Anacostia section of Washington. The fort was manned by a brigade under the command of Colonel William L. Tidball of the 59th New York Volunteer Infantry.

When Dr. Mudd tried to retrieve the two little boys, the soldiers refused to let them go. A new law had just gone into effect prohibiting the military from returning escaped slaves to their owners. Frustrated, Dr. Mudd wrote the following March 18, 1862 letter to his cousin Henry Alexander Clarke, a Washington businessman:

Cousin Alex,

Pa has two little boys in one of the encampments on Good Hope Hill - their names are Hillary, a black boy son of old Leck, the other is a yellow boy named Ambrose, son of old Miley of Aunt Reeve's estate. We have sent after them twice and they will neither give them up or drive them from the camp, nor will they permit you to enter the lines to take them yourself. My object in addressing this to you is to find out the means under the present state of affairs to reclaim my servants, or slaves. I have offered a reward of fifty dollars, which I am in hopes will compensate for any trouble, without the hazard of life. I would go to the War Department & enquire of Mr. Stanton, if the people of Maryland are to be treated as Secessionist, after

paying a tax of $2,500,000 to carry on the war & pay a prospective tax of
three cents per pound on leaf tobacco.

  Pa, Jim, & my family are all very well with the exception of myself. I
am in bed sick as a horse at this time. Remember me to cousin Em and
family & believe me yours most truly, etc.

  Sam A. Mudd

A month later, on April 16, 1862, President Lincoln signed a bill abolishing slavery in Washington, D.C. From then until the end of the war, Washington was a magnet for Southern Maryland slaves who ran away from their owners. *"These stampedes are becoming common,"* reported the June 19, 1862 issue of the Port Tobacco Times.

Three months later, July 17, 1862, Washington became an even greater magnet for Maryland slaves when Congress passed the Second Confiscation Act which declared that slaves owned by disloyal masters were free. Many Maryland slaves thought their masters fit that description exactly. As a result, fugitive Maryland slaves now routinely claimed that their former owners were disloyal when they appeared at Army encampments seeking safe haven.

In August 1863, the Union government established Camp Stanton in Benedict, Maryland, just 10 miles from Dr. Mudd's farm. Camp Stanton recruited and trained free blacks and runaway slaves for the Union Army. This provided an unparalleled opportunity for more Southern Maryland slaves to escape their masters. The 7th, 9th, 19th, and 30th regiments of the U. S. Colored Troops, totaling over 4,000 African-American soldiers, were trained at Camp Stanton.

On Saturday night, August 29, 1863, with a full moon to guide their way, forty slaves ran away from the farms of Dr. Mudd, his father Henry Lowe Mudd, and Jeremiah Dyer. They timed their escape well. Slaves weren't expected to be at work on Sunday, and it was not unusual for slaves to be out Saturday night as they went to visit family members on other farms. Escaped slaves tended to be men, so these escapees were probably all male field hands.

The escaping slaves included Elzee Eglent and Dick Washington from Dr. Mudd's farm, and Sylvester Eglent, John Henry Eglent, and

Henry Simms from the farm of Dr. Mudd's father. Jeremiah Dyer complained afterwards that because he lost so many slaves, he had to pay free workers to finish his tobacco harvest.

The slaves testified at the Lincoln assassination trial that they ran away after Sylvester Eglent overheard Dr. Mudd and Jeremiah Dyer discussing plans to send a number of them to Richmond to help the Confederate Army build fortifications for Richmond's defense. At the trial, Sylvester Eglent testified:

Last August a twelvemonth ago, I heard him say he was going to send me, Elzee, my brother Frank, and Dick Gardner and Lou Gardner to Richmond to build batteries... That was the last Friday in the August before last, and I left the Saturday night following... Forty head of us went in company.

Elzee Eglent testified that Dr. Mudd "*...told me the morning he shot me that he had a place in Richmond for me.*" Jeremiah Dyer denied that he and Dr. Mudd had talked about sending slaves to Richmond.

Two days after the great escape, some of the 40 slaves who ran away filed complaints with the military in Washington, claiming that their owners were disloyal and were planning to send slaves to Richmond to help in the defense of that city. Richard Washington, one of Dr. Mudd's slaves, filed one of the complaints:

Headquarters, Provost Marshal's Office
Washington, D.C. August 31, 1863
Richard Washington
Henry Simms
Colored
Make statements that Dr. Samuel Mud, Henry Burch, and Henry Mud, residents of Brientown, Charles Co., Md. are now and have been for a month past enrolling the colored slaves of that District and vicinity for the Rebel Army and that they have to their certain knowledge harbored, aided, and comforted Rebel officers and soldiers ever since the rebellion commenced. They further state that these parties have carried away colored persons, both free and slave into the Rebel lines and that they are

*now engaged in this work - that these parties caught a slave named George
Hawkins while trying to make his escape to the city of Washington, and
carried him back to Brientown, beat him in a most unmerciful manner, and
then carried him into the rebel lines. This slave was from the farm of James
Mudd, who is, and has been a long time in the Rebel army.*

*Simms and Washington state that they were to be carried into the
Rebel army. Simms belongs to Henry Mud and Washington to Samuel
Mud, and state that there is a quantity of arms and accoutrements buried
in the ground in the vicinity of Samuel Mud's house and that as some
cavalry were making a search in the vicinity, Samuel Mud's wife ran into
the kitchen and threw a bundle of Rebel mail into the fire and Henry Mud
said after the cavalry had gone that he had hid a lot of arms under the bed
and that as they were not found, he considered himself a smart man.*

*Richard Washington states that Dr. Samuel Mud, his master, is one of
the parties who assisted in enrolling the names of the slaves, amongst
whom was himself and Elsey Engley, for the purpose of sending them south
to go in the Rebel army as soldiers.*

*Mud lives in St. Charles Co., Md. - Brientown District, 3 miles above
the town - has been in the habit of harboring Rebel soldiers.*

*These parties convey the slaves in wagons to landing in St. Mary's
county, keep them in the woods until an opportunity presents itself to carry
them off. Henry Burch watches and reports when the way is clear.*

The Army's report of investigation of the slaves' claims said:

Capt:

*I have the honor to report on investigating the case in regards to certain
parties in the State of Maryland charged by the contrabands with enrolling
the slaves for the Rebel Army and various other charges.*

*The colored people both free and slave, also white people of undoubted
loyalty, in Charles and Talbot counties, state the charge is without foundation. There is (I learn) a patrol composed of citizens who patrol the country
around for the purpose of apprehending fugitive slaves, which, when
caught, are placed in jail, until such time as their owners shall call for
them, and then being considered unsafe to roam at large, are taken and sent*

south, to make their escape more uncertain. This, I find, are the grounds upon which the charges are founded.

Rufus McKinney living near Mt. Pleasant Ferry is now, and has been recruiting for the Confederate Army. I understand the Military Authorities of Baltimore have been trying to accomplish his arrest for some time but he had eluded their vigilance. I was informed McKinney was now at his place and that his arrest might be easily accomplished. Some information might be obtained of the Military Authorities at Baltimore, I think, if desired.

Birdy Mason and Benjamin Green in the vicinity of Marbry's Landing, Charles Co., Md., have been seen to carry groceries, clothing, and men over the river to Virginia for the Confederate Army. They secret their boat in the marsh. Mr. Marbry is a loyal man, and could give some information in the matter.

J. Jarboe of Long Old Fields, Prince George Co., Md. has been confined in the Old Capitol Prison twice, but is still to all accounts a rebel. On the 6th of July 1863, Jarboe urged two young men of the same place to make an attack on a party of Col. Baker's detectives who were passing through the village, saying he would assist them, that he was prepared. These young men, two brothers, are the young men alluded to. They will give statements to the case if so required.

Jarboe has a son in the Confederate Army who has been there since the commencement of the rebellion. He came home some time since and went back again.

I am of the opinion that the majority of the people in the lower part of the state of Maryland, especially Charles County, are disloyal, and that the loyal people are deterred from giving information through fear. It is my impression it would be a good remedy to station a negro Regiment in their midst.

Your obedient servant,
John D. Johnson, Capt. Military Detec.

In 1864, the Union began drafting slaves into the army, further depleting the supply of slave labor. Dr. Mudd and other Southern Maryland farmers were unable to raise a crop in the summer of 1864 due to the lack of slave labor. As a result of the loss of slave labor, farm income and land values in Southern Maryland fell sharply. Several people testified at the conspiracy trial that Dr. Mudd wanted to sell his farm. Dr. William T. Bowman testified:

> *I heard him say last summer when he could get no hands, that he could not till his land and he would like to sell it and would do so. I asked him what he expected to do in case he sold his land. He said he thought of going into the mercantile business in Benedict... Benedict is in an easterly direction from Bryantown, and is our usual port for Charles County... on the Patuxent River.*

Farmers brought their produce to Benedict for sale. Steamboats transported produce and passengers between Benedict, Baltimore, and ports on the Rappahannock and Potomac rivers. Benedict also prospered from the new Union Army encampment at nearby Camp Stanton.

Dr. Mudd probably got the idea of a mercantile business from his brother-in-law, Jeremiah Dyer. Jere, as he was called, had gotten out of farming the previous year, 1863, and moved to Baltimore where he was in the mercantile business selling grain, tobacco, and other farm products. Others testified similarly. Dr. J.H. Blanford testified:

> *During the last eighteen months, I have several times heard Dr. Mudd speak, in general terms, of being dissatisfied with his place, and that he would sell if an advantageous offer were made to him.*

And Marcellus Gardiner testified:

> *I have heard Dr. Samuel Mudd, on several occasions during the past two years, state that he wanted to sell out.*

In 1862, to help pay for the enormous cost of the war, Congress passed the Internal Revenue Tax Act of July 1, 1862. This new tax was the first on the incomes of individual U.S. citizens. It was assessed on annual incomes over $600. Businessmen, including physicians, were also required to pay an annual $10 business license. 1864 tax assessment records show that Dr. Mudd paid his $10 physician's license fee, but do not show that he was assessed any income tax. It therefore appears that Dr. Mudd's 1864 income was below $600 (about $12,000 in today's dollars). The Civil War and the end of slavery had brought hard times to Dr. Mudd and the people of Southern Maryland.

Dr. Mudd's financial situation was not helped by the addition of another mouth to feed. His fourth child, Samuel A. Mudd II, was born January 30, 1864. He now had to provide for a wife and four children from a small rural medical practice and a farm which produced little income.

His situation almost got worse when, on July 19, 1864, he was drafted into the Union army. However, he did not serve. A draftee could escape serving if he failed the physical exam, or hired a substitute, or paid a $300 commutation fee. Dr. Mudd's father had paid for substitutes for his brothers Henry and James when they were drafted. Dr. Mudd's name does not show on lists of draftees who obtained a substitute, or who failed a physical exam. Most likely, Dr. Mudd or his father paid the $300 commutation fee.

Three months after Dr. Mudd's draft scare, on November 1, 1864, the final nail in the coffin of the slave-based Southern Maryland economy was driven in when a new Maryland state constitution abolishing slavery took effect. In Baltimore that morning, church bells rang and Fort McHenry's 65 guns boomed in celebration. (Lincoln's January 1, 1863 Emancipation Proclamation freed the slaves in the rebellious states, but not in loyal border states such as Maryland which had stayed in the Union.) Article 24 of the new Maryland constitution said:

> *Hereafter, in this state, there shall be neither slavery nor involuntary servitude, except in punishment of crime, whereof the party shall have been duly convicted; and all persons held to service or labor as slaves are hereby declared free.*

In Charles County where Dr. Mudd lived, only 13 people voted for the new constitution. Nine hundred ninety-one, probably including Dr. Mudd, voted against it.

Later that month, as Dr. Mudd pondered whether to continue working his farm by himself, or sell it and move, he was introduced to someone who said he might be interested in buying his property, a 26-year-old actor by the name of John Wilkes Booth.

JOHN WILKES BOOTH

The famous actor John Wilkes Booth had the wholly impractical idea that if he could somehow kidnap President Lincoln, the Union government would exchange a large number of Confederate prisoners for Lincoln, or perhaps even force the Union Government into discussions ending the war on terms favorable to the Confederacy.

Booth's kidnapping idea involved transporting a captured Lincoln in a carriage from Washington, D.C. to the Confederate government in Richmond. He planned to bypass the Union Army presence in Northern Virginia by leaving Washington over the Eastern Branch (now the Anacostia River) bridge, go down the eastern side of the Potomac River through Confederacy-friendly Southern Maryland for 30 miles or so, ferry across the Potomac River into Virginia, and then travel to Richmond, somehow eluding General Grant's entire Army of the Potomac which blockaded Richmond.

Booth went to Southern Maryland two or three times in the fall of 1864 to familiarize himself with the road network and river-crossing points. On a couple of these occasions he stayed with a local physician, Dr. William Queen. Dr. Queen's son-in-law John C. Thompson described introducing Booth to Dr. Mudd during his testimony at the conspiracy trial:

I reside in Charles County, Maryland. I had a slight acquaintance with a man named Booth; I was introduced to him by Dr. Queen, my father-in-law, about the latter part of October last, or perhaps in November. He was brought to Dr. Queen's house by his son Joseph. None of the family, I believe, had ever seen or heard of him before; I know that I had not. He brought a letter of introduction to Dr. Queen from some one in Montreal, of the name of Martin, I think, who stated that this man Booth wanted to see the county.

Booth's object in visiting the county was to purchase lands; he told me so himself, and made various inquiries of me respecting the price of land there, and about the roads in Charles County. I told him that land varied in price from $5 to $50 per acre; poor land being worth only about $5; while land with improvements, or on a river, would be worth $50; but I could not give him much information in regard to these matters, and referred him to Henry Mudd, Dr. Mudd's father, a large landowner.

He also inquired of me if there were any horses for sale in that neighborhood. I told him that I did not know of any, for the government had been purchasing, and many of the neighbors had been taking their horses to Washington to sell.

Booth told me, on the evening of his arrival at Dr. Queen's, that he had made some speculations or was a share-holder in some oil lands in Pennsylvania; and as well as I remember, he told me that he had made a good deal of money out of it, and I did not know but that he came down there for the purpose of investing.

On the next morning, Sunday, I accompanied him and Dr. Queen to Church at Bryantown. I happened to see Dr. Samuel A. Mudd in front of the Church before entering, and spoke to him, and introduced Mr. Booth to him. Mr. Booth staid at Dr. Queen's that night and the next day. About the middle of the December following, if my memory serves me, Mr. Booth came down a second time to Dr. Queen's; he staid one night and left early next morning. I never saw him but on these two occasions, and do not know whither he went when he left Dr. Queen's.

Booth told Dr. Mudd at the church that he was visiting the area to look for land and a horse to buy. Dr. Mudd told him he might be interested in selling his farm, and that his neighbor had a good horse for sale. He invited Booth to stop by.

That evening, Booth went to the Mudd farm, had dinner, and stayed the night. The next day he looked over the farm and offered to buy it. He then purchased a horse from Dr. Mudd's neighbor, and left.

A month later, just before Christmas, Dr. Mudd went to Washington to meet Booth again, presumably to further discuss the sale of the farm. They had drinks and conversation with two other people - John Surratt and Surratt's friend Louis Weichmann. During conversation, Booth mentioned to the group that he had offered to buy Dr. Mudd's farm, which Dr. Mudd affirmed. Surratt became a co-conspirator in the kidnap plot. Weichmann became a prosecution witness at the conspiracy trial.

Friday, April 14, 1865

On Good Friday evening, April 14, 1865, at a little after 10 o'clock, Dr. Mudd and his wife Sarah checked to see that their four young children, Andrew, Lillian, Thomas, and baby Samuel were asleep, and went to bed themselves in their first floor bedroom at the back of the house.

At about the same time, John Wilkes Booth crept up behind President Abraham Lincoln in his box at Ford's Theatre in Washington, D.C., and shot him in the head.

Shouting *"Sic semper tyrannis"* (death to tyrants), Booth leaped from Lincoln's box onto the stage, breaking a bone in his left leg. Hobbling across the stage and through a back door to the alley, Booth got onto his horse and rode hard out of the city, across the Eastern Branch (Anacostia River) bridge, and shortly met up with an accomplice, David Herold, who had crossed the bridge shortly before.

The two men rode quickly south through the dark Maryland countryside, following the escape route Booth had originally planned for his kidnap plot. A third-quarter moon was setting in the west, but gave no light through a solid cloud cover. A cold drizzle dampened Booth and Herold, and made the dirt road slippery. The leg Booth had broken when jumping to the stage at Ford's Theatre was beginning to ache.

Around midnight, Booth and Herold arrived at the Surratt Tavern in Surrattsville, Maryland, where they obtained a carbine, cartridges, field glass, and a bottle of whiskey from the tavern keeper, John Lloyd. Lloyd would later be a key witness against Mrs. Surratt, who owned the tavern. Booth decided he had to find a doctor to treat his aching leg, and asked Herold to lead him to Dr. Mudd's farm.

Saturday, April 15, 1865

Dr. Mudd opened his front door to the loud knocking at 4 a.m., and saw John Wilkes Booth, who said he and a companion were on their way to Washington when his horse fell and he broke his leg.

With no radio, TV, smartphone, or internet to inform him, Dr. Mudd had no knowledge of the assassination. He helped Booth up the stairs to the guest bedroom on the second floor. Working quietly in order not to awaken his four young children sleeping in the adjoining bedroom, Dr. Mudd cut the boot off Booth's swollen left leg and examined it. He found a broken bone about two inches above the left ankle, fashioned a splint for the leg, and told Booth to rest.

President Lincoln died in Washington at 7:22 a.m. He had lived through the night without regaining consciousness. About 9 a.m., Dr. Mudd had breakfast with his wife and David Herold. At mid-day, after checking Booth's condition, he had lunch. Then he and Herold rode to his father's adjoining farm to see if there was a buggy Herold could use to carry his injured companion. There wasn't, so he and Herold started to ride to Bryantown to see if one could be obtained there. Herold soon changed his mind and decided to return to Dr. Mudd's farm. Dr. Mudd continued to Bryantown alone to shop for his wife.

Dr. Mudd found Bryantown full of soldiers. Lieutenant David Dana, who was in charge of the soldiers, had informed the townspeople that President Lincoln had been assassinated, and that John Wilkes Booth was the assassin. This was the first that Dr. Mudd learned of the assassination. He later claimed that he didn't immediately tell the soldiers in Bryantown that Booth was at his farm because he didn't know that the man with the broken leg was Booth.

Dr. Mudd did not immediately return home. Perhaps hoping Booth and Herold would be gone by the time he got back home, he first finished his shopping and on the way back stopped to chat with neighbors Francis Farrell and John Hardy. He told them he had heard in Bryantown that the president had been assassinated. At the trial, Farrell testified that Dr. Mudd said "*he was very sorry this thing had happened, very sorry.*" Hardy testified that Dr. Mudd said there was "*terrible news*" - that the president had been assassinated, and that "*it was one of the most terrible calamities that could have befallen the country at this time.*"

Dr. Mudd arrived home just before sundown to see Booth and Herold leaving.

In a statement Mrs. Mudd later made about Booth's visit, she said that neither she nor her husband recognized that the man with the broken leg was Booth, but that upon returning from Bryantown, Dr. Mudd told her he was suspicious of the two men. She wrote that he then decided to return to Bryantown:

> He then sent for his horse to go to Bryantown and tell the military authorities about those two men. I begged him not to go himself, but to wait till church next day and tell Doctor George Mudd or some one else living in Bryantown all the circumstances and have him tell the officers at Bryantown about it. He was very unwilling to delay and warned me of the danger from a failure to tell of these men at once. I told him if he went himself, Boyle who was reported to be one of the assassins and who had killed Captain Watkins last fall in that county might have him assassinated for it, and that it would be just as well for the authorities to hear it next day, because the crippled man could not escape.

Shortly after leaving Dr. Mudd's farm at sundown, Booth and

Herold became lost in the darkness. They then ran into a local resident, Oscar Swan (aka Oswald Swan), and asked him to guide them to Samuel Cox's farm. Swan was later arrested and brought to the Old Capitol Prison in Washington, where he gave the following statement:

Oscar Ausy Swan: Live about two miles from Bryantown, Md. I know Capt. Saml. Cox. I met two men on Sat night 15 April about 9 o'clock. I had heard of the murder of the president. These men asked me the way to Mr. Burtle's; dark and could not see their faces. I was on foot when they asked. They told me to get my horse and show them the way. They asked me if I had any whiskey. I gave them some and some bread. They offered me $2 to take them to Mr. Burtle's. Before I got to Burtle's they asked me if I could take them to Capt. Cox. If so, they would give me $5 more. I took them.

One man was a small man. The other was lame and had a crutch. The small man said the other man broke his leg. I saw it was the left leg that was broken. When they got to Cox they got off. It was near midnight. Cox came out with a candle. he said "How do you do." They went in and remained 3 or 4 hours. I staid outside. When they came out they were alone. Cox did not come out with them. The small man went some little distance, when the lame man called and said "Don't you know I can't get on?" The small man then came and helped. The small man told me to put my hand under his foot & lift him up, which I did. One said when they were mounted "I thought Cox was a man of Southern feeling."

They did not come out of the gate as far as I saw. The gate is 1/4 of a mile from Cox's house. Before I got to Cox's the small man said "Don't you say anything. If you tell that you saw anybody you will not live long." I saw nothing more of them. I got back home which is 12 miles from Cox's about sunrise. In all they paid me $12.00.

After traveling about 12 miles from Oscar Swan's home, Booth, Herold, and Swan arrived around midnight at Rich Hill, the farm of Samuel Cox, a prosperous farmer, slave owner, and Southern sympathizer. He suspected his visitors were the assassins everyone was looking for. While sympathetic to them, he was afraid of later being accused of giving them refuge. He told them to hide in the woods while he decided how to help them.

Sunday, April 16, 1865

The next morning was Easter Sunday. Dr. Mudd had the choice of two churches: St. Peter's, the small country church about two miles north of their farm, and St. Mary's, about five miles south of their farm in Bryantown, where he had first met Booth.

Instead of going to church in Bryantown where he could have reported the two strangers to the authorities, Dr. Mudd instead went in the opposite direction, to St. Peter's. Sarah stayed home with their four small children.

The president's assassination was a topic of great discussion at St. Peter's that morning. After church, Dr. Mudd caught up with his cousin Dr. George Mudd, who was riding back to his home in Bryantown. At the trial, Dr. George Mudd testified:

I had very little conversation with Dr. Mudd at church. He remarked that he regarded the assassination of the president, to use his own expression, was a most damnable act. He overtook me on the road after church, and stated to me that two suspicious persons had been at his house; that they came there on Saturday morning a little while before daybreak; that one of them had a broken leg, or a broken bone in the leg, which he bandaged; that they got while there something to eat; that they seemed laboring under some degree, or probably quite a degree, of excitement - more excitement than probably should necessarily result from the injury received; that they said they came from Bryantown, and were inquiring the way to Parson Wilmer's; that while there one of them called for a razor, and shaved himself; I do not remember whether he said shaved his whiskers or moustache, but altered somewhat, or probably materially altered, his features; he did not say which it was that had shaved himself; that he himself, in company with the younger one, or the smaller one of the two, went down the road toward Bryantown, in search of a vehicle to take them away from his house; that he arranged or had fixed for them a crutch or crutches (I do not remember which) for the broken-legged man; and that they went away from his house, on horseback, in the direction of Parson Wilmer's. I do not think he stated what time they went.

When I was about leaving him, he turning into his house, I told him that I would state it to the military authorities, and see if any thing could be made of it. He told me that he would be glad if I would, or that he particularly wished me to do it; but he would much prefer if I could make the arrangement for him to be sent for, and he would give every information in his power relative to the matter; that, if suspicions were warrantable, he feared for his life on account of guerrillas that were, or might be, in the neighborhood. This was about half-past 11 o'clock in the forenoon, and when I parted with him, I was within fifty yards of his house.

As I left Dr. Samuel Mudd, I went toward Bryantown. I dined at his father's house that day, and on my way toward Bryantown I stopped to see a patient, and it was nightfall before I got to the village of Bryantown. What Dr. Samuel Mudd had told me I communicated to the military authorities at Bryantown the next morning.

Dr. Mudd clearly did not give his cousin George the impression that alerting the authorities to the visit of the two strangers was a matter of any great importance. Instead of going immediately to Bryantown with the news, George Mudd had a leisurely lunch at Dr. Mudd's father's home, visited a patient on his way back to Bryantown, and then went home for the night. The next morning, when he finally got around to telling the military authorities about Dr. Mudd's visitors, he obviously didn't lend any sense of urgency to the story, since the military didn't begin to look into the story until the next day, Tuesday.

About the same time that Dr. Mudd was attending church Easter Sunday morning, Samuel Cox sent his son to see his foster-brother and neighbor, Thomas A. Jones. Jones had been employed by the Confederate Government during the war to transport Confederate agents and mail across the Potomac between Maryland and Virginia. Jones later wrote:

The next morning, which was Easter Sunday, soon after breakfast, Samuel Cox, Jr, adopted son of my foster-brother, Samuel Cox, came to my house, Huckleberry, and told me his father wanted to see me about getting some seed-corn from me. He added, in an undertone, "Some strangers were at our house last night."

Even had I not heard the evening before of the assassination of Mr. Lincoln, knowing Cox as I did, I would have been sure he had sent for me to come to him for something of more importance than to talk about the purchase of seed-corn. But putting together the intelligence I had the evening before received from the two soldiers, the fact that strangers had been at Cox's the previous night and that Cox had now sent for me, I was convinced that he wanted to see me in reference to something connected, in some way, to the assassination.

When Jones arrived at Cox's house, Cox told him that Lincoln's assassins had come to his farm during the night, and that his farm overseer, Franklin Robey, had hidden them in a pine thicket about a mile away. He asked Jones to help them get across the Potomac into Virginia, and Jones agreed. For the rest of that week, until Friday, April 21st, Jones would bring food and supplies to Booth and Herold in the pine thicket, asking them to be patient until it was safe to cross the Potomac.

Booth and Herold would remain in hiding in the pine thicket until Friday night, with food and supplies provided by Thomas Jones.

Monday, April 17, 1865

On Monday morning, Dr. George Mudd finally told Lieutenant Dana about the two strangers. The story apparently was not presented to Dana as an urgent matter, since he didn't bother to assign detectives to investigate until the next day.

Also on Monday, five of the alleged conspirators were arrested. Samuel Arnold was arrested at Fortress Monroe, Michael O'Laughlen was arrested in Baltimore, Mary Surratt and Lewis Powell were arrested at the Surratt boarding house in Washington, and Edman Spangler was arrested at his boarding house a few blocks away.

Late Monday evening, Major James R. O'Beirne, Washington's Provost Marshal, ordered Lieutenant Alexander Lovett to proceed to Southern Maryland and arrest anyone suspected of being implicated in the assassination of President Lincoln. Nine cavalrymen and two Special Officers (military detectives) of Major O'Beirne's force, Simon Gavecan and William Williams, were assigned to assist Lovett.

Booth and Herold remained in the pine thicket a mile from Thomas Jones' home, and would stay there until Friday, when they would try to cross the Potomac.

Tuesday, April 18, 1865

En route to Bryantown, another of Major O'Beirne's Special Officers, Joshua Lloyd, joined Lieutenant Lovett's group. Around noon on Tuesday, Lieutenant Lovett and his men arrived in Bryantown, where Lieutenant Dana told him of Dr. George Mudd's report of two strangers at Dr. Samuel Mudd's farm. Lieutenant Lovett immediately interviewed George Mudd, who repeated the story Dr. Mudd had told him. Lovett then took George Mudd and his men to Dr. Mudd's farm.

When they arrived, Dr. Mudd was out working in the fields. While waiting for Dr. Mudd to return from his fields, Lieutenant Lovett interviewed Mrs. Mudd. She told about the two strangers coming to their house early Saturday morning, and how Dr. Mudd set the broken leg of one man. She also mentioned that the man with the broken leg had shaved off his mustache, and that as he was coming down the stairs to leave the house in the afternoon, his chin whiskers became detached. She said she thought his beard was false. When asked about this later, Dr. Mudd said he didn't know if the beard was real or false.

When Dr. Mudd came in from the fields, his cousin George Mudd told him why Lieutenant Lovett and his men had come to see him. Lovett then proceeded to interview Dr. Mudd about his visitors. At the trial, Lieutenant Lovett testified that Dr. Mudd told him that he didn't recognize either of the two men, that they had stayed but a short time, leaving that same morning, and that he first learned of President Lincoln's assassination on Easter Sunday morning at church. None of these claims later proved to be true.

After interviewing Dr. Mudd for about an hour, Lieutenant Lovett and his men left. He wrote in his report:

Dr. Mudd seemed to be very much reserved and did not care to give much information. I was then satisfied that it was Booth and Herold, and made up my mind to arrest Doctor Mudd when the proper time came.

Wednesday, April 19, 1865

While Dr. Mudd worked quietly on his farm, the government still had no definite idea where Booth was. Some thought Booth was hiding in Washington. Others thought he had escaped north to Canada, or west to Chicago, or east to the Chesapeake Bay, or even to London. Several men resembling Booth's description had been arrested in error. The two strangers who had been at Dr. Mudd's farm may or may not have had something to do with the assassination. Dr. Mudd had said he didn't recognize them.

Near Washington, George Atzerodt was found at the home of a relative, and arrested as a suspected conspirator in the assassination of President Lincoln. Six of the eight persons who would stand trial for conspiring to assassinate President Lincoln had now been arrested. Only David Herold and Dr. Mudd remained free.

Thursday, April 20, 1865

On Thursday, the Federal Government posted a $100,000 reward ($2 million in today's dollars) for information leading to the arrest of Booth ($50,000), John Surratt ($25,000), and David Herold ($25,000). The government's reward poster included the following statement:

All persons harboring or secreting the said persons, or either of them, or
aiding or assisting their concealment or escape, will be treated as accom-
plices in the murder of the president and the attempted assassination of the
Secretary of State, and shall be subject to trial before a Military Commis-
sion and the punishment of DEATH.

Dr. Mudd worked on his farm Thursday, hoping he had seen the
last of detectives hunting for Booth. But he hadn't.

Friday, April 21, 1865

On Friday morning, Lieutenant Lovett procured a fresh squad of
mounted men of the 16th New York Cavalry and returned to Dr.
Mudd's farm. Lovett was again accompanied by Special Officers
Simon Gavecan, William Williams, and Joshua Lloyd.

At the trial, Lieutenant Lovett testified:

When he found that we were going to search the house he said something
to his wife, and she brought down a boot and handed me the boot.

He said that he had to cut it off the man's leg in order to set the leg. I
turned down the top of the boot and saw some writing on the inside, saw
the name "J. Wilkes" written in it. I called his attention to it, and he said he
had not taken notice of that before.

Lovett took Dr. Mudd back to Bryantown where Colonel Henry H.
Wells interviewed him about Booth's visit. He signed a statement in
which he described Booth's visit to his home in November, and
Booth's visit after the assassination. He said that he had not seen
Booth between those two visits. This latter statement was not true. He
was trying to hide his meeting with Booth in Washington.

Meanwhile, Thomas Jones decided it was time to try to get Booth
and Herold across the Potomac. That night, he led the two men from
their hiding place to the Potomac shore, and helped them into a
small boat. Booth and Herold then set off on the dark Potomac, but
the current prevented them crossing to the Virginia shore. They

wound up on the Maryland shore again, some distance from where they started, and found a place to hide until they could try to cross again the next night.

Saturday, April 22, 1865

Colonel William P. Wood arrived in Bryantown from Washington, where he was the superintendent of the Old Capitol Prison. He had been sent to Bryantown by Secretary of War Stanton to assist in the hunt for Booth. Colonel Wood went to the Mudd farm where Dr. Mudd told him what had happened there. Afterwards, he wrote a report that said "*Dr. Mudd's statement I now believe to be true.*"

Later that Saturday night, Booth and Herold set out again in their small boat. This time they successfully crossed the Potomac, arriving about sunrise Sunday morning on the Virginia shore at the mouth of Machodoc Creek near the home of Elizabeth Quesenberry.

Sunday, April 23, 1865

Elizabeth Quesenberry had sheltered Confederate agents crossing the Potomac during the war, but she didn't know who these two strangers were, didn't trust them, and told them to move on, suggesting that the man with the broken leg find Dr. Richard Stuart who lived a few miles away. When they arrived at Dr. Stuart's later in the day, Stewart refused to admit the two men to his house, only allowing them to spend Sunday night in his slave quarters.

Dr. Mudd had a normal day that Sunday. He went to church in the morning and spent the rest of the day at home with Sarah and his four children. He may have thought he was finished with Booth, but that night was the last night he would spend at home with his family for almost four years.

Monday, April 24, 1865

Colonel Henry L. Burnett, the military prosecutor assigned by Secretary of War Stanton to build criminal cases against the alleged conspirators, had been following reports concerning Dr. Mudd, including his statement to Colonel Wells. Burnett ordered that Dr. Mudd be transferred from the Bryantown jail to the Old Capitol Prison in Washington.

Dr. Mudd, Frank Washington, Thomas Davis, and Alexis Thomas (aka Electus Thomas) were taken together to the Old Capitol Prison in Washington, D.C. to join other witnesses. Frank Washington was a black farmhand who cared for Booth's and Herold's horses while they were at Dr. Mudd's farm. Thomas Davis was a white farmhand who was living at the Mudd farm house when Booth and Herold arrived. Alexis Thomas was a black farmhand of Dr. Mudd's father, Henry Lowe Mudd. Herold had asked directions of Thomas after he and Booth had left Dr. Mudd's farm.

In Virginia, Booth and Herold continued their flight, finally arriving at the Richard Garrett farm where Booth, using a false name, was allowed to spend the night indoors for the first time since leaving Dr. Mudd's farm. Herold continued down the road to Bowling Green, Virginia, where he spent the night.

Tuesday, April 25, 1865

Herold rejoined Booth at the Garrett farm where they rested for the day. That night, becoming suspicious of the two men, the Garretts did not let them sleep in their home, making them sleep in the barn.

Wednesday, April 26, 1865

Union soldiers hunting for Booth had learned he was at the Garrett farm. About 2 a.m., they arrived at the farm, cornering Booth and Herold in the barn. The soldiers set fire to the barn in hopes this would flush the two men out. Herold came out of the barn and surrendered, but Booth defiantly stayed in the burning barn.

One of the soldiers, Sergeant Boston Corbett, watched Booth through the slats in the barn, outlined by the fire. Corbett took aim, and shot Booth with his revolver, mortally wounding him. Booth was pulled from the barn, still alive but in great pain. He died soon afterwards, about 7 a.m.

The 12-day hunt for John Wilkes Booth was finally over.

The Conspirators, Illustration by Benn Pitman

THE CONSPIRATORS

The Conspirators illustration on the previous page is from *The Assassination of President Lincoln and the Trial of the Conspirators*, 1865, by Benn Pitman, who was the official court stenographer with the title Recorder to the Commission. Pitman's book was the government-approved official record of the Lincoln assassination trial, and remains one of the primary reference works for the Lincoln assassination trial.

Those in the Conspirators illustration are John Wilkes Booth, Lewis Powell (aka Lewis Payne, David Herold, Michael O'Laughlen, John Surratt, Edman Spangler, Samuel Arnold, George Atzerodt, and Mary Surratt.

Note that Pitman places Mrs. Surratt, not Booth, at the center of the ring of alleged conspirators, and includes her son John Surratt who was not on trial. Also note that Pitman does not include Dr. Mudd as one of the conspirators. He explains his decision to omit Dr. Mudd in a letter to Dr. Mudd's lawyer, General Thomas Ewing:

Phonographic Institute
Cincinnati
August 24, 1865

Dear Sir:

Red'd your corrected remarks. I will for your sake as well as for my own reputation do the best I possibly can for you. The whole is in type, but I think all can be corrected, though it may be attended with some expense & trouble.

The book is 7/8 done. I think you will be pleased with it. I am conscious of having done the work carefully and fairly.

It has been a prodigious labor. If we are not disappointed with the engravers the book will be ready in three weeks.

The accused will be engraved in the highest style of cut.

I intended to omit Dr. Mudd from the illustration - without consulting with anyone about it - partly, perhaps mainly from consideration to his family. The publishers now think and half demand that I should give the likeness of the Dr. with the rest of the accused.

I have written to Dr. G.D. Mudd about it. Can you assist me to a photograph? If I cannot obtain one there is danger of the publisher using one of the vile caricatures that have appeared in the illustrated papers.

Very resp.
Benn Pitman

Dr. G.D. Mudd is Dr. George Dyer Mudd, who trained Samuel Mudd in medicine, and who was active in helping General Ewing organize defense witnesses for Dr. Mudd at the trial. Many years after the trial, Dr. George Mudd told an interviewer "*it became necessary for us to raise witnesses down here who would take the edge off these facts.*" Was he hinting that some of the defense witnesses committed perjury?

Pitman apparently never obtained a photograph of Dr. Mudd, or decided to keep him out of the illustration anyway, or the publisher didn't press the matter. And apparently neither Secretary of War Stanton nor any other government official noticed the omission. Whatever happened, Dr. Mudd does not appear in the illustration of the accused conspirators in the U.S. Government's officially approved report of the Abraham Lincoln assassination trial.

The eight persons arrested for conspiracy in the assassination of President Abraham Lincoln were David Herold, George Atzerodt, Samuel Arnold, Michael O'Laughlen (also known as Michael O'Laughlin), Edman Spangler (also known as Edmund, Edward, or Ned Spangler), Lewis Powell (also known as Lewis Payne), Mary Surratt, and Dr. Mudd.

There was little question as to the guilt of David Herold, Mary Surratt, Lewis Powell, and George Atzerodt.

David Herold, found guilty and hanged, had accompanied Booth during the entire twelve-day escape attempt, from the night of the assassination until he was captured at the Garrett farm.

Mary Surratt, found guilty and hanged, was the owner of the Washington boarding house where Booth and his fellow conspirators plotted against Lincoln, and of the Surrattsville tavern where she stored supplies for Booth's escape from Washington. Her guilt or innocence remains a matter of debate today.

Lewis Powell, found guilty and hanged, freely admitted that he was part of the plot against Lincoln, and that he tried to kill Secretary of State William H. Seward.

George Atzerodt, found guilty and hanged, admitted that he had agreed to murder Vice President Andrew Johnson, but lost his nerve and failed to do so.

The court did not believe the remaining four defendants, including Dr. Mudd, had anything to do with planning or carrying out the assassination of President Lincoln, but thought they were either part of Booth's original plot to kidnap the president, or had aided Booth's escape attempt.

Edman Spangler

Edman Spangler was born on August 10, 1825 in York, Pennsylvania. He worked his whole life as a carpenter. He first met John Wilkes Booth as a young man while working on a carpentry job for Booth's father, the famous actor Junius Brutus Booth. In 1861, Spangler moved to Washington to work as a carpenter at the new Ford's Theatre. There, he became reacquainted with John Wilkes Booth, who was now a famous actor like his father.

Spangler's boss, John T. Ford, considered Spangler a valued employee, and a man innocent of any involvement in Lincoln's assassination. To his everlasting credit, John Ford continued to assert Spangler's innocence and fight for his release during the entire four years Spangler was in prison.

Spangler lived frugally. He slept at Ford's Theatre, taking his meals at a nearby boardinghouse. He was a friendly, good-hearted, hard-working, and dependable man. His only vice was drinking with his friends, but it never interfered with his work. His spare-time passion was crabbing in the nearby Chesapeake Bay.

In a classic case of being in the wrong place at the wrong time, Spangler was in the alley behind Ford's Theatre when Booth rode there to assassinate the president. Booth dismounted, asked Spangler to hold the reins of his horse, and went inside the theater. Spangler, who had scene-shifting duties to perform, asked another person to hold the reins and went inside to perform his duties during the play *Our American Cousin.*

In the confusion and pandemonium that reigned after Booth shot the president, jumped to the stage, and ran from the theater, observers mistakenly thought Spangler had assisted Booth, and reported this to the authorities. The unfortunate carpenter was arrested and ultimately convicted of helping Booth escape, although the military judges signaled their uncertainty of his guilt by giving him the relatively light sentence of six years.

In prison, Spangler and Mudd would become friends. Spangler taught Mudd carpentry, and Mudd credited Spangler with saving his life during the 1867 yellow fever epidemic. Spangler spent the last few months of his life at the Mudd farm, where he died in 1875.

Samuel Arnold and Michael O'Laughlen

Samuel Arnold and Michael O'Laughlen (aka O'Laughlin) were both born in 1834 and both grew up in Baltimore. Arnold's father owned one of Baltimore's largest bakeries. In 1848 he attended St. Timothy's Hall boarding school near Baltimore where he became friends with another student by the name of John Wilkes Booth. When the Civil War broke out, Arnold and two brothers joined the Confederate Army, fighting with the First Maryland Infantry. Discharged for medical reasons, Arnold worked for a while with his brother in Georgia, but returned to Baltimore in 1864.

In 1845, the Booth family bought a house across the street from the O'Laughlens. John and Mike soon became good friends. As they grew older their paths took them in separate directions, with Booth pursuing his acting career and O'Laughlen working in the family hay and feed business. When the Civil War started, O'Laughlen joined the Confederate First Maryland Infantry. He was discharged in June 1862, and then divided his time between Baltimore and his brothers' family business in Washington, D.C..

Although Arnold and O'Laughlen both grew up in Baltimore and both had served in the same Confederate Army unit, they had never met. That changed in August 1864 when John Wilkes Booth invited both men to a meeting at his Baltimore hotel room. Booth proposed to the two men a plan to capture President Lincoln and exchange him for Confederate prisoners needed to replenish the Confederate Army's ranks. Union General Grant had stopped prisoner exchanges as a way to starve the South of fighting men. To their ultimate regret, the two men agreed to join Booth's plan.

Several months passed without Booth taking any action to carry out his plan. Then, in a Washington, D.C. restaurant on March 15, 1865, Booth brought Arnold and O'Laughlen together for the first time with his other kidnap conspirators, Lewis Powell, David Herold, George Atzerodt, and John Surratt. Booth proposed that the group handcuff Lincoln in his box at Ford's Theatre, lower him by rope from the box to the theater stage, carry him out of the theater to a waiting carriage, and then flee from the city with the captured Lincoln.

Arnold, who had agreed to help capture Lincoln in a country setting, was stunned by the complete impracticality of Booth's plan, and said so. Besides, he argued, since General Grant had resumed prisoner exchanges, what was the point of continuing the kidnap plot? The meeting broke up with nothing planned.

Two days later Booth learned the president was scheduled to attend a play at Campbell Hospital on the outskirts of the city. This was more of the country setting Arnold had in mind. Booth quickly assembled the conspirators, but Lincoln had a change of schedule and never went to Campbell Hospital. At this point, Arnold and O'Laughlen concluded that the idea of kidnapping Lincoln was going nowhere, told Booth they were finished with the plot, and returned to Baltimore.

Booth assassinated President Lincoln a month later on Good Friday evening, April 14, 1865. Tracking Arnold through a letter he had written to Booth, detectives arrested Arnold at his new job at Fortress Monroe the following Monday morning. Arnold implicated O'Laughlen, who was arrested at his sister's house in Baltimore.

Arnold and O'Laughlen were as surprised as everyone else at Booth's assassination of Lincoln. They admitted they were part of Booth's original plot to kidnap Lincoln, but denied having anything to do with Lincoln's assassination. The court believed them. It spared them from hanging, but sentenced them to life imprisonment. O'Laughlen would not survive prison as the others did. He died in the prison's great 1867 yellow fever epidemic. After Mike O'Laughlen's death, Dr. Mudd said of him:

I never met with one more kind and forbearing, possessing a warm friendly disposition and a fine comprehensive intellect. I enjoyed greater ease in conversational intercourse with him than any of my prison associates.

〜

THE SIX MEN arrested as conspirators in the assassination - David Herold, Lewis Powell, George Atzerodt, Samuel Arnold, Michael O'Laughlen, and Edman Spangler - were held under close military guard on the Navy ironclads Montauk and Saugus anchored in the Eastern Branch (now Anacostia River) of the Potomac River, near the Navy Yard. A short distance downstream from the Navy Yard, where the Eastern Branch joined the main Potomac River, was the Washington Arsenal, the present-day site of Fort Lesley J. McNair.

Others arrested in connection with the Lincoln assassination were held at the Old Capitol Prison, located opposite the U.S. Capitol on the present-day site of the U. S. Supreme Court. One of those was Mary. Surratt, owner of the boardinghouse where John Wilkes Booth and his co-conspirators often met. She had been arrested on April 17th, three days after the assassination.

On April 29th, Secretary of War Edwin Stanton ordered that Mrs. Surratt and the six men being held on the Navy vessels be transferred to the penitentiary on the grounds of the Washington Arsenal. The men were transferred later that night and Mrs. Surratt the next day. Seven of the eight persons who would be tried for conspiracy were now incarcerated at the Arsenal, which would also be the site of their trial.

Dr. Mudd arrived at the Old Capitol Prison from Bryantown on April 24th. While seriously annoyed with Dr. Mudd and other Southern Marylanders who had not fully cooperated in the hunt for Booth, the government wanted to put on trial only those persons who had actually conspired with Booth to assassinate the president. Dr. Mudd was being held as a witness, not as a conspirator. But that was about to abruptly change with the arrest and interrogation of Louis Weichmann.

Louis Weichmann was arrested and brought to the Old Capitol Prison on April 30th, the same day Mrs. Surratt was moved from there to the Arsenal. Weichmann had been a boarder at Mrs. Surratt's boarding house, and was a long-time friend of her son John. Because of his closeness to the Surratts, Weichmann was terrified that the government would try him as a conspirator. John T. Ford, the owner of Ford's Theatre where President Lincoln was shot, was also under arrest at the Old Capitol Prison. A few years later, Ford recalled conversations he had with Weichmann at the prison:

It was about the 20th or 21st of April [Note: Ford's recollection was off by about 10 days] that I was accosted by a young man who said his name was Weichmann and that he had been a school mate at Charlotte Hall, Maryland with Mrs. Surratt's son, that he was holding a government position in Col. Hoffman's Commissary of Prisoners Office and that he boarded at Mrs. Surratt's house. He was greatly agitated and begged my advice as to how he should act and said that he had been away with the officers in pursuit of John H. Surratt for the purpose of identification but the trip had no result and further that he was to go before Secretary Stanton to be interrogated.

... When he urged me to advise him, he said he had no others accessible to go to who could realize his situation. I answered, simply tell the truth, be right in all you say - don't be frightened or influenced any other way.

... It was two days afterwards when we had another conversation and in the meanwhile it was known in the prison that Weichmann and others had been taken to the War Department and had an interview with Secretary Stanton. He told me of it and seemed unnerved and beyond the power to control his terror. He said Mr. Stanton had told him that the blood of the murdered president was as much on his hands as on Booth's, that his association with the other conspirators and various other incidents were sufficient to justify at least the suspicion, and he had not told the government all, which he must do for his own safety. He was during this recital shaking with freight and I could say nothing to him except a few assuring words that Mr. Stanton was a harsh lawyer and evidently had in his mind to frighten him thoroughly for a purpose. His nervous condition was so pitiful that the wags among the prisoners took advantage of it.

... It was probably two days later I met him again. He exhibited considerable self control and said he had been again to the War Department and had made up his mind to stand by the government - which he repeated several times within the few minutes we were together.

Weichmann had calmed down because he realized the government needed him as a witness against the alleged conspirators, and he knew that a person appearing as a witness could not also be tried as a defendant. If he fully cooperated with the government and truthfully told them all he knew, he had nothing to fear.

When Dr. Mudd saw Weichmann at the Old Capitol Prison, he must have become very worried. Weichmann had been at the December 1864 meeting in Washington that Dr. Mudd had with John Wilkes Booth, John Surratt, and Weichmann. Dr. Mudd had signed a sworn statement that this meeting did not happen. Booth was dead and John Surratt was in hiding. Weichmann was the only person who could tie Dr. Mudd to this meeting, and Weichmann was now under arrest and being grilled by the government.

Because of his intimate knowledge of what took place at the Surratt boarding house, Weichmann was interrogated personally by Secretary of War Edwin Stanton. In a book Weichmann wrote after the trial, he recounted Stanton's reaction when he told Stanton of Dr. Mudd's meeting with Booth:

> He [Stanton] now requested me to state who had introduced me to John Wilkes Booth. "Dr. Samuel A. Mudd," answered I. "Did you say Dr. Mudd?" queried Mr. Stanton. "Yes, sir." And then I related the story of the meeting of Booth, Mudd, Surratt, and myself...
>
> Then Stanton, half rising from his desk, and bringing down his clenched hand on the table with much force, exclaimed with great earnestness to General Burnett, "By God, put that down Burnett; it is damned important."

This changed everything. Dr. Mudd had been caught in a lie of major proportions. The government now considered Dr. Mudd to be a conspirator, not a witness. On May 4th, he was transferred to the Arsenal Penitentiary and placed in cell 176. Like the others before him, he surrendered his personal effects, was handcuffed, and had chains put on his feet. An armed guard was posted outside his cell, and the iron door shut. This cell would be his home for the next two and a half months.

DR. MUDD and the other alleged conspirators were the first prisoners the forty-year-old penitentiary had seen for three years. In 1862, the prison had been converted to a war-time storage depot for ordnance supplies. The prison contained 224 cells. One hundred and sixty of these were in a four-tier central cellblock. The other 64 were in a three-tier adjoining cellblock. The three-tiered cellblock also contained office space and quarters for the warden. Dr. Mudd and the others were held in this cellblock. The trial courtroom was conveniently located on the third floor of the warden's section.

Brevet Major-General John F. Hartranft was appointed Military Governor, or Warden, of the Arsenal Penitentiary for the duration of the trial. To avoid fraternization between guards and prisoners, a different set of soldiers was assigned to the prison each day. The soldiers were chosen from among the best in Washington, and were not told their assignment until they arrived at the prison. Guards were rotated to a different post every two hours, and were never assigned to the same post during their 24 hours of service. Prisoners were forbidden to talk to the guards, and were not allowed to have knives, spoons or other articles they might use to escape, or take their own life.

Each prisoner was manacled and confined in a separate cell, attended by a guard; and the heads of the male prisoners were enveloped in mufflers, as one of them, while on board the monitor, had endeavored to commit suicide by dashing out his brains.

During their first month at the Arsenal prison, whenever they were in their cells, the prisoners were required to wear a padded hood that covered their entire head. There was an opening at the mouth to allow for eating, but no openings to see out of. The hood was tied around the neck and induced a terrible feeling of claustrophobia. After Edman Spangler was pardoned in 1869, he wrote about the use of the hood in an article for the *New York World* newspaper, dated June 24, 1869:

"Spangler, I've something that must be told, but you must not be fright-
ened. We have orders from the Secretary of War, who must be obeyed, to
put a bag on your head." Then two men came up and tied up my head so
securely that I could not see daylight. I had plenty of food, but could not eat
with my face so muffled up. True, there was a small hole in the bag near
my mouth, but I could not reach that, as my hands were wedged down by
the iron. At last, two kind-hearted soldiers took compassion on me, and
while one watched the other fed me.

... The next morning someone came with bread and coffee. I remained
there several days, suffering torture from the bag or padded hood over my
face. It was on Sunday when it was removed and I was shaven. It was then
replaced.

... On every adjournment of the court, I was returned to my cell, and
the closely-fitting hood placed over my head. This continued until June 10,
1865, when I was relieved from the torture of the bag, but my hands and
limbs remained heavily manacled.

In his *Reminiscences of the Civil War*, General August V. Kautz, a
member of the Military Commission that tried the eight prisoners,
recalled his shocked reaction when the prisoners were brought into
court the first time on May 9th wearing hoods, chains, and black
cloaks:

The prisoners in the number of eight were brought in behind a railing.
They were masked and chained, and clad in black dominos so that we
could not identify the prisoners. The Commission decided that they must be
brought in so that we could recognize the different prisoners and be able to
identify them. The mystery and apparent severity with which they were
brought into the court room partook so much of what my imagination
pictured the Inquisition to have been, that I was quite impressed with its
impropriety in this age. The prisoners were never again brought into court
in this costume.

At some point that day, either in the courtroom or afterwards, Dr.
Mudd was not hooded like the other prisoners. General Hartranft's

superior, General Winfield Hancock, asked why he wasn't hooded. General Hartranft replied:

> *Dr. Mudd has been treated since he has been in this prison precisely the same as each of the other prisoners, except that he has not been hooded, which was in accordance with your instructions. I disclaim all intention of granting to Dr. Mudd any privileges.*

No further mention is made in the prison records of Dr. Mudd not being hooded like the other prisoners. Although the prisoners no longer wore the hated hoods in the court room, the hoods were replaced as soon as they left the court room and returned to their cells. On June 6th, General Hartranft wrote to his superior:

> *The prisoners are suffering very much from the padded hoods, and I would respectfully request that they be removed from all the prisoners except 195. This prisoner does not suffer as much as the others, and there may be some necessity for his wearing it, but I do not think there is for the others.*

Four days later, on the evening of June 10th, the hoods were removed from all the prisoners except Lewis Powell in cell 195, and never used again.

∽

THE LINCOLN CONSPIRACY TRIAL

T he public was clamoring for the government to act, and it did - with breath-taking speed. President Lincoln was shot on April 14, 1865. Two weeks later, on May 1st, President Johnson ordered creation of a Military Commission. The members of the Commission were:

MAJOR-GENERAL DAVID HUNTER, U.S. Volunteers
 Major-General Lewis Wallace, U.S. Volunteers
 Brevet Major-General August V. Kautz, U.S. Volunteers
 Brigadier-General Albion P. Howe, U.S. Volunteers
 Brigadier-General Robert S. Foster, U.S. Volunteers
 Brevet Brigadier-General James A. Ekin, U.S. Volunteers
 Brigadier-General T.M. Harris, U.S. Volunteers
 Brevet Colonel C.H. Tompkins, U.S. Army
 Lieutenant-Colonel David R. Clendenin, Eighth Illinois Cavalry

BRIGADIER-GENERAL JOSEPH HOLT, Judge Advocate General, was appointed the Judge Advocate and Recorder of the Commission.

Congressman John A. Bingham of Ohio and Brevet Colonel Henry L. Burnett were designated as Assistant Judge Advocates.

When the Commission opened the trial on May 9th, the prisoners were still frantically trying to secure defense attorneys. Dr. Mudd tried to secure the services of attorney Robert James Brent, a former Maryland Attorney General, but this was unsuccessful. At his wits end, he asked several non-lawyers to represent him.

These included his cousin Henry Alex Clarke, who owned a Washington coal company; his physician cousin, Dr. George Mudd; and another physician, Dr. James Morgan. All of these non-attorneys wisely declined to act as Dr. Mudd's legal counsel. Finally, the Mudd family was able to find legal counsel, and it was very good legal counsel. On May 11th, two powerhouse attorneys, Frederick Stone and Thomas Ewing, Jr. appeared as defense counsels for Dr. Mudd and were accepted by the court.

Frederick Stone was a highly respected lawyer from Port Tobacco, Maryland. Born in 1820, he grew up in Charles County, Maryland and graduated from St. John's College in Annapolis. He was admitted to the bar in 1841. Frederick Stone was the grandson of Michael J. Stone, the younger brother of Thomas Stone, a signer of the Declaration of Independence. He was a member of the Maryland House of Delegates in 1864 and 1865, and a Member of Congress from 1867 to 1871, representing Maryland's Fifth Congressional District where Dr. Mudd lived. From 1881 to 1890 he was an Associate Judge of the Maryland Court of Appeals.

Thomas Ewing, now a civilian attorney, had served with great distinction as a Union Major-General during the Civil War. He was born to a prominent Ohio family in 1829. His father was a U.S. Senator, and his brothers Hugh and Charles were also Union generals. His brother-in-law was Union General William Tecumseh Sherman.

At the age of 19, young Thomas Ewing Jr. worked as private secretary to President Zachary Taylor. He studied law at Cincinnati Law School and was admitted to the bar in 1855. He subsequently married and practiced law in Leavenworth, Kansas. In 1861 he was elected the first Chief Justice of the Supreme Court in the new state of Kansas.

When the Civil War broke out, he resigned as Chief Justice to serve as a Colonel in the Eleventh Kansas Volunteers. He was soon promoted to Brigadier-General, and then to Major-General. He would take the lead role in Dr. Mudd's defense.

Counsels for Mary Surratt also appeared and were accepted by the court on May 11th. Defense counsels for the other defendants were arranged shortly thereafter.

~

WITH THE TRIAL UNDERWAY, an observer described the scene in the courtroom:

A large room in the north-east corner of the third story of the old Peniten-tiary, near the cells in which the prisoners were confined, was fitted up for the trial. It is about thirty by forty-five feet square, with a ceiling about eleven feet high, supported by three wooden pillars. Four windows, with heavy iron gratings, afforded tolerable ventilation; and there are two ante-rooms for the accommodation of the court and of the witnesses. The room was whitewashed and painted for the occasion, a prisoner's dock was constructed along the western side. The floor was covered with cocoa-nut matting, and the tables and chairs were new. Gas was introduced, in case the court should protract its sittings until after dark.

The members of the Court, who were all in full uniform, took their seats around a large table parallel with the north side of the room... At the foot of the table at which the Court sat was another, occupied by Judge Advocate General Holt, with his Assistants, Hon. Mr. Bingham and Colonel Burnett. On this table, as the trial progressed, were deposited the weapons deposited by witnesses, the machine used by the Rebel War Department as a key to communications written in cipher, the articles found on the dead assassin's person, with a mass of law-books, notes of testimony, &c.

In the center of the room was a stand for witnesses... Behind the witness-stand, and parallel with the southern side of the room, was a long table, which was occupied by reporters and correspondents during the public sessions of the court. At the foot of this table sat the counsel for the prisoners after they had been introduced.

The prisoner's "dock" was a platform raised about one foot from the floor, and about four feet broad, with a strong railing in front of it. Along this "dock" sat the prisoners. Mrs. Surratt had the left-hand corner to herself; a passage-way to the door leading to the cells intervening between her and the seven male prisoners, who sat sandwiched with six soldiers who wore the light-blue uniform of the Veteran Reserve Corps. Dr. Mudd wore handcuffs connected with chains; but the "bracelets" of the other male prisoners were joined by wide bars of iron ten inches long, which kept their hands apart. All of the prisoners, including Mrs. Surratt, wore anklets connected by short chains, which hamper their walk; and heavy iron balls were also attached by chains to the limbs of Payne and Atzerodt, attendants carrying them as they go to and from their cells. As the prisoners entered and left the room, their fetters clanking at every step, they formed an impressive procession. As seen by the court and the gentlemen of the press, they sat in the following order:

Samuel Arnold, a young Baltimorean, had a rather intelligent face, with curly brown hair and restless dark eyes. He was a schoolmate of the president's assassin; and, at the breaking-out of the Rebellion, he joined the rebel army. An original conspirator, his courage failed him; and he went some weeks before the assassination to Fortress Monroe, where he was clerk to a sutler when arrested.

Samuel A. Mudd, M.D., was the most inoffensive and decent in appearance of all the prisoners. He was about forty years of age, rather tall, and quite thin, with sharp features, a high forehead, astute blue eyes, compressed pale lips, and sandy hair, whiskers, and mustache. He took a deep interest in the testimony, often prompting his counsel during the cross-examinations.

Edward Spangler was a middle-aged man, with a large, unintelligent-looking face, evidently swollen by an intemperate use of ardent spirits, a low forehead, anxious-looking gray eyes, and brown hair. He was born in the interior of Pennsylvania, where he has respectable connections; and, after having been employed in Ford's Theater in Baltimore as a stage-carpenter, came to Washington with Mr. Ford when he built the house in *which Mr. Lincoln was assassinated. Doleful as Spangler looked when in court, the guards declared that he was the most loquacious and jovial of the prisoners when he was in his cell.*

Michael O'Laughlin, like Arnold, was a Baltimore friend of the principal assassin, and at one time a soldier in the rebel army. He was a rather small, delicate-looking man, with rather pleasing features, uneasy black eyes, bushy black hair, a heavy black mustache and imperial, and a most anxious expression of countenance, shaded by a sad, remorseful look.

George B. Atzerodt was a type of those Teutonic Dugald Dalgettys who have taken an active part in the war for the suppression of the Rebellion, - sometimes on one side, and sometimes on the other, as bounties, or chances to pillage, were presented. He was born in Germany, but was raised and lived among the "poor white trash" in Charles County, Md.; working as a blacksmith until the war broke out, when he became a blockade-runner. He was a short, thick-set, round-shouldered, brawny-armed man, with a stupid expression, high cheek-bones, a sallow complexion, small grayish-blue eyes, tangled light-brown hair, and straggling sandy whiskers and mustache. He apparently manifested a stoical indifference to what was going on in the Court, although an occasional cat-like glance would reveal his anxiety concerning himself. Evidently crafty, cowardly, and mercenary, his own safety was evidently the all-absorbing subject of his thoughts.

Lewis Payne was the observed of all observers, as he sat motionless and imperturbed, defiantly returning each gaze at his remarkable face and person. He was very tall, with an athletic, gladiatorial frame; the tight knit shirt, which was his only upper garment disclosing the massive robustness of animal manhood in its most stalwart type. Neither intellect nor intelligence was discernible in his unflinching dark gray eyes, low forehead, massive jaws, compressed full lips, small nose with large nostrils and stolid, remorseless expression. His dark hair hung over his forehead, his face was beardless, and his hands were not those of a man who had been accustomed to labor. Report said that he was a Kentuckian by birth, and one of a family of notorious desperadoes; one of his brothers having been such a depraved criminal, that the rebels hung him. But, for weeks after the trial commenced, all that was certainly known of him was, that he was the ruffian who made the ferocious series of assaults on Secretary Seward and his family.

David E. Herold was a doltish, insignificant-looking young man, not much over one and twenty years of age, with a slender frame, and irreso-lute, cowardly appearance. He had a narrow forehead, a somewhat Israelitish nose, small dark hazel eyes, thick black hair, and an incipient mustache which occupied much of his attention. Few would imagine that any villain would select such a contemptible-looking fellow as an accomplice.

Mrs. Mary E. Surratt, who was a belle in her youth, had borne her five and forty years or more bravely; and, when she raised her veil in court that some witness might identify her, she exposed rather pleasing features, with dark gray eyes and brown hair... Whether she was guilty or innocent, it was easy to perceive that she desired to make a favorable impression upon the court, and to inspire feelings of pity.

The trial lasted from May 9, 1865 to June 30, 1865. Testimony concerning Dr. Mudd was presented intermittently during the course of the trial. The prosecution called 16 witnesses to testify against Dr. Mudd. The defense, led by General Ewing, called more than 60 witnesses to testify in his defense. The government's charge against Dr. Mudd alleged that he was part of the plot to assassinate the president, and that he aided Booth's escape after the assassination. It said:

And in further prosecution of said conspiracy, the said Samuel A. Mudd did, at Washington City, and within the military department and military lines aforesaid, on or before the 6th day of March, A.D. 1865, and on divers other days between that day and the 20th day of April, A.D. 1865, advise, encourage, receive, entertain, harbor, and conceal, aid and assist, the said John Wilkes Booth, David E. Herold, Lewis Payne, John H. Surratt, Michael O'Laughlin, George A. Atzerodt, Mary E. Surratt, and Samuel Arnold, and their confederates, with knowledge of the murderous and treacherous conspiracy aforesaid, and with the intent to aid, abet, and assist them in the execution thereof, and in escaping from justice after the

murder of the said Abraham Lincoln, in pursuance of said conspiracy in
manner aforesaid.

March 6, 1865 was the date of Lincoln's second inauguration. April
20, 1865 was the day the government offered a $100,000 reward for
the capture of John Wilkes Booth, David Herold, and John Surratt,
and threatened the death penalty for anyone aiding their escape.

TESTIMONY at the trial failed to show that Dr. Mudd was part of the
plot to assassinate the president, but did convince the Commission
that Dr. Mudd aided Booth's escape by misleading the authorities
about Booth's visit. General August V. Kautz, one of the nine
members of the Military Commission that tried the eight alleged
conspirators, said:

> *Dr. Mudd attracted much interest and his guilt as an active conspirator*
> *was not clearly made out. His main guilt was the fact that he failed to*
> *deliver them, that is, Booth and Herold, to their pursuers.*

General Kautz's judgement would be echoed in President Johnson's 1869 pardon of Dr. Mudd, which said in part:

> *I am satisfied that the guilt found by the said judgment against Samuel A.*
> *Mudd was of receiving, entertaining, harboring, and concealing John*
> *Wilkes Booth and David E. Herold, with the intent to aid, abet and assist*
> *them in escaping from justice after the assassination of the late President of*
> *the United States, and not of any other or greater participation or*
> *complicity in said abominable crime.*

When the trial was over on June 30th, all eight defendants were
convicted. The official records of the trial contain no information
about how each of the nine military judges voted as individuals.
However, six or more of the military judges must have voted Guilty

for David Herold, George Atzerodt, Lewis Powell, and Mary Surratt since a two-thirds or greater majority vote was required for the death penalty. Five of the nine judges must have voted Guilty for Dr. Mudd, Edman Spangler, Samuel Arnold, and Michael O'Laughlen since a 5-4 vote would have convicted them, but not resulted in execution.

On July 5th, President Johnson approved the sentences of the Military Commission and issued the following Executive Order:

Executive Mansion, July 5, 1865.

The foregoing sentences in the cases of David E. Herold, G. A. Atzerodt, Lewis Payne, Michael O'Laughlin, Edward Spangler, Samuel Arnold, Mary E. Surratt, and Samuel A. Mudd, are hereby approved, and it is ordered that the sentences of said David E. Herold, G. A. Atzerodt, Lewis Payne, and Mary E. Surratt be carried into execution by the proper military authority, under the direction of the Secretary of War, on the 7th day of July, 1865, between the hours of 10 o'clock, A.M., and 2 o'clock, P.M., of that day. It was further ordered, that the prisoners, Samuel Arnold, Samuel A. Mudd, Edward Spangler, and Michael O'Laughlin be confined at hard labor in the Penitentiary at Albany, New York, during the period designated in their respective sentences.

Andrew Johnson, President.

Lewis Powell, David Herold, George Atzerodt, and Mary Surratt were quickly hanged as ordered on July 7th.

A week after the executions, President Johnson issued a second Executive Order, changing the location where Dr. Mudd, Spangler, O'Laughlen, and Arnold would be imprisoned from the penitentiary at Albany to the military prison in the Dry Tortugas islands of Florida. The four men were not told of the change of plans. The second Executive Order read:

Executive Mansion July 15, 1865

The Executive Order, dated July 5, 1865, approving the sentences in the cases of Samuel Arnold, Samuel A. Mudd, Edward Spangler, and Michael O'Laughlin is hereby modified, so as to direct that the said Arnold, Mudd,

Spangler, and O'Laughlin, be confined at hard labor in the military prison at Dry Tortugas, Florida, during the period designated in their respective sentences.

The Adjutant-General of the Army is directed to issue orders for the said prisoners to be transported to the Dry Tortugas, and to be confined there accordingly.

Andrew Johnson, President

Two days later, July 17, 1865, the *New York Tribune* carried a story about Dr. Mudd and his three companions following the end of the trial. About Dr. Mudd, it said:

Mudd seems in very good spirits over his escape from the gallows. He says very little about the trial. He acknowledged that the testimony of the witness Weichmann in reference to himself is correct.

If Dr. Mudd was quoted correctly, his statement that Weichmann's testimony was correct is his first admission that he lied about not seeing Booth between November 1864 and the morning after the assassination. He would make the same admission to others during his trip to the Dry Tortugas.

FORT JEFFERSON

Fort Jefferson

At 1 o'clock in the morning on Monday, July 17, 1865, a soldier awakened Dr. Mudd, Spangler, Arnold, and O'Laughlen in their cells at Washington's Arsenal prison and ordered them to get up. The four men were taken in irons to a nearby wharf on the Potomac River where they were put aboard a former Army hospital ship, the steamer State of Maine.

About 2 o'clock in the morning, the State of Maine quietly pulled away from the wharf and picked up speed as it slipped through the night down the Potomac River. By dawn the ship was in the Chesapeake Bay, and by afternoon it arrived at Fortress Monroe, located at Hampton, Virginia, where the Chesapeake Bay empties into the Atlantic Ocean.

One of the ships lying at anchor off Fortress Monroe that afternoon was the U.S.S. Florida, a 1,261-ton wooden side-wheel steamship the Navy had used to help enforce the blockade of the Atlantic coast of the Confederacy. It was used to carry Union supplies down the Atlantic coast to the Gulf of Mexico, and to transport Confederate prisoners to New York. The Florida's commander, Captain William Budd, had orders to take on some very special passengers.

Once Dr. Mudd and the other prisoners had been transferred to the Florida, the anchor was pulled up and the Florida steamed out into the Atlantic Ocean, where it turned due south. As the ship continued in its southerly direction, the prisoners began to realize they were not going to Albany.

In a 1902 newspaper article, Samuel Arnold wrote:

No sooner were we upon the gunboat than we were ordered into the lower hold of the vessel. It required, in our shackled condition, the greatest care to safely reach there, owing to the limited space, eight inches of chain being allowed between our ankles. After leaving the second deck we were forced to descend upon a ladder whose rounds were distant so far apart that the chains bruised and lacerated the flesh and even the bone of the ankles. We remained in the sweltering hole during the night in an atmosphere pregnant with disagreeable odors, arising from various articles of subsistence stored within, and about 8 o'clock next morning we passed through another ordeal in our ascent to the deck, which was attended with more pain than the descent, owing to the raw condition of our wounds.

All intercourse with the crew was prohibited, guards being stationed around us, and we were not permitted to move without being accompanied by an armed marine. Subsistence of the grossest kind was issued, in the shape of fat salt pork and hard-tack. We remained on deck during the day, closely watching, as far as we were able, the steering of the vessel by the sun, and found we were steaming due South. The course was unchanged the next day and I began to suspect that fatal isle, the Dry Tortugas, was our destined home of the future.

From this time out we remained on deck, our beds being brought up at night and taken between decks in the morning. Arriving off Hilton Head, S.C., and whilst lying in port, we were informed by General Dodd that he was sailing under sealed orders, but as soon as we left the port he would announce our destination. We remained there during the night, having received some guests on board, and the officers amused themselves with dancing and carousing. About 12 o'clock in the day we were informed that the Dry Tortugas was our destination. Of it I had no idea beyond that gathered through the columns of the press, in which it had been depicted as a perfect hell, which fact was duly established by imprisonment on its limited space. After the second day on the ocean the irons were removed from our feet during the day, but replaced at night, and we were permitted from this day out the privilege of being on deck on account of the oppressive heat of the climate, where we could catch the cool sea breeze as it swept across the deck in the ship's onward track over the bounding ocean.

During the voyage to Fort Jefferson, Edman Spangler wrote a short letter to a friend that was printed in the Washington Evening Star:

A gentleman in this city received a letter from Spangler, written previous to his arrival at the Dry Tortugas, written with a lead pencil, as follows:

On Board St'r Florida, bound to the Island of Dry Tortugas, Fla. — Friend: Still thinking of old times, and wishing I was seated in your saloon drinking a nice glass of whiskey, instead of in this hot and sunny clime. The last drink I had was in your house, and you may put it down as a settled fact it will be the last for six long years to come, and may be forever before I get another. You must not forget me now in my sunny home. When joy shall swell your heart, and the welkin is made to ring with the light and

*cheerful voices of yourself and my former companions, stop for a moment
to cast a lingering but bright thought upon him who was life, all life,
amidst you, wish him a companion of your festival, and I will feel happy in
my exile – banished and in a burning clime – Dry Tortugas, thirteen
hundred miles from you. Extend your hospitality to the gentleman who
brings this to you. Good bye: sometimes think of me and my companions,
though they are unknown to you personally. – Edward Spangler*

CONSTRUCTION OF FORT JEFFERSON had begun in 1846, and was still
underway when Dr. Mudd and his companions arrived. Inside the
fort there was a large central parade ground surrounded by soldiers'
living quarters, gunpowder magazines, storehouses, and other buildings necessary for construction. The Army employed civilian
machinists, carpenters, blacksmiths, masons, general laborers, military prisoners, and slaves to help construct the fort. Slaves were no
longer employed after the 1863 Emancipation Proclamation.

Fort Jefferson's peak military population was 1,729. In addition, a
number of officers brought their families, and a limited number of
enlisted personnel brought wives. There were also a lighthouse
keeper and his family, cooks, and many others. In all, there were close
to 2,000 people at Fort Jefferson during its peak years. It was a
crowded place, in a small space.

With the war over, the population began to quickly decline. It had
dropped to 1,013 by the time Dr. Mudd arrived in July 1865. Of these,
486 were soldiers or civilians and 527 were prisoners. The military
prisoners at Fort Jefferson were a rough crowd. Their offenses
included murder, manslaughter, robbery, grand larceny, and deser-
tion. Standing orders said:

*If a prisoner refuses to obey orders the sentinel must shoot him, and then
use his bayonet, at the same time calling for the guard.*

Construction of Fort Jefferson continued throughout the time he was imprisoned there and for several years thereafter, but was never completely finished.

Sam Arnold described the arrival of the U.S.S. Florida at Fort Jefferson:

We arrived in sight of Fort Jefferson, Dry Tortugas, Fla., on July 24, 1865. When nearing the grim-looking walls, a signal gun was fired from the gunboat, which was responded to by the officer in command of the fort, and soon the officer of the day made his appearance on board, and was informed of the object of the visit of the boat, etc. Within a very short time we were placed within a small boat, were conveyed to the fort, and placed within one of the many casemates existing there.

The officers who had had us in charge remained at the fort a sufficient length of time to have, as it is called, a lark. After three months of torture both of body and mind, we thought that we had at last found a haven of rest, although in a government Bastile, where, shut out from the world, we would dwell and pass the remaining days of our life. It was a sad thought, yet it had to be borne.

We were now left under the charge of Col. Charles Hamilton, 110th New York Volunteers, who was at that period commandant of the post. He gave us instructions relative to the rules in force, stating the consequences which would attend any breach in discipline, finally impressing upon our minds that there was a dark and gloomy dungeon within the fort, to which offenders against the rules were consigned, over whose entrance was inscribed the classic words: Whoso entereth here leaveth all hope behind.

Each new prisoner was given a number. Arnold was prisoner 1523, Dr. Mudd was prisoner 1524, O'Laughlen was prisoner 1525, and Spangler was prisoner 1526.

Dr. Mudd and his companions were assigned to work according to their skills. Dr. Mudd was assigned to work in the prison hospital. Arnold was assigned to clerical work. Spangler was assigned to the carpentry shop. O'Laughlen was assigned to work as a laborer helping with construction of the fort.

Following is the first letter Mrs. Mudd received from her husband after his arrival at Fort Jefferson. Her family called her Frank, short for Frances, her middle name.

Fort Jefferson, Dry Tortugas, Florida, August 24, 1865

Dearest Frank:

To-day one month ago we arrived here. Time passes very slowly and seems longer than that period - years gone by, apparently no longer. What do you think? I have received no letter or news whatever from home since being here. One or two of those who came down with me have received letters, containing no news, and do not advert to the possibility or the subject of release.

You know, my dear Frank, that that subject is the all absorbing one of my mind. Frank must be sick — the little children are sick — some may be dead, or some other misfortune has happened, are questions frequently revolving in my mind and heart, and the dear ones at home are unwilling to break the cruel intelligence to me.

My dear Frank, were it not for you and those at home, I could pass the balance of my days here perfectly content or satisfied. Without you and the children, what is life for me - a blank, a void. Then, my dear Frank, if you have any regard for me, which you know I have never doubted, let me hear from you and often. I have written to you by every mail that has left this place, and surely some have been received. I wrote to you aboard the boat before arriving here. Mail, sometimes, arrives here in five days from New York.

This place continues to be unusually healthy, and the only fear manifested is that disease may be propagated by the arrival of vessels and steamers from infected ports. At this time there is a vessel lying at quarantine with all hands aboard sick with fever of some description, — several have died, and there is not one well enough to nurse the sick — no volunteers from among the prisoners going to them, so the chances of life are small.

I am now in the hospital. I have little or no labor to perform, but my fare is not much improved. My principal diet is coffee, butter and bread three times a day. We have had a mess or two of Irish potatoes and onions, but as a general thing vegetables don't last many days in this climate before decomposition takes place.

Pork and beef are poisonous to me; and molasses when I am able to buy it, and occasionally (fresh) fish, when Providence favored, are the only articles of diet used. I am enjoying very good health, considering the circumstances.

Sweet, dearest Frank, write to me soon on the receipt of my letter. I am afraid letters have been intercepted from either you or myself. If I don't hear from you soon, I am afraid I will become alike indifferent and careless. I have written to Jere, Ewing, Stone, Ma and Papa some several letters - others, one or two, and not one syllable have I received.

I am afraid when the silence is broken, the news will be so great as to endanger the safety of the boat. My dear Frank, I have nothing to interest you — several hundred prisoners have been released and gone home recently to their families.

My anxiety increases upon the arrival of every boat and mail, and I envy the departing homeward bound.

Give my love to all - kiss the children and believe me,

Truly and sincerely, your husband, S.A. MUDD

THROUGHOUT HIS ENTIRE IMPRISONMENT, Dr. Mudd experienced a dizzying roller coaster ride of rising hopes for imminent release followed by sinking drops to the depths of despair as such hopes were dashed. His hopes for release were fed by well-wishing family members, various friends, and lawyers. In letters home he would often speak hopefully of his imminent release based on their encouragement. When such hopes were routinely dashed, he finally asked that people stop telling him he was going to be released. But of course they didn't stop, and Dr. Mudd's roller coaster ride of hope and despair continued for almost four years.

President Andrew Johnson was the source of much of the optimism for Dr. Mudd's release. From the very beginning of Dr. Mudd's imprisonment, President Johnson made regular private promises to

Mrs. Mudd and others that he would release Dr. Mudd as soon as he could politically do so. One of Johnson's promises was recounted in a letter that Jeremiah Dyer wrote to his sister, Mrs. Mudd.

In the letter, John Ford, owner of Ford's Theatre, said President Johnson thought that Dr. Mudd *was a mere creature of accident, and ought not to have been put there.* Nevertheless, Johnson did keep him there because, as he told Ford, he feared his political enemies would use Dr. Mudd's release against him. Dr. Mudd's pardon would surely have provided the basis for more political attacks against Johnson, and could conceivably have cost him the presidency.

THE ATTEMPTED ESCAPE

In September 1865, two months after Dr. Mudd arrived, control of Fort Jefferson was transferred from the 161st New York Volunteers to the 82nd U. S. Colored Infantry. Prisoners had received good treatment under the 161st, but as a recent slave owner and a person convicted of conspiring to kill the president who had freed the slaves, Dr. Mudd was fearful of his treatment by the incoming black troops. On September 25, 1865, he attempted to escape from Fort Jefferson by stowing away on the visiting Army transport ship Thomas A. Scott. He was discovered, returned to the fort, and placed at hard labor.

Fort Jefferson's commanding officer, Major George E. Wentworth, filed a report on Dr. Mudd's escape attempt:

Hdqrs Fort Jefferson Fla., September 27, 1865.

Sir:

I have the honor to report that this morning upon searching the U. S. Transport Thos A Scott before her departure for New York, Dr Saml A Mudd was found secreted in the Lower Hold of the vessel under some planks. I immediately placed him in the dungeon in irons. From the position in which he was found I thought that he must have secured aid from some Party or Parties on board the steamer.

I went to the dungeon in which Dr Mudd was confined, and threatened him with some punishment unless he disclosed the name of the parties who assisted him.

He at last stated that a man by the name of Kelly, one of the crew of the steamer, assisted him. I immediately ordered his arrest and now have him confined in irons.

From the evidence of one James Healy, Coal Passer on the Steamer Scott whose deposition has been taken, I am of the opinion that Kelley was bribed by Dr. Mudd as I understand that he Mudd has offered money to parties here to get them to do him favors.

Henry Kelley is a young man. I should think about 18 years old. I would respectfully request that orders be given me in regard to the disposition of this man Kelly.

I am Very Respectfully

Your Obt. Serv't, George E. Wentworth, Major 82d. U.S.C. Infty, Commanding

Dr. Mudd apologized to Major Wentworth for having tried to escape. He wrote:

To the Major Commanding

Sir,

I acknowledge to having acted contrary to my own judgment & honor, in my attempted escape. I assure you it was more from the impulse of the moment & with the hope of speedily seeing my disconsolate wife & four little infants. Mr. Kelly did not secrete me aboard, but, promised to do so only. Before I was detected I had made up my mind to return if I could do so without being observed by the guards. I am truly ashamed of my conduct, & if I am restored again to the freedom of the Fort & former position, no cause shall arise to create your displeasure, & I shall always counsel subordination to the ruling authorities. By complying or relieving me from my present humble locality - you will merit the gratitude of your humble servant, a devoted wife & four dear little children. I do not

*complain of the punishment, but I feel that I have abused the kindness &
confidence reposed, & would be glad exceedingly to comply with any other
honorable acquirement, whereby, I may be able to wash away, the folly of
my weakness.*

> *TRULY & RESPECTFULLY YRS &c*
> *SAML. A MUDD*

DR. MUDD DESCRIBED his attempted escape and its aftermath in three
letters to his wife's brother Jeremiah Dyer. The first letter said:

Fort Jefferson, Tortugas Island, Fla., September 30, 1865.

> *My dear Jere:*
>
> *I wrote to you and Frank by the last steamer, but at the same time
> intended to arrive before it. Providence was against me. I was too well
> known and was apprehended five or ten minutes after being aboard the
> steamer. They were so much rejoiced at finding me, they did not care to
> look much farther; the consequence was, the boat went off and carried
> away four other prisoners, who no doubt will make good their escape. I
> suppose this attempt of mine to escape will furnish the dealers in newspa-
> pers matter for comment, and a renewal of the calumnious charges against
> me. Could the world know to what a degraded condition the prisoners of
> this place have been reduced recently, they, instead of censure, would give
> me credit for making the attempt. This place is now wholly guarded by
> negro troops with the exception of a few white officers. I was told by
> members of the 161st N.Y.V. Reg., that so soon as they departed, the pris-
> oners would be denied many of their former privileges, and life would be
> very insecure in their hands. This has already proved true; a parcel of new
> rules and regulations have already been made and are being enforced,
> which sensibly decreases our former liberties.*
>
> *For attempting to make my escape, I was put in the guard-house, with
> chains on hands and feet, and closely confined for two days. An order then
> came from the Major for me to be put to hard labor, wheeling sand. I was
> placed under a boss, who put me to cleaning old bricks. I worked hard all*

day, and came very near finishing one brick. The order also directs the Provost Marshal to have me closely confined on the arrival of every steamer and until she departs. I know not how long this state of things will continue. I have arrived at that state of mind at which I feel indifferent to what treatment I am subjected. The 161st N.Y. Reg. were very kind and generous to me, and I was as much induced by them to make the attempt to take French leave as my own inclination and judgment dictated. I am now thrown out of my former position, chief of dispensary, and not likely to be reinstated. I know not what degree of degradation they may have in store for me. I was forced, under the penalty of being shot, to inform on one of the crew who promised to secrete me aboard. They have him still in close confinement, and will likely try him before court martial for the offense. I have written a note to the Major and have seen the Provost Marshal, and have taken upon myself the whole blame and responsibility of the affair, yet they pay little or no attention, and the young fellow is still kept in close confinement.

I don't regret the loss of my position. Take away the honor attached, the labor was more confining than any other place or avocation on the island. At the same time it relieved me of the disagreeable necessity of witnessing men starve for the nutriment essential for a sick man, when it could be had with no trouble and but a little expense. Four prisoners have died during the short time I have been here; the last one died the morning I made my attempt to escape. Not a single soldier or citizen laborer has died or suffered with any serious sickness; thereby showing something wrong, something unfair, and a distinction made between the two classes of individuals. Every case of acute dysentery or diarrhea among the prisoners, either dies in the onset or lingers on and terminates in the chronic, which eventually kills.

We have a disease here which is termed bone fever, or mild yellow fever, which has attacked at least three-fourths of the inmates of the Fort. It lasts generally but two or three days; during the time, the patient imagines every bone will break from the enormous pain he suffers in his limbs. None has died with it.

I have not been a day sick or unwell, owing no doubt to the fact of my thoughts being concentrated upon home, my dear Frank, and the children. Little did I think I would ever become the veriest slave and lose the control of my own actions, but such, unfortunately, is too true, and God, I suppose, only knows whether these misfortunes will terminate with my frail existence, or that after being broken down with cares and afflictions of every kind, I be returned to my family a burden, more than a help and consoler. My only hope now is with you and the influence you can bring to bear. To be relieved from my present situation, I would be willing to live in poverty the balance of my days with Heaven my only hope of reward. If money be necessary, sell everything that I possess, and what might be allotted by poor Papa from his already exhausted means.

I feel that I am able now, and have resolution to make a decent living in any section of the world in which I am thrown by the Grace and Providence of the Almighty.

It strikes me that the Hon. Reverdy Johnson, Montgomery Blair, and many others whose principles and opinions are growing daily more popular - their influence could be easily brought to bear in my behalf. You fail to give me any idea of what was being done or any reasons for me to hope for relief by any certain time. You may have omitted this for prudential reasons. I have been too careless in my language among the evil disposed. They have never failed to misinterpret my language and meaning, and to omit everything having a tendency to exonerate me.

Knowing this, I shall be the keeper or guardian of my own thoughts and words for the future. I never knew how corrupt the world was before being visited by my recent calamities and troubles. They have shamefully lied and detracted everything I have said or done - a privilege for the future they shall never have.

No doubt they will get up a great sensation in regard to my attempted escape. Some thirty or forty have made their escape, or attempts to do so, since I have been here, and there never was anything thought of them. Since my unlucky attempt, everything seems to have been put in commotion, and most unfounded suspicions, rumors, etc., started.

My only object for leaving at the time I attempted, was to avoid the greater degradation, and insecurity of life, and at the same time be united again with my precious little family. I don't perceive why there is so much *odium attached, as the authorities, by their harsh and cruel treatment, endeavor to make believe.*

I will soon be returned to some duty more compatible with my qualifications. In the mean time, assure Frank and all that I am well and hearty, and as determined as ever. Write soon. Give my unbounded love to all at home, and believe me most truly and devotedly,

    Yours, etc., S.A. MUDD

DR. MUDD's second letter to Jeremiah Dyer said:

Oct. 1st. -

I am constrained before mailing this, to acquaint you with the following: The young man Kelly, and Smith who was locked up with him, and bound with chains and thrown in a place they denominate the dungeon, on my account, freed themselves from their chains, broke out the iron-grated window, let themselves down from the window by the chains with which they were bound, stole a boat, and made good their escape last night.

Smith was one of the most outrageous thieves that ever walked. You would marvel to hear him tell of his wonderful feats and thefts. Kelly promised to secrete me aboard the steamer, and to save my life, I was necessitated to inform on him. He was brought to the same room in which I was locked. He excused me, and said that the Commandant was a fool to think that they could hold him upon this island, which has proved too true. The authorities are no doubt much disappointed and chagrined at this unexpected occurrence. I feel much relieved.

    Yours as ever, etc., SAM

DR. MUDD's third letter to Jeremiah Dyer said:

Fort Jefferson, Dry Tortugas, Fla., October 5, 1865.

    My dear Jere:

A vessel is about leaving port. I take advantage of it to drop you a few hasty lines. I forgot to mention, in the letters previously written, to inform you that none of the drafts, that I drew upon you, will be presented for payment. I was fortunate in being able to borrow twenty-five dollars; the check, so soon as I can obtain the money, will go to liquidate it. I shall endeavor to be as economical as possible, knowing to what straits my family has been already reduced. The only need I have for money is to purchase a few vegetables, and supply myself with tobacco. The only article of clothing I need is shirts. The Government furnishes flannel shirts, which I find very pleasant in damp weather, but very disagreeable and warm in dry sunshine.

If the friends of Arnold and O'Laughlin should send a box of clothing to them, you may put in a couple of brown linen, or check linen, shirts and a couple pairs cotton drawers. You may not bother yourself to this extent if you anticipate an early release. My clothing is sufficient to come home in. I will need no more money before the first of December, or latter part of November. It generally takes a letter ten or twelve days to reach this place, so anticipate the period, and send me twenty-five dollars in greenbacks. Address your letters to me, and not in care of anyone, and I will get them without fail. Write me soon and let me know whether my attempted escape caused much comment in the Northern papers. I fear it will have the effect to again agitate the question. I had written so often and desired information and council, that I became truly impatient and vexed. I expected to hear something from Ewing or Stone, but not a word have I received from either. I received a letter a few days ago which gave me more consolation and hope than any yet come to hand, from Henry. Had I received such a letter earlier I would have been content, and would never have acted as I did. I would have succeeded, only for meeting a party aboard, who knew me, before I could arrive at my hiding-place. I was informed on almost immediately, and was taken in custody by the guard. I regret only one thing, being necessitated to inform on the party who had promised to befriend me. It was all done by the mere slip of the tongue, and without reflection; but perhaps it was all providential. He is now free, having made good his escape with a notorious thief with whom he was locked up. I understand, after escaping from the dungeon in which they were confined, they robbed *the sutler of fifty dollars in money, as much clothing as they needed, and a plenty of eatables in the way of canned fruits, preserves, meats, etc. Six prisoners made good their escape on the same boat upon which I was so unfortunate. It seems they were too much elated to look farther after my apprehension.*

I am taking my present hardship as a joke. I am not put back in the least. I will soon assume my former position, or one equally respectable. The only thing connected with my present attitude is the name, and not the reality. I have no labor to perform, yet I am compelled to answer roll-call, and to sleep in the guard-house at night. This will not last longer than this week. Write soon, give me all the news, and continue to send me papers. I have received several from you, Frank, and some have been sent from New York by unknown parties, which afforded me considerable recreation. Give my love to all at home, and send this, after reading, to Frank, so that she may know that I am well, etc. I am sorry Tom is going to leave so early. I am under the greatest obligations to him for interest and kindness manifested. I am in hopes my release won't be long deferred, when I shall be able to see you all.

SAMUEL MUDD

Dr. Mudd also wrote to his wife about his escape attempt:

Oct. 1st. - I am constrained before mailing this, to acquaint you with the following: The young man Kelly, and Smith who was locked up with him, and bound with chains and thrown in a place they denominate the dungeon, on my account, freed themselves from their chains, broke out the iron-grated window, let themselves down from the window by the chains with which they were bound, stole a boat, and made good their escape last night.

Smith was one of the most outrageous thieves that ever walked. You would marvel to hear him tell of his wonderful feats and thefts. Kelly promised to secrete me aboard the steamer, and to save my life, I was necessitated to inform on him. He was brought to the same room in which I was locked. He excused me, and said that the Commandant was a fool to think that they could hold him upon this island, which has proved too true. The authorities are no doubt much disappointed and chagrined at this unexpected occurrence. I feel much relieved.

Yours as ever, etc., SAM

THE DUNGEON

Following Dr. Mudd's failed escape attempt he was placed in a small cell in the guardhouse, located next to the Sally Port entrance. After a couple of days, he was allowed outside to work during the day, but was required to sleep in the guardhouse at night.

On October 18th, he was transferred along with Arnold, O'Laughlen, Spangler, and Colonel George St. Leger Grenfell to a large empty ground-level gunroom in the bastion at the south end of the Sally Port wall. This was the *"dark and gloomy dungeon"* Dr. Mudd and his companions were warned about when they arrived at Fort Jefferson.

Spangler, Arnold, and O'Laughlen were transferred to the dungeon along with Dr. Mudd because the authorities had heard, incorrectly, that there was a plan under way to free the four men.

The fifth man in the dungeon was Colonel George St. Leger Grenfell, a former officer in the Confederate Army.

The dungeon was the most secure place in the fort. It had a locked wooden door, a slate floor, slimy wet brick walls and ceiling, and two gun ports. Although one port was open, the other was closed with metal shutters. As a result, there was no cross ventilation and the light admitted by the single open port was insufficient to brighten the room. Immediately outside the small open port was an area where the fort's toilets, called sinks, emptied into the 70-foot wide moat. The architects had assumed the moat would be flushed clean by tidal action, but that often didn't happen. Inside the dungeon, the smell from the moat was inescapable. In a letter he wrote from the dungeon, Dr. Mudd said:

> *The atmosphere we breathe is highly impregnated with sulphuric hydrogen gas, which you are aware is highly injurious to health as well as disagreeable. The gas is generated by the numerous sinks that empty into that portion of the sea enclosed by the breakwater, and which is immediately under a small port hole – the only admission for air and light we have from the external port.*

The food in the dungeon was as bad as the air. Sam Arnold wrote:

> *The rations issued at this time were putrid, unfit to eat, and during these three months of confinement I lived upon a cup of slop coffee and the dry, hard crust of bread. This is no exaggeration, as many others can testify to its truthfulness. Coffee was brought over to our quarters in a dirty, greasy bucket, always with grease swimming upon its surface; bread, rotten fish and meat, all mixed together, and thus we were forced to live for months, until starvation nearly stared us in the face.*

Six days a week Dr. Mudd and the others were let out of the dungeon to work at hard labor. On Sundays and holidays they were confined all day inside the noxious cell. The men wore leg irons while working outside, but the irons were removed when inside the dungeon. Dr. Mudd suffered quite a bit both mentally and physically during his time in the dungeon. In a letter to his wife he said:

> *My legs and ankles are swollen and sore, pains in my shoulders and back are frequent. My hair began falling out some time ago, and to save which I shaved it all over clean, and have continued to do so once every week since.*

It is now beginning to have a little life. My eyesight is beginning to grow very bad, so much so that I can't read or write by candlelight.

John Ford, Spangler's boss at Ford's Theatre, described Dr. Mudd's condition at this time in a letter he wrote to General Ewing. He said:

I am anxious to get a settlement with the Govt and then take measures with you looking to Spangler's pardon.

I heard from him the other day by a returned prisoner. He is doing well and is a general favorite but is compelled to wear irons. Dr. Mudd looks very badly. His hair is nearly all out and he is nearly half crazy. With Arnold he is compelled by a Negro guard to sweep the Sally Port continually. I believe that is the name. He is ironed, as well as Arnold.

On January 26, 1866, following a complaint by Mrs. Mudd to President Johnson, Dr. Mudd and the other men were no longer required to wear leg irons. Shortly thereafter they were released from the dungeon and moved into the empty casemate directly above the Sally Port entrance. The casemates on this second tier of the Sally Port wall were never fitted out with cannons, and instead were used to house the general prisoner population. The casemate cell above the Sally Port entrance would be the home for Dr. Mudd, Spangler, Arnold, and O'Laughlen during the remainder of their time at Fort Jefferson.

∾

COLONEL GEORGE ST. LEGER GRENFELL

The other man in the dungeon with Dr. Mudd and his companions was Colonel George St. Leger Grenfell. Born in London on May 30, 1808, Grenfell was a British soldier of fortune who claimed to have fought in Algeria, in Morocco against the Barbary pirates, under Garibaldi in South America, in the Crimean War, and in the Sepoy Mutiny. He came to America in 1862 and became an officer in the Confederate Army, serving with General John H. Morgan, General Braxton Bragg, and General J.E.B. Stuart. He resigned from the Confederate Army in 1864 to join a plot to take over the governments of Ohio, Indiana, and Illinois and establish a Northwestern Confederacy.

When the plan to take over Chicago was discovered, Grenfell and some 150 others were arrested. In what became known as the "*Chicago Conspiracy*," Grenfell was tried, convicted, and sentenced to hang. Through the efforts of the British Minister in Washington, his sentence was commuted to life imprisonment at Fort Jefferson.

Shortly after Grenfell arrived, Dr. Mudd wrote to his brother-in-law Jere Dyer:

We are all at this moment in chains. Neither Colonel Grenfel nor myself has been taken out to work the past two or three days, but suffered to remain passively in our quarters. He is quite an intelligent man, tall, straight, and about sixty-one or two years of age. He speaks fluently several languages, and often adds mirth by his witty sarcasm and jest. He has been badly wounded and is now suffering with dropsy, and is allowed no medical treatment whatever, but loaded down with chains, and fed upon the most loathsome food, which treatment in a short time must bring him to an untimely grave. You will confer an act of kindness and mercy by acquainting the English Minister at Washington, Sir F.A. Bruce, of these facts.

In an April 16, 1867 letter to Tom Dyer, his wife's brother in New Orleans, Dr. Mudd writes of Grenfell again:

Colonel St. Ledger Grenfel is kept in close confinement under guard. A few days ago, being sick, he applied to the doctor of the Post for medical attention, which he was refused, and he was ordered to work. Feeling himself unable to move about, he refused. He was then ordered to carry a ball until further orders, which he likewise refused. He was then tied up for half a day, and still refusing, he was taken to one of the wharves, thrown overboard with a rope attached, and ducked; being able to keep himself above water, a fifty pound weight was attached to his feet. Grenfel is an old man, about sixty. He has never refused to do work which he was able to perform, but they demanded more than he felt able, and he wisely refused. They could not conquer him, and he is doing now that which he never objected doing.

In a 1926 Saturday Evening Post article, author George Allan England provided a description of Colonel Grenfell, as told to him by a former Fort Jefferson lighthouse keeper:

All sorts and conditions were herded into the prison of Dry Tortugas. The greatest mystery man of them all was a fiery swashbuckler known as Col. St. Leger Grenfell.

"He was a queer bird altogether," one William Felton told me at Key West. Felton was long a custodian at the fort, and can rock on his front porch and spin yarns about it by the hour. "Grenfell was sure one tough lookin' customer, six foot tall, black-haired, an' with black eyes under big, bushy eyebrows. He had a tremendous black beard, too, an' wore a red flannel shirt open at the neck, an' his pant legs tucked in high boots. Folks said he was a son of Sir Roger Grenfell, a earl, or somethin' swell like that."

Colonel Grenfell was afflicted with yellow fever during the height of the epidemic in September 1867. In letters to his wife, Dr. Mudd wrote *"Colonel Grenfel is quite sick with the disease; he was taken yesterday. I will do all that is possible to save him... Colonel Grenfel is quite sick; his case is doubtful."* But in the end, Dr. Mudd was able to save his life and Colonel Grenfell recovered.

GRENFELL WROTE of the epidemic in a letter to H.L. Stone, brother of Major Valentine H. Stone, commander of Fort Jefferson in 1867. Grenfell and H.L. Stone had served together under Confederate General John Hunt Morgan during the Civil War. The letter said:

Fort Jefferson, Wednesday, Sept. 25, 1867
  To: Mr. H.L. Stone
  Dear Sir:
  It is a disagreeable task to have to communicate evil tidings, but I think it is my duty to inform you that the yellow fever has been making sad ravages here, and that among its victims were first your brother's wife, and then the Major himself. After Mrs. Stone's death, he left for Key West, with his little boy, intending to go North; but he was seized with the fever on board, and died there, the quarantine laws preventing his being landed.
  I deeply regret that his leaving this place prevented my nursing him throughout the malady; care does more than doctors, and he had great confidence in my nursing. I write only a few lines. I am tired and grieved, having been now 21 days and nights by the bedsides of the sick. Last night

was my first night passed in bed! grieved on account of your brother's death, who was the only officer that has ever shown me any kindness since I came here.

I wish I could say that they had not been positively inimical and cruel. Bt your brother's arrival put an end to all that. I am much afraid that the old system will soon be in force.

We have had some one hundred and eighty yellow fever cases and upward of thirty deaths. Two companies have been sent to other islands, so that our whole force, prisoners included, only amounts to some one hundred and eighty men. Dr. Smith is dead and his son; your poor brother and his wife; Lieut. Orr is dead; Lieut. Gordon is very low, indeed, and Lieut. Leginskin also. The only officer left for duty is Lieut. Rounce, who has had the fever, and recovered. Major Andrews, who was in command, ran away when the fever broke out, and has only returned once since, not then to land, but to inquire at a distance how things were progressing, and to set sail two hours afterward.

Altogether we are in a nice state; Dr. Mudd doing physician's duty, Colonell head nurse. Only one prisoner, Michael O'Laughlen, one of the Lincoln conspirators; a fortunate escape, I think, from life imprisonment.

Excuse this brief letter, and believe me, my dear sir, yours very sincerely, G. St. L. Grenfell.

(Letter courtesy Filson Historical Society, Special Collections Department, Louisville, Kentucky)

IN MARCH 1868, Colonel Grenfell and three others escaped from Fort Jefferson in a small boat. The military report of the escape said:

...Private William Noreil of Company I 5th US Arty who had been on duty posted as a sentinel over the boats within the boom, did between the hours of 11 o'clock P.M. and 1 A.M. desert his post, taking possession of a small boat and carrying with him the following named prisoners – G. St. Leger Grenfell, J.W. Adare, James Orr and Joseph Holroya.

I am impressed with the belief that Grenfell had considerable money in his possession by and through which he bribed the sentinel. The surveying steamer Bibb which was lying in the harbor was dispatched in pursuit of them about 8 o'clock the same morning but after cruising the whole day failed either to overhaul or hear anything concerning them.

Dr. Mudd's final mention of Colonel Grenfell is in an April 14, 1868 letter to his wife. In it he says

We have heard nothing from Grenfel since he escaped on the 6th of last month.

All hands may have perished, it being quite stormy at the time.

Most assumed that Grenfell and the others perished at sea, but there were persistent rumors he had survived. On June 5, 1868, the following announcement, originally published in the Mobile Alabama Advertiser, appeared in the New York Times:

St. Leger Grenfell - The public was greatly gratified not long since to learn that this gallant English soldier had escaped his prison at the Dry Tortugas, and in his love of liberty at the risk of life, he had trusted himself to the mercies of a frail boat in an attempt to cross the Florida Straits to Cuba. We have the pleasure of stating that his voyage was made in safety, and that a letter has been received from him in Havana, sending his thanks and acknowledgements for kind treatment to some of the army officers at Tortugas, and stating that he was just about to sail for Old England. We do not doubt that every gentleman officer belonging to the garrison of his prison guard rejoices at his escape.

～

PRISON LIFE

Daily life at Fort Jefferson was dictated by the rhythm of a busy army post. In the morning, bugle calls announced the time to rise and shine, to assemble for morning roll call, and for breakfast. The morning gun was fired as the flag was raised over the fort. Lunch, supper, and various events in between were announced by bugle calls. In the evening, bugle calls announced retreat, evening roll call, and bedtime taps. The evening gun was fired as the flag was lowered for the night. During the night, fort sentries loudly announced the regular changing of the guards.

Unfortunately for Dr. Mudd and his companions, they had front row seats to the sights and sounds of all this activity. For most of their time at Fort Jefferson, they lived in a casemate cell directly over the Sally Port near the area where most of this activity took place. One wonders how they ever got a good night's sleep.

Dr. Mudd wrote:

We have three sentries within ten feet of our door that cry out the hours of the night at the pitch of their voices, which awakens us and destroys our sleep.

The casemate cells at Fort Jefferson were not like cells in a normal prison. There were no bars or locked doors on the cells. Prisoners were generally able to freely go about the island to attend to the jobs they were assigned. There was no way to escape from Fort Jefferson except by stealing or stowing away on a boat, and these were closely watched, as Dr. Mudd found out when he tried to escape.

Dr. Mudd and his companions were an exception, probably due to Dr. Mudd's having attempted to escape. He wrote:

We can't move five steps from our door without permission of the sergeant of the guard, and followed by the sentry. When we are at work or walking, we can't move faster than the guard is disposed to walk himself, so you see all running, fast walking, wrestling, etc., is excluded. This is now our principal grievance, which has been brought about by no word or act of ours. All the rest of the prisoners, except those confined to the guardhouse, are allowed the freedom of the island; we ask no more.

Dr. Mudd's main problem with prison life, however, was the separation from his wife and children. In various letters, he wrote:

... My heart almost bleeds sometimes when I think of you and our dear little children.

... I have now, my darling wife, but one affliction, viz : uneasiness of mind regarding you and our precious little children. Imprisonment, chains and all other accompaniments of prison life, I am used to. I believe I can stand anything, but the thought of your dependent position, the ills and privations consequent, pierce my heart as a dagger, and allow me no enjoyment and repose of mind.

... My heart yearns to be with you and our precious little children. How much I need your consoling and soothing voice, and the happy and innocent pranks and glee of our dear little ones, to cheer me up. In being separated from you, my dear Frank, I am parted with all that I desire to live for in this world.

... How anxious I feel concerning your welfare and our dear little children; it is the only pain I suffer.

Living Quarters

Dr. Mudd, Spangler, Arnold, and O'Laughlen lived in a casemate cell located just above the Sally Port entrance. The moat and Gulf of Mexico could be seen from one side of the casemate. The other side opened to the interior of the fort. Immediately outside was a small cottage, surrounded by a white picket fence. Behind the cottage was a 65-foot lighthouse. It was tended by William Felton, the lighthouse keeper who lived in the cottage with his family. The lighthouse had been in operation before Fort Jefferson was established, and continued in operation while Fort Jefferson was built around it.

Whenever it rained, water seeped through the walls and ceiling, pooling on the floor of the casemate. The men gouged a series of small trenches into the floor to channel the water to a hole in the floor where they could scoop the water up and throw it outside. In a letter home, Dr. Mudd wrote:

> *After every rain, our quarters leak terribly, and it's not unusual to dip up from the floor ten and twelve large buckets of water daily. We have a hole cut into the floor and little trenches cut, so as to concentrate the aqueous secretion, which facilitates the dipping process and freeing the room from noxious miasma.*

Sam Arnold wrote of the same problem:

> *Often during our confinement in the place buckets were used to bail out the collected water, it having been found necessary to dig deep holes and gutters to catch the water, thereby preventing our quarters becoming flooded all over. For months - yes, over a year - were we quartered in this filthy place, having as companions in our misery every insect known to abound on the island, in the shape of mosquitoes, bedbugs, roaches and scorpions, by which, both night and day, we were tormented.*

The Climate

Hurricanes were a constant threat. One struck on Sunday, October 22, 1865, while Dr. Mudd was imprisoned in the dungeon. Trees were uprooted. The cattle pen in the middle of the parade ground collapsed and the cattle roamed free in frightened confusion. With the wind still howling in the darkness before dawn the next morning, the upper story of the south section of the officers quarters blew out, killing Lieutenant John W. Stirling in his bed and injuring Captain R.A. Stearns. The walls and roofs of many other buildings were severely damaged. It would take months to repair the damage.

The Baltimore Daily Commerce newspaper of November 1, 1865 reported the hurricane:

New York, October 31, 1865 - The steamer John Rice, from New Orleans on the 19th, reports having experienced a hurricane on the 22nd. On the 24th she stopped at Fort Jefferson, and found that the hurricane had blown down a large brick building, and killed the post quartermaster and severely injured several others. The buildings inside the fort were unroofed, and trees were torn up, etc.

Summertime temperatures at Fort Jefferson hovered in the 90s. Temperatures over 100 degrees were not uncommon. The high temperatures combined with the high humidity produced a broiling sensation that could not be escaped. The winter months provided some relief, but could still be uncomfortable. On January 22, 1866, in the middle of his first 'winter' at Fort Jefferson, Dr. Mudd wrote to his wife:

During the day, owing to the overpowering light and heat, my eyes are painful and irritated.... The weather here since the beginning of winter has been as warm as summer with you.... It sounds strange to read of heavy snows and persons freezing to death, in the papers.

Trying to ease his wife's concerns about the tropical climate, Dr. Mudd wrote to her:

> *You seem to manifest some uneasiness on my account, apprehending the injurious effects of the heat upon my feeble constitution. In this regard I must remark that the climate being more moist and equable, is not liable to the evil and depressing effects, as with you. Heat in the sun here is very great, yet rarely attended with "sun stroke"; no fatal case from this cause having occurred since I have been here.*
>
> *Whenever there is a breeze, which is generally the case, it is always pleasant. A strict eye is kept to the cleanliness of the place, and being remote from the main land we have no fears of any infectious or epidemic disease. Unsuitable diet, beef, pork, etc. are more frequent causes of disorders and disease than locality or climate. We stand in need of a vegetable and fruit diet, of which this place is woefully deficient.*

The damp tropical conditions also provided a prefect breeding ground for insects of all kinds. At one point, Dr. Mudd wrote:

> *I am nearly worn out, the weather is almost suffocating, and millions of mosquitoes, fleas, and bedbugs infest the whole island. We can't rest day or night in peace for the mosquitoes.*

He had no way of knowing that the mosquitoes were not just pests, but potential killers that could transmit the deadly yellow fever virus.

Work

Before his attempted escape Dr. Mudd had been working in the prison hospital. After his attempted escape he was assigned to manual labor — sweeping down various parts of the fort. However, he was eventually assigned to the carpentry shop where he worked with Edman Spangler until the yellow fever epidemic began in August 1867.

As he became more proficient at carpentry under Spangler's guidance, Dr. Mudd made larger, more intricate items such as walking canes, cribbage boards, jewelry boxes, and items of furniture, some of which contained intricate inlaid patterns. He sold some of these items to the soldiers and their wives who lived at Fort Jefferson, and sent others to his family back home. Several of the items have survived and are on display at the Dr. Samuel A. Mudd House Museum near Bryantown, Maryland.

A few months after the end of the epidemic, probably as recognition for his work during the epidemic, Dr. Mudd was assigned to work as a clerk in the Provost Marshall's office, where he remained until his pardon.

Food and Water

There was no fresh water on the Dry Tortugas islands, but large cisterns built into the fort's foundation caught and stored rainwater for the fort. The fort also had steam condensers for converting sea water into fresh water.

Food and other supplies arrived on a military steamer twice a month from New Orleans. The quality of the food was a source of constant complaint. But it was bad for everyone, prisoners and soldiers alike, since everyone ate the same food.

Watermelons, bananas, and pineapples sometimes arrived on ships from Cuba, but at exorbitant prices. Fresh vegetables were rare. Canned tomatoes and beans were sometimes available. Bread, butter, molasses, and coffee were a staple. Sea turtles, some weighing as much as two or three hundred pounds, were sometimes caught by the soldiers and added variety to the diet.

Dr. Mudd was mostly a vegetarian at Fort Jefferson. Meat was of such bad quality he never ate it. He said *"All articles of meat, salt and fresh, are repulsive. I can't bear the sight of them."* In the final year of his imprisonment, Dr. Mudd was allowed to tend a small vegetable garden. In April 1868, he wrote lovingly of his garden, saying:

There are a great quantity of ripe tomatoes, peas, beans, and collards in the garden, now suitable for table use. The corn is in silk, and soon there will be roasting ears.

Here is what Sam Arnold thought of the food:

Food issued was horrible in the extreme. Many were suffering dreadfully from scurvy and chronic troubles. The bread was disgusting to look upon, being a mixture of flour, bugs, sticks and dirt. Meat, whose taint could be traced by its smell from one part of the fort to the other; in fact, rotten, and to such an extent that dogs ran from coming in contact with it, was served. No vegetable diet was served of any description, and the coffee, which should have been good, as good quality was issued, was made into a slop by those who had charge of the cookhouse.

Arnold was apparently not exaggerating. A soldier serving at Fort Jefferson at about the same time wrote:

I have just been to dinner we had boiled Pork Potatoes & a piece of Bread & a dish of Rain water with wiggles in it we drink lots of wiggles & the Bread is well filled with Black Bugs about 1/4 of an inch long we pick out some of them & eat the rest there is scarcly anything that turns my stomach now it has got to be proof against dirt & nastiness.

The bad food and living conditions affected everyone's health. Scurvy was a major medical problem at Fort Jefferson, resulting from the lack of fruits and vegetables containing vitamin C. Arnold and Dr. Mudd both suffered from rheumatism. Dr. Mudd lost weight – he normally weighed about 150 pounds. Shortly before his release, Dr. Mudd wrote to his wife that his hair was much thinner than when he left home, and that he had shaved off his mustache and trimmed his goatee quite short. He said he scarcely recognized himself when he looked in a mirror.

The Sutler Store

Many military posts, including Fort Jefferson, had convenience stores run by civilian businessmen known as sutlers. Soldiers complained that the prices were high and the quality low, but they had nowhere else to go. There was no competition at isolated Fort Jefferson. Sutlers sold clothing, ink, pencils, writing paper, preserves, tobacco, canned food, pins, mirrors, pocketknives, toothbrushes, hairbrushes, and a wide variety of other everyday items.

Emily Holder, the wife of a Fort Jefferson assistant surgeon, wrote that she was able to buy a stove and other necessities for setting up housekeeping from the sutler's store. Whiskey was also available from the sutler's store, and drunkenness on the part of soldiers was a common disciplinary problem at the fort.

The store at Fort Jefferson was located outside the walls of the fort. Prisoners could purchase items at the store with the three dollars per month credit they were given there. Some prisoners also received money from home, or earned money doing odd jobs at the fort.

Dr. Mudd received some spending money from his family, and also earned some money by making and selling small boxes ornamented with sea shells.

Spangler also made extra spending money. Dr. Mudd wrote:

Spangler made money by trafficking with the soldiers, and we are mainly indebted to him for something extra to the crude, unwholesome, and sometimes condemned Government ration that was issued to us.

Prisoners also received food and other items in packages from home. Dr. Mudd and his fellow prisoners received clothing, canned fruit and vegetables, tobacco, and sometimes even whiskey, although the whiskey often mysteriously disappeared from the packages before being given to the prisoners.

Mail and Reading Material

Friends and family supported Dr. Mudd during his imprisonment by sending him letters, newspapers, spending money, and food. Two mail boats a week normally arrived at Fort Jefferson, but sometimes the boats were delayed due to quarantine procedures designed to protect against yellow fever and other diseases. Dr. Mudd's mail usually encountered additional delays as it passed through the fort's military censor. While the mail from family and friends was usually upbeat about his chances for release, the newspapers allowed him to form a more realistic view of the political climate and his likelihood of release.

Fort Jefferson also had a small library that both prisoners and soldiers could use. Samuel Arnold, who usually worked as a clerk in the office of the fort's commanding officer, was sometimes placed in charge of the library when the regular military librarian was away. Records show that the small library had over 250 books, and subscribed to newspapers such as the New York Herald, the Washington Chronicle, and the London Illustrated News. A soldier wrote:

We have a good library, pretty well stocked with books, and receive also some New York papers, besides other publications; so that in this respect we are very fortunate, isolated as we are from the outer world.

Entertainment

There was obviously little opportunity for entertainment at a military prison located on a desert island. However, although neither Dr. Mudd nor Samuel Arnold mentioned it in their writings, the officers and civilians at the fort did organize plays for entertainment. Both soldiers and prisoners were able to attend.

Alfred O'Donoghue, a soldier at Fort Jefferson, wrote that the fort had:

...a very good theatre, gotten up entirely, at very great cost and labor and well supported, by the present battalion. There are performances nearly every week. The plays are sent on from New York, and the dramatic

company is kept pretty well informed in theatrical matters. The great difficulty that the managers labor under is the want of female characters,
personated by real women. Soldiers do not, as a rule, make good lady characters, and especially here, the face of every man being so well known, their
employment in the female department destroys the illusion of reality so
necessary to good playing. A shout of derisive laughter often greets the false
woman in expansive crinoline; the awkwardness of the figure and long
stride betray the deception. Besides, despite of care, very ridiculous acci-
dents in the dress arrangement will sometimes occur, pins will get out of
place, and skirts will fall, betraying the masculine trowsers.

For a brief period we had indeed a real live woman character; the very
pretty and very talented wife of a non-commissioned officer, since promoted
to another department, consented to act with the boys. Her acting and
deportment were both excellent, and the enthusiasm on such occasions
among the audience was unbounded. On the evening previous to her departure a benefit was given her, and a goodly pile of greenbacks raked in.

Colonel Grenfell didn't agree with O'Donoghue that the fort had
"*a very good theater.*" A grumpy Grenfell wrote in a January 15, 1868,
letter to his Confederate Army friend Colonel Henry Lane Stone that:

A learned physician, Dr. Mudd, has descended to playing the fiddle for
drunken soldiers to dance to or form part of a very miserable orchestra at a
still more miserable theatrical performance.

Baseball was also a popular form of entertainment at the fort. The
large grassy center of the fort, known as the Parade Ground, made an
ideal playing field. Army records show that the soldiers played, but
are silent on whether prisoners also played. Dr. Mudd's letters never
mentioned baseball.

∾

THE 1867 YELLOW FEVER EPIDEMIC

Yellow fever is a viral infection transmitted from an infected person to a healthy person by mosquito. If there is no infected person around, mosquitoes can bite people all day and no one will become infected. At Fort Jefferson, any incoming ship suspected of carrying a yellow fever victim was not allowed to dock. It would have to remain quarantined at anchor in the harbor until deemed safe to discharge passengers. In the late summer of 1867, the system failed.

In the initial stages of yellow fever the victim suffers headache, muscle aches, fever, loss of appetite, vomiting, jaundice, kidney failure, and bleeding. Those who do not recover from this stage can then experience multi-organ dysfunction including liver and kidney failure, brain dysfunction, seizures, coma, shock, and death. Yellow fever gets its name from the jaundice that affects many patients, causing yellow eyes and yellow skin.

In the mid-1800s neither the cause nor the proper treatment of yellow fever was understood. It would not be until 1900 that Dr. Walter Reed and his assistants would prove that yellow fever was caused by the bite of an infected Aedes Aegypti mosquito, and not by person-to-person transmission. Dr. Reed found that eradicating mosquitoes eradicated yellow fever.

Today, in addition to mosquito eradication, a safe and effective vaccine is available to prevent contracting yellow fever. However, there is still no cure for yellow fever once it is contracted. All that can be done is to treat the symptoms. Treatment today is essentially the same as it was in the mid-1800s — complete bed rest accompanied by lots of fluids.

The 1867 yellow fever epidemic at Fort Jefferson was part of a wider yellow fever epidemic that killed thousands of people along the Gulf Coast from Texas to Florida, and northward up the Mississippi valley to Memphis, Tennessee.

DR. JOSEPH SIM SMITH assumed his duties as the new Fort Jefferson doctor on July 31, 1867. A couple of weeks later, August 18, 1867, he wrote a letter saying all was well at Fort Jefferson - especially no annoying mosquitoes. That very same day, a soldier in Company K fell ill. Dr. Smith had no idea that the great yellow fever epidemic at Fort Jefferson had just begun. His letter said:

> Fort Jefferson, Florida, August 18, 1867 - I arrived here, safe and sound, after a not very pleasant trip. The thermometer keeps steadily between eighty-five and ninety, but with a steady breeze. I do not feel the heat as much as I did in Washington. The quarters are excellent and plenty of them, and I have not slept under a mosquito bar, nor nave I been annoyed by the mosquito at all. I amuse myself fishing, and it is the finest I have ever enjoyed; coraling and collecting shell.
>
> Our greatest drawback is the irregularity of the mails. Our mail reaches us by way of Havana. It comes out from New York, in one of the Havana line of steamers, and we send a schooner over for it.
>
> There are but few prisoners here now, forty-five in all, and two-thirds of them, if not more, are United States soldiers, who have been sent here for various crimes, principally desertion.

The conspirators are lodged like the other prisoners, in the second tier of casemates. Their quarters are cool, dry, and airy, and command quite as pleasant view as there is. They manage to live pretty well with their Government rations, and what their friends send them.

Arnold is employed as a clerk, and seems satisfied. Arnold and O'Laughlin work at their trade as carpenters. Mudd works now in the carpenter shop, and is getting quite handy with the tools. They are all in excellent health, but are a little thinner than is natural for them.

They have the benefit of the library, and Mudd and Arnold read some. On the whole they are much better off than they would be somewhere else. I believe certainly they are better off than any prisoners I ever saw. A reporter of the New York Herald visited the post this morning, and Mudd expressed some fears that he would publish something concerning them, and said that they would much rather be left alone, as they already suffered a good deal from newspaper accounts. (Washington Evening Star, August 30, 1867)

On August 22nd, Private James Forsythe was the first to die. Private Joseph Enits died next, on August 30th. The fever spread to Company L and to the officers' servants. Company I, housed in the barracks adjoining the hospital, was then attacked. Company M escaped the plague until September 7th when 30 men were stricken.

When Dr. Smith himself contracted the disease on September 5th, the post's commanding officer, Major Valentine H. Stone, asked Dr. Mudd to take over caring for the sick until a replacement for Dr. Smith arrived, and he agreed. Dr. Smith died on September 8th. The next day, Dr. Daniel W. Whitehurst arrived from Key West to help Dr. Mudd.

For the next month, Drs. Mudd and Whitehurst worked day and night to treat those afflicted with yellow fever, which included nearly everyone at the fort, soldiers and prisoners alike. Samuel Arnold and Michael O'Laughlen both contracted the disease. Arnold survived, but O'Laughlen died on September 23rd. On October 1st, Dr. Whitehurst was relieved by Dr. Edward Thomas, a civilian contract doctor from New York. Dr. Mudd himself contracted the disease on October 4th, 47 days after the epidemic had begun.

~

FRIENDS OF SPANGLER shared two letters he wrote during the epidemic with the Baltimore Sun, which published them on October 11, 1867. His first letter said:

Fort Jefferson, Florida, September 23, 1867

I have received the barrel of potatoes and am very thankful for them. We have drawn but a half bushel of potatoes from the government since the first of last January. We have bought some at Key West, for which we paid seven and eight dollars per barrel. There are some seven of us in one mess; we do not eat with the other prisoners.

We have the yellow fever here very bad. We had a doctor that came from Washington; he got it and died; his name was J. Sim Smith. He has a wife and two children. Dr. Mudd was in charge for a few days, and was very successful, and then they got a doctor from Key West; but Dr. Mudd is still in the hospital attending to the sick, and I am in the carpenter shop making coffins for those that die.

While I am writing, they have burned all the beds that belonged to every one that got sick, and all their clothing. We have a dreadful time of it here. There is no use of getting frightened of it; we must stand up and face the music.

Since writing the above, one of Dr. Smith's children has died. Lieutenants Solam and Orr, Major Stone's wife, and Michael O'Laughlin.

Spangler's second letter said:

Fort Jefferson, Florida, Sept. 24, 1867

Poor Michael O'Laughlin, my friend and roommate died at 7 o'clock yesterday, of yellow fever, and during the past 24 hours, seven others have passed from life to eternity. The fever has assumed a more malignant type. There is but one officer for duty at the post, the others having died now

lying ill with the fever. Lieut. Gordon, taken two days ago, is now lying in
critical condition. From all I can learn, we have had 280 cases, out of which
so far thirty have died.

Some are even taken with it the second time, and from appearances,
and from what the Doctor says, we shall always have it here - the ther-
mometer never falling below 63 degrees.

I have not been attacked yet, but may be at any moment, in which case
I thought it best to forward to you and my family small mementoes, should
I die of the fever. Arnold has had it, and has fully recovered, yet remains in
a very weak condition. Something should be done, if possible, towards
removable from this den of pestilence and death to some more healthy
place. Nearly all the late cases are of a very malignant type, scarcely any
recovering.

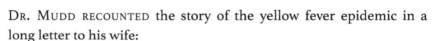

DR. MUDD RECOUNTED the story of the yellow fever epidemic in a
long letter to his wife:

October 27, 1867
I will now, as near as I can, by a pen description, give you an idea of
the embarrassment I labored under upon assuming the duties as surgeon of
the post, that were unexpectedly thrust upon me, and the track followed by
the germs or poison, as evidenced by the appearance of disease.

Thus on the 4th of September, seventeen days after the epidemic of
yellow fever had broken out, the surgeon, Dr. J. Sim Smith, a gentleman
much respected and beloved by the garrison, was himself attacked with the
fever, and by his illness, the Post was left without a physician in the midst
of a fearful pestilence. The thought had never before entered my mind that
this contingency might arise, and consequently I found myself unprepared
to decide between the contending emotions of fear and duty that now
pressed to gain ascendancy. Memory was still alive, for it seemed as yester-
day, the dread ordeal through which I had passed. Tried by a court not
ordained by the laws of the land, confronted by suborned and most
barefaced perjured testimony, deprived of liberty, banished from home,

family and friends, bound in chains as the brute and forced at the point of the bayonet to do the most menial service, and withal denied for a time every luxury, and even healthy subsistence, for having exercised a simple act of common humanity in setting the leg of a man for whose insane act I had no sympathy, but which was in the line of my professional calling. It was but natural that resentment and fear should rankle in my heart, and that I should stop to discuss mentally the contending emotions that now rested upon a horrid recollection of the past. Can I be a passive beholder? Shall I withhold the little service I might be capable of rendering the unfortunate soldier who was but a tool in the hands of his exacting officer? Or shall I again subject myself to renewed imputations of assassination? Who can read the motives of men? My motive might be ever so pure and praiseworthy yet one victim of the disease might be sufficient to start up the cry of poison and murder.

Whilst these disagreeable thoughts were revolving a fellow-prisoner remarked, saying: "Doctor, the yellow fever is the fairest and squarest thing that I have seen the past four or five years. It makes no distinction in regard to rank, color, or previous condition - every man has his chance, and I would advise you as a friend not to interfere." Another said it was only a little Southern opposition to reconstruction, and thought the matter ought to be reported to Congress in order that a law might be passed lowering the temperature below zero, which would most effectually put an end to its disloyalty.

But I must be more serious; and you will perceive that the time had now arrived in which I could occupy no middle ground. I felt that I had to make a decision, and although the rule of conduct upon which I had determined was not in accord with my natural feelings, yet I had the sanction of my professional and religious teachings and the consciousness of conforming to that holy precept, "Do ye good for evil," which alone distinguishes the man from the brute.

It being our breakfast hour on the morning of the 5th, and thinking it required some condescension on the part of the commanding officer to call upon an humble prisoner to serve in the honorable position of surgeon of the post, I concluded to spare him this disagreeable duty, and instructed Mr. Arnold, a fellow prisoner and roommate, who was acting clerk at head-

quarters, to inform Major Stone, then commanding, that should my services be required, I had no fear of, nor objection to, performing whatever aid was in my power toward the relief of the sick. On approaching head-quarters, Mr. Arnold met Major Stone coming to my quarters to inquire whether I would consent to attend the sick of the Post until the arrival of a regular surgeon.

When informed that I had offered my services, the Major seemed much pleased and had me forthwith detailed. Fortune favored me, and it so happened that during the intervals, amounting to nearly three weeks, that I had the exclusive care of the sick, not one died. Time will not permit me further digression. I shall pass over many incidents of interest connected with hospital management, difficulties I had to overcome in breaking up the prior arrangement of sending away the sick in open boats over a rough sea two miles and a half distant and also in obtaining an opposite order from the commander to send to one of the islands near by as many of the well soldiers as could be spared from the garrison. This latter measure, though I had advised it on the day I took charge of the hospital, was not carried out until the arrival of Dr. D. W. Whitehurst of Key West, Florida; a noble, kind-hearted gentleman, who superseded me on the 9th of September.

The first case of yellow fever at the Dry Tortugas, in the epidemic of which I now speak, occurred on the 18th of August, 1867, in Company K, which was located in the casemates on the south side of the Fort immedi-ately over the unfinished moat, which at low tide gave rise to quite offen-sive odors. To this circumstance the surgeon of the Post attributed the cause of the disease, and at his request the company was removed and the port-holes ordered to be closed, to prevent the supposed deadly miasma from entering the Fort.

Having the honor at this time of being a member of the carpenter's shop, it fell to my lot to aid in the work of barricading against the unseen foe, and it was during this patriotic service the 22nd of August, that I made my first note of the epidemic. The places occupied by the beds of the four men, one on the 18th, one on the 20th, and two on the 21st, that had gone to the hospital sick with yellow fever, were all contiguous. The Fort was hexagonal in shape with a bastion at each corner, and the company, after its removal, was placed on the east side, the bastion forming the center with several casemates above and below boarded up separating it from Company L on the north and the prisoners on the south, and in the most eligible position for the spread of the poison, owing to the prevalence of the wind, which from early in April up to this period had blown continuously from the southeast, varying only a few degrees.

There was a lull or temporary suspension of the activity of the poison on the 22d and 23d. For two days the company remained without any new cases, but on the 24th day one man was taken from the same company on stretchers, being unable to walk. The fever then rapidly extended right and left until it reached Company L, which was nearest the point where it arose this second time, and later the prisoners' quarters, which were more remote, were attacked. To show and to prove to you that the germs, or cause, spreads by continuity of matter, and not with the disease, the first two cases that occurred in Company L, and the first two cases among the prisoners, were immediately next the boarded partition that separated them from Company K, where the fever was raging, having followed along the rows of beds, up to this line of division, and then passed through the open spaces between the plank, which were loosely nailed.

There were at this time two hospitals, the Post Hospital within the Fort, and Sand Key Hospital on an adjacent island about two miles and a half distant, which latter was fitted up as soon as the fever began to assume an epidemical form. The sick that occurred during the night and following day were immediately taken to the Post Hospital, and from thence at 4 o'clock P. M. they were carried in boats by the surgeon, on his accustomed visit, to Sandy Key Hospital. Notwithstanding the fact that most of the sick walked from their beds to the Post Hospital, and no effort or pains on the part of the surgeon to isolate the disease were taken, owing to the belief in its miasmatic character, the germs or cause had not up to this time, September 12, viz: 25 days, reached either of the hospitals, if we may judge from the circumstance that not one of the many nurses, who waited upon the sick day and night and even slept in the same room, were stricken down with the fever.

The disease after extending into Company L, and to the prisoners' quarters, next made its appearance into Company I, located in the inner *barracks, a building about three hundred feet long, thirty feet wide, and four stories high on the east side, running north and parallel with the Fort, and immediately in front of Company K and Company I, and distant about sixty feet.*

I was called into this company on the morning of September 8, and found Sergeant Sheridan and a private that slept in the next bed ill with the fever. Sergeant Sheridan and the first sergeant of Company K were great friends, and when off duty were constantly in each other's quarters. Sheridan generally wore a heavy cloak during the showers of rain that were frequent at this period, and I feel satisfied that the poison was carried by the ferment set up in the cloak, or mechanically, by adhering formites, though it is possible for it to have been wafted across from Company K, the two beds in Company I being near the window facing that company. Then the fever gradually worked its way along through the whole company without a skip in regular succession as they slept.

At the northern extremity of the barracks two rooms were set apart, thirty feet square, as the Post Hospital. On the 7th we were necessitated by the increasing number of sick to provide other hospital quarters, and for convenience four casemates opposite on the ground tier, under Company L, were boarded up as a temporary hospital, with our kitchen and dispensary inter-mediate. On the 8th our hospital supply of beds and bedding gave out, and on the 9th we were compelled to bring the bed along with the patient into the hospital. Two days after the admission of the infected beds, our nurses began falling sick, three being attacked during the day and night of the 11th of September. Then the three laundresses, families who did the washing for the hospitals and separate quarters on the west side of the Fort, sixty or seventy yards apart, were all simultaneously attacked upon the first issue of soiled clothing - after our hospital became infected.

Then again, upon the breaking up of the Sand Key Hospital, and the return of the nurses to the Fort, they were all speedily stricken down with the fever upon their being placed on similar duty. These nurses had remained free from all disease up to their return to the Fort, although the majority of the cases whom they nursed at Sand Key died with the fever.

But the most remarkable spread of the disease occurred on the night of the 16th of September in Company M, which was quartered in the case-

mates immediately above the hospital and Company L, and notwithstanding the proximity up to this date, twenty-nine days since the epidemic began, had remained entirely exempt from the fever, owing no doubt to the fact that it laid behind the bastion, which, with the prevailing southeast wind, produced a downward or opposing current. However, on the morning of the above date, about nine o'clock, a small rain cloud common to that locality, arose to the south of the fort, which came up rapidly with a heavy wind, lasting about twenty minutes, and which blew directly from the hospital and Company L, toward Company M, and the night following every man went to bed in his usual health, yet between eleven and one o'clock nearly one-half of the company, or thirty men, were attacked with the most malignant form of the disease - beginning at the point nearest the hospitals and extending thirty beds without missing or skipping a single occupant.

It had been my custom to remain at the hospital every night until eleven o'clock to see that every patient received the medicine prescribed and was quiet. On this occasion I had not retired more than fifteen minutes before I was sent for by the sergeant of Company M to come to his quarters, that several of his men were sick. Feeling much fatigued, I did not attend the summons, but referred the messenger to Dr. Whitehurst and the steward of the hospital.

At one o'clock the sergeant himself came down to my room and begged me for God's sake to get up, that one-half of his company were attacked with the fever, and that he did not know what to do with them, as the hospitals were already full. I went along with the sergeant, and found his statement fully correct, and the wildest alarm and confusion prevailing.

As the hospitals were already crowded, we concluded, for convenience, to enclose the six casemates nearest the regular hospitals, which was speedily executed with canvas, and in less than two hours all moved back and were quiet under comfortable treatment. The next night or two after, the balance of the company, in the order of their beds, were attacked with the disease without an exception.

The disease did not extend among the officers at headquarters until it had at first reached the negro prisoners, several of whom were employed by the officers as servants, and who were in the daily habit of carrying to and *fro their blankets. The humble individual who now addresses you was not attacked until the 4th of October, forty-seven days after the beginning of the epidemic, though constantly at the bedside of the sick, and in the midst of the infected hospitals and quarters. One evening, at our usual supper hour, feeling much depressed and exhausted from the unaccustomed duties I went over to my mess, where I was besieged with many questions concerning the sick, and notwithstanding the solemnity of the occasion, a hearty laugh was frequently indulged at the expense of our ready wit, Edward Spangler.*

The debilitating effects of the climate, added to the condition conse-quent upon the excitement, very much depressed me, and after finishing my bowl of coffee and slice of bread, I fell upon my rude cot to spend a few minutes of repose. The customary sea breeze at this hour had sprung up, and I was shortly lulled into sweet sleep. My faithful and ever solicitous roommate, Edward Spangler, who on former occasions had manifested so much concern when the least indisposition was complained of, seemed to anticipate my every want, was not unguarded at this time. As soon as he found me quiet, he closed the door and turned back several intruders, stating that the Doctor was feeling unwell, and had laid down to rest himself. In the course of an hour, he said, he will be through his nap, when he will return to the hospital, where all who desire can see him. Spangler made money by trafficking with the soldiers, and we are mainly indebted to him for something extra to the crude, unwholesome, and sometimes condemned Government ration that was issued to us. He was not generally select in his epithets toward those whom he disliked, yet if he saw them in suffering, it excited the liveliest sympathy, and he would do anything that laid in his power for their relief. At a later period he, in conjunction with Mr. Arnold, watched over me in my illness as attentively as if their own brother, and I owe my life to the unremitting care which they bestowed.

The reader, I am in hopes, will excuse this little digression from the subject - a tribute of thanks is due, and I know no more fitting place to give it expression. I may perhaps be doing injustice by omitting another name equally deserving of my esteem, Michael O'Loughlin. He, unfortunate young man, away from his family and friends, by whom he was most tenderly loved, fell a victim to the pestilence in spite of every effort on our part to save him. He had passed the first stage of the disease and was apparently convalescent, but, contrary to my earnest advice, he got out of bed a short time after I left in the morning, and was walking about the room looking over some periodicals the greater part of the day. In the evening, about five o'clock, a sudden collapse of the vital powers took place, which in thirty-six hours after terminated his life. He seemed all at once conscious of his impending fate, and the first warning I had of his condition was his exclamation, "Doctor, Doctor, you must tell my mother all!" He called then Edward Spangler, who was present, and extending his hand he said, "Good-by, Ned." These were his last words of consciousness. He fell back instantly into a profound stupor and for several minutes seemed lifeless; but by gently changing his position from side to side, and the use of stimulating and cold applications, we succeeded in restoring him to partial strength and recollection.

I never met with one more kind and forbearing, possessing a warm friendly disposition and a fine comprehensive intellect. I enjoyed greater ease in conversational intercourse with him than any of my prison associates. He was taken sick whilst my kind friend, Dr. D. W. Whitehurst of Key West, Florida, had charge of the Post; from him he received prompt medical attention from the beginning of his illness to his death.

The news had spread around through the garrison of the neat and comfortable appearance of the hospital and the improved condition of the sick, which had the effect to gain for me a reputation, and the confidence of the soldiers - all I could desire to insure success. It was not long before I discovered I could do more with nine cases out of ten by a few consoling and inspiring words, than with all the medicine known to me in the materia medica.

EDMAN SPANGLER also wrote about the yellow fever epidemic. His letter appeared in the September 22, 1867 issue of the New York Times:

Fort Jefferson Fla., Sept, 6, 1867.

I am well at present, but don't know how long it will last, for we have had the yellow fever here, and there are two or three dying each day, and I am busy working in the carpenters' shop, making coffins day and night, and don't know when my time will come. They don't last longer than a few hours. I will enclose a few moss pictures for you, and I will send you a barrel of coral if I don't get the yellow fever and die; but there are ten chances to one if I ever see you again. It is very desperate here. The doctor of the post is very sick with it, and there is no doctor here but Dr. Mudd, and he volunteered his services, and has made a good hit of it. We have lost no cases with him yet. - With love to all, Edward Spangler

Spangler was one of the few at Fort Jefferson who never contracted yellow fever during the epidemic. Sam Arnold contracted yellow fever, but lived to tell about it.

SAMUEL ARNOLD also wrote of the yellow fever epidemic at Fort Jefferson:

In the brief space of a month after the killing of Winters (an imprisoned soldier shot while running from his guards) our small island and inclosure was visited by yellow fever. It made fearful ravages among the limited number stationed there, sweeping nearly every officer at the post away. It struck from earth our best officers and permitted the heartless ones to recover, to repeat again, I suppose, more of their cruelties upon humanity under their command. The ways of Providence are mysterious, and no doubt it was done for some good and wise purpose.

Among the first to succumb to the dread disease was Brevet Major J. Sim Smith, surgeon in charge. Dr. Smith, on his arrival at the post, which was but a few months before, corrected in various instances the abuse and reigning terrors which abounded there. He was, indeed, a man of humanity and kindness, a gentleman by birth and culture the soldiers' and prisoners' friend and protector, and, his memory lives in the mind and the heart of all by whom he was then surrounded as all that was good, pure, upright, and noble. He worked with untiring zeal whilst the fever raged, until the fatal malady struck him down upon the bed of sickness, where he lingered but three days and died. He received every attention from Dr. Mudd, who, at that period, had charge.

Mrs. Smith was lying in an adjacent room, sick with the fever. Dr. Mudd paid her every attention and worked unfalteringly to save her life. His efforts were crowned with success and she recovered from the disease. During the period of the sickness of Dr. Smith and family there was neither an officer nor an officer's wife that came near them to administer to their wants, their cases devolving upon the care of Dr. Mudd, and faithfully did he perform all that lay within his power.

In a short time the fever proved epidemic, and men could be seen falling down in every section of the fort, as the dread malady seized them. When in former times officers were parading about devising plans wherewith to torture the soldiers and prisoners nothing was seen or heard of them, they keeping themselves closely closeted, a pall like unto death seemingly hanging over the officers' quarters. Fear was depicted upon the countenance of everyone on the island, each looking for his turn next.

Two of the companies were removed to the adjacent islands, thereby being saved from the fever's fearful ravages. Two companies were retained to guard the fort and prisoners. Prisoners had to stand the brunt of the fever, their only safety being in an overruling Providence. Out of the 52 prisoners confined there but two died, whereas the garrison lost in officers and men 37.

Men at first, when taken sick, were carried to the small key termed Sand Key, upon which a small temporary shed had been erected as a hospital, the commanding officer thinking thereby to prevent the garrison from being infected. Sick patients, seated in a small boat, were conveyed over, confronted by coffins which were piled up in the bow of the boat. This of itself was sufficient to cause alarm, and even to kill the fainthearted, of whom there were quite a number collected on that small area of seven and a half acres.

With but a few exceptions those who were conveyed to the key in the small boat fell victims to the disease, and are buried beneath the sandy soil. When Dr. Mudd was given charge he stated to the commanding officer that it would be advisable to discontinue this practice; that the fever was in our midst, and that it could not be dislodged until the poison had expended itself, advising that all cases be brought to and treated at the hospital. This was acceded to, and, from his manner of treatment in the disease, a great change was soon to be noted.

From this period until the arrival from Key West of Dr. Whitehurst everything was progressing favorably, no death occurring. Dr. Whitehurst, perfectly conversant with the mode of treatment, he having had immense practice in the disease, approved Dr. Mudd's manner of treatment, and it was continued throughout the period the fever raged in our midst. The fever began to assume a more virulent type, and in spite of the untiring exertion of both began to make sad inroads into our numbers.

Everyone now thought of self alone. There was not respect shown by the attendants, they being soldiers taken from different companies, to either the dead or the dying. No sooner had the breath left the body than it was coffined and hurried over to its last resting place, there being a boat, with a crew detailed as the burying party, always awaiting. In many instances coffins were brought into the hospital and placed alongside of the bed to receive the body of some one expected to die, and had to be removed again, the patient still tenaciously clinging to life.

Men less sick were startled viewing these proceedings, it having a tendency to cause their own condition to become worse. During the terrible ordeal of the fever the garrison kept itself, duties being neglected by both officers and soldiers. During its progress the island assumed a different aspect. The island, which before was more like a place peopled by fiends than anything else it could be compared with suddenly became calm, quiet and peaceful. Fear stood out upon the face of every human being.

Some attempted to assume the tone of gaiety and indifference, but upon their faces could be read traces of other feelings. For two months the fever raged in our midst, creating havoc among those dwelling there. During this time Dr. Mudd was never idle. He worked both day and night, and was always at post, faithful to his calling, relieving his sufferings of humanity as far as laid within his power. The fever having abated through the want of more subjects, a contract physician from New York arrived at the post and relieved Dr. Whitehurst of his duties. When the new doctor took charge there were but two or three sick, and they were in a state of convalescence.

Soon thereafter Dr. Mudd was taken down with the fever in his quarters, and during the entire period of his illness was never visited by the New York doctor, the surgeon in charge, he remaining closeted in his room. The only medical treatment received by Dr. Mudd during his illness was administered at the hands of Spangler and myself. True, neither of us knew much about the disease or its treatment, all the experience either possessed being derived from observation during its prevalence, and the mode of treatment having been learned from personal experience in the nursing of patients under our charge.

Dr. Mudd was watched over by us both day and night in turns. We adopted the same method of treatment in his case as had been administered by him in ours, through which he happily recovered. He stated upon his recovery that had it not been for our care and watchfulness he would have died, and, and thanked each of us in unmeasured terms for our friendly consideration.

Dr. Mudd had worked during the prevalence of the yellow fever with an unfaltering zeal, until nature was well-nigh exhausted, relieving in every way at his command and knowledge the sufferings of humanity, but when afflicted himself he was left entirely to the mercies of his God and the limited knowledge of his two companions, which fact had the appearance of a desire for his death on the part of those at the head of affairs.

We all felt from the first that we had been transported to Dry Tortugas to fall victims to the many dreadful poisons of malaria generated in that climate. Happily we lived through it all, and I am permitted to give to the world at large some inkling of the many wrongs, tortures and sufferings inflicted upon us during the period of nearly four long years of exile. In the month of October, 1867, the fever having exhausted itself and finally stamped out, and with it, to a great extent, the harsh and rigorous measures which had heretofore been adopted in the manner of our imprisonment, some of the privileges which we had taken during its prevalence were curtailed, but for the most part the others were not countermanded by the officers in command.

The officers who garrisoned the fort at this time, with the exception of two, fell victims to the disease. A lieutenant recovered alone through the kind care and watchful nursing and attention of Colonel Grenfell who remained with him day and night, administering to his slightest want. The officers died of the disease were coffined and borne to their last resting place by the prisoners of the post, no respect being shown by the other officers. Even wives were carried in like manner, the husband remaining in his quarters.

∿

IN HIS 1926 Saturday Evening Post article, author George Allan England reported the following excerpt from a letter written by the wife of a Fort Jefferson officer:

The whole island became one immense hospital. The silence was oppressive beyond description. There were no soldiers for drill or parade, and the gloom was indescribable. Five hundred at one time would scarcely cover the list of sick.... Those able to move about looked like ghosts. The mercury was 104 in the hospital.... We seemed in some horrible nightmare. It was terrible beyond description to be hemmed in by those high, literally red-hot brick walls, with so much suffering. I could see the beds brought out, hoping for a breath of air to fan the burning brow and fever-parched lips. There was nothing to brighten the cloud of despair that encompassed the island.

Drs. Mudd and Whitehurst applied the standard treatment for yellow fever used at the time, including the use of powdered opium and powdered mercury. Dr. Mudd was also credited with using a procedure called blanketing, in which the patient was first submerged to his chin in a hot bath until he sweated profusely, and then put into bed between blankets.

∿

ALFRED O'DONOGHUE, a Union soldier from Ireland who served at Fort Jefferson during the yellow fever epidemic, wrote in the February 1869 issue of Galaxy magazine that:

During the prevalence of the yellow fever at the fort last year, when the garrison suffered terribly, Dr. Samuel Mudd, sent hither for complicity in the assassination of President Lincoln, was at one time our only physician. It is simple justice and gratitude to acknowledge the skillful and self-sacrificing service he rendered. I may add that nothing can be more exemplary than the conduct of the three political prisoners now on the island (Michael O'Loughlin having died of yellow fever last year). They perform the work assigned them without complaint, and with apparent cheerfulness; if the iron sometimes enter their souls, or the bitterness of their situation be felt, it is never exhibited. This, at least, if not much more, must in justice to them be told.

O'Donoghue and 300 other surviving Fort Jefferson soldiers signed a petition asking the government to release Dr. Mudd in recognition of his services in saving so many lives during the course of the epidemic. President Johnson ignored the petition, but in his 1869 pardon, a year and a half after the epidemic, he cited Dr. Mudd's work during the epidemic as one of the reasons for the pardon. The petition of the soldiers said:

It is with sincere pleasure that we acknowledge the great services rendered by Dr. S. A. Mudd (prisoner) during the prevalence of yellow fever at the Fort. When the very worthy surgeon of the Post, Dr. J. Sim Smith, fell one of the first victims of the fatal epidemic, and the greatest dismay and alarm naturally prevailed on all sides, deprived as the garrison was of the assistance of any medical officer, Dr. Mudd, influenced by the most praiseworthy and humane motives, spontaneously and unsolicited came forward to devote all his energies and professional knowledge to the aid of the sick and dying. He inspired the hopeless with courage, and by his constant presence in the midst of danger and infection, regardless of his own life, tranquillized the fearful and desponding.

By his prudence and foresight, the hospital upon an adjacent island, to which at first the sick were removed in an open boat, was discontinued. Those attacked with the malady were on the spot put under vigorous treatment. A protracted exposure on the open sea was avoided, and many now strong doubtless owe their lives to the care and treatment they received at his hands. He properly considered the nature and character of the infection and concluded that it could not be eradicated by the mere removal of the sick, entailing, as it did, the loss of valuable time necessary for the application of the proper remedies, exposure of those attacked and adding to the general fear and despondency. The entire different system of treatment and hospital arrangement was resorted to with the happiest effect.

Dr. Mudd's treatment and the change which he recommended met with the hearty approval and warm commendation of the regularly appointed surgeons, with whom, in a later stage of the epidemic, he was associated. Many here who have experienced his kind and judicious treatment, can never repay him the debt of obligation they owe him. We do, therefore, in consideration of the invaluable services rendered by him during this calamitous and fatal epidemic, earnestly recommend him to the well-merited clemency of the Government, and solicit his immediate release from here, and restoration to liberty and the bosom of his family

- Edmund L. Zalinski, 1st Lieutenant, 5th U.S. Artillery

BENJAMIN F. BUTLER was a Union General during the Civil War, and after the war was elected to the U.S. House of Representatives where he chaired a congressional committee to investigate the assassination of Abraham Lincoln. Butler sent William H. Gleason to Fort Jefferson to obtain statements from Dr. Mudd, Spangler, Arnold, and O'Laughlen.

Gleason arrived at Fort Jefferson immediately after the yellow fever epidemic was over. He found that O'Laughlen had died in the epidemic, but he was able to get statements from Dr. Mudd, Arnold, and Spangler. See the Documents section for Gleason's report and the three men's statements.

THE PRISONER OF SHARK ISLAND

I n 1936, Twentieth Century Fox Pictures produced a movie called *The Prisoner of Shark Island*, produced by Darryl F. Zanuck, directed by John Ford, and starring Warner Baxter and Gloria Stuart. It purportedly told the story of Dr. Mudd's imprisonment at Fort Jefferson.

Two years later, in 1938, Lux Radio Theater produced a radio broadcast version of the movie using the same script as the movie. It starred Gary Cooper and Fay Wray. The broadcast was hosted by Cecil B. DeMille. During an intermission, DeMille introduced Dr. Mudd's daughter, Nettie Mudd Monroe. He said:

We've completed the second act of The Prisoner of Shark Island. In this intermission, before Gary Cooper and our all-star cast return in Act 3, a remarkable privilege is ours. The tragic circumstances which gave us the story of tonight's play seem to belong to a dim and distant past. This is a new world, and for our reflections on the 1860s we are accustomed to rely upon ancient records and books of history. Yet tonight, a human link binds us to the time and to the hero of our play, for with us in the Lux Radio Theater is the daughter of The Prisoner of Shark Island. She is Mrs. Nettie Mudd Monroe of Baltimore, Maryland. Better than any other person she

can tell us of that noble American who was her father. I'm honored to introduce the daughter of Dr. Samuel A. Mudd, who speaks to us from New York
City, Mrs. Nettie Mudd Monroe.

Nettie then said:

Thank you Mr. DeMille. I wish to extend to the Lux Radio Theater both
my gratitude and congratulations for devoting this splendid hour to my
father's memory. I'm amazed by your play, for with some exceptions, The
Prisoner of Shark Island is proving to be a most accurate portrayal. In my
possession are many letters which my father wrote to my mother from Fort
Jefferson. They tell of how, upon his arrival there in 1865, he served for a
time on the wharf, carrying bricks. There is one letter I want to read to you.
It tells better than all others what my father was like. He says:
  "I endure the severest privations, for the most part patiently, and can
stand anything my dear wife but the thought of your dependent position,
your ills and privations."
  This thought undoubtedly drove him to attempt his escape. He hoped to
reach some spot where he could surrender and get a civil trial. He was
certain that a civil court would prove his innocence. But, as the play points
out, he was caught, chained hand and foot, and put in a dungeon. My
father had magnificent courage, He took on not only the ordeal of being
imprisoned, but the ordeal of being free. As far as I know, my father never
referred to his four years on the Dry Tortugas, and my mother too was
always silent on this subject. The world will never know what she felt. All
of these details, I suppose, are best forgotten. For after all, justice did
triumph. Furthermore, my father felt no malice, for if he had, the events
that you will hear in the next act of your play could never have come to
pass.
  Father's unfortunate life, strangely enough, taught me a very beautiful
lesson. It made me realize that out of great suffering can come something
glorious. Through injustice the world becomes more just. Through cruelty
the world gains kindness. Through inhumanity we find mercy.
  Thank you Mr. DeMille for asking me to be a guest tonight in your Lux
Radio Theater.

The Prisoner of Shark Island is excellent entertainment, performed by Hollywood's top actors, but wildly inaccurate as history. Dr. Samuel A. Mudd was indeed the name of the doctor who treated John Wilkes Booth's broken leg, and the doctor was indeed sent to an island prison. Other than that however, not much else in the movie is historically accurate. Nevertheless, it is freely available on the internet, and one should see it if possible.

~

PARDONS

D r. Mudd, Arnold, and Spangler had not been forgotten in prison. From the first days of their imprisonment, their families and friends had worked diligently for their release. Mrs. Mudd wrote several letters to President Johnson and went to see him often, begging for her husband's release. In her last public statement, in the *Baltimore News* newspaper of February 11, 1909, she said:

> I called on President Johnson a great many times. He always treated me courteously, but impressed me always as one shrinking from some impending disaster. He conveyed to me always the idea that he wanted to release my husband, but said more than once "the pressure on me is too great."

General Thomas Ewing, who was Dr. Mudd's attorney during the conspiracy trial, continued to provide legal and moral support to Dr. and Mrs. Mudd during the years of his imprisonment.

Others continued their direct appeals to President Johnson for Dr. Mudd's pardon. On January 31, 1869, a month before he would leave office, President Johnson received a high-powered delegation of men from Maryland.

The delegation consisted of Maryland Governor Oden Bowie, three justices of the Maryland Court of Appeals - Chief Justice James Bartol, Justice John Robinson, and Justice Richard Grayson - and two Maryland congressmen - Hiram McCullough and Frederick Stone. Mr. Stone had been one of Dr. Mudd's defense counsels during the conspiracy trial.

The six men asked Johnson to pardon Dr. Mudd before he left office. They also asked him to pardon Samuel Arnold and Edman Spangler. Everyone considered Spangler to be innocent, but he seemed to be comparatively friendless. Johnson said he would seriously think about it.

A week later, February 8, 1869, President Johnson summoned Mrs. Mudd to the White House and personally handed her Dr. Mudd's pardon. He apologized for not keeping his earlier promises to release Dr. Mudd, but now that his political enemies could no longer harm him, he was setting Dr. Mudd free. The pardon mentioned Dr. Mudd's work during the 1867 yellow fever epidemic, but the primary reason Johnson gave for the pardon was:

I am satisfied that the guilt found by the said judgment against Samuel A. Mudd was of receiving, entertaining, harboring, and concealing John Wilkes Booth and David E. Herold, with the intent to aid, abet and assist them in escaping from justice after the assassination of the late President of the United States, and not of any other or greater participation or complicity in said abominable crime.

Following the pardon, the War Department ordered the commanding officer of Fort Jefferson to release Dr. Mudd. The order was carried out on March 8, 1869, and Dr. Mudd's long ordeal was over. He had been in government custody just six weeks shy of four years, from April 21, 1865 when he was arrested at his farm, until March 8, 1869 when he was released from custody at Fort Jefferson.

He was still a young man, just 35 years old, but must have felt much older.

Although free, Dr. Mudd had to wait three days for a ship that would carry him away from Fort Jefferson. On March 11th, he finally left Fort Jefferson on the Navy schooner Matchless for Key West.

In Key West, Dr. Mudd secured passage on the steamship Liberty as it sailed up from Havana on its way to Baltimore. The Liberty had just finished a six-month overhaul, which included upgrading all the passenger accommodations. This included new painting and carpeting throughout, and installation of a splendid new piano from the Baltimore piano factory of Knabe & Co. in the main salon. The contrast between the prison cell where he had lived for the past four years and the luxurious accommodations aboard the Liberty must have overwhelmed Dr. Mudd.

The Liberty arrived in Baltimore at 4 o'clock in the morning on Thursday, March 18, 1869. With no one to meet him at the dock at that time of the morning, Dr. Mudd left the ship and secured a room at Barnum's City Hotel, where he rested and waited for morning to arrive. When it did, he left Barnum's and went to his brother-in-law Jeremiah Dyer's house, where he was finally reunited with his wife after almost four years.

Later in the day, Dr. Mudd was visited by several prominent Marylanders who had worked for his release, including the Governor of Maryland, Oden Bowie. On Saturday, March 20, 1869, Dr. Mudd and his wife arrived back home at their farm, where there was a joyful reunion with his four children.

Dr. Mudd's mother, Sarah Ann Mudd, was no longer alive, having died shortly before his release from prison. His father Henry Lowe Mudd lived until 1877, but in ever-declining health.

On the evening of March 2, 1869, three weeks after he pardoned Dr. Mudd, President Johnson pardoned Edman Spangler and Samuel Arnold. The next day, March 3rd, Arnold's father, who lived in Baltimore, called at the White House, where he received his son's pardon from the hands of President Johnson. The next day, March 4th,

Ulysses S. Grant was sworn in as the 18th president of the United States.

Historians generally agree that Spangler had nothing to do with the assassination of Lincoln. However, he was philosophical about his sentence. Spangler is quoted by Emily Holder, the wife of a Fort Jefferson assistant surgeon, as saying:

> *They made a mistake in sending me down here. I had nothing to do with Booth or the assassination of President Lincoln; but I suppose I have done enough in my life to deserve this, so I make the best of it.*

Arnold and Spangler were released from confinement at Fort Jefferson on March 21, 1869. Sam Arnold's father went to Fort Jefferson to bring his son back home. Sam, his father, and Spangler traveled back to Baltimore together on the steamship Cuba. The *Baltimore Sun* of April 7, 1869 reported their arrival this way:

> *Local Matters. Return of Arnold and Spangler, the Dry Tortugas Prisoners. - Samuel B. Arnold and Edman Spangler, the prisoners recently released from the Dry Tortugas, under pardon of President Johnson, the former having been sentenced for life and the latter for six years, by the military commission that tried the assassination conspirators, reached this city yesterday. They came passengers on the steamship Cuba, from Key West. Arnold appears in rather delicate health, but Spangler is well, and both seem in good spirits. They are set free now, after three years and eight months in durance vile.*
>
> *After their trial and sentence, they reached the Dry Tortugas with Dr. Mudd, their late fellow-prisoner, and O'Laughlin, who died during imprisonment, on the 24th of July, 1865, and were released on the 22nd of March 1869. Both Arnold and Spangler reply readily to the queries concerning their imprisonment and the treatment they received from the different commanders of the post.*
>
> *During the season of the fearful rage of the yellow fever in 1867 at the fort, they state that after nearly all the troops had been attacked and either recovered or died, Dr. Mudd, who had so faithfully and advantageously*

labored among the sick, was taken down with the disease, and there being no medical man left fit for duty, was nursed solely by themselves, his only remaining companion, O'Laughlin, having previously died. During its prevalence there were thirty-seven deaths in that limited community, two of whom were prisoners and the balance officers and soldiers. They speak highly of the late Major Stone, who commanded at the time. His wife having died of the epidemic of which he had recovered, he carried his little child over to Key West, with the intention of sending it to his relatives in the North, and shortly after reaching there he was taken with a relapse and died. Their treatment depended much on the commander of the post, but after the season of yellow fever they fared much better than previously.

They received a telegram on the 9th of March, informing them of their pardon, and Spangler says it appeared to him that from that time until the 21st, when Arnold's father reached there with the pardons, he gained in flesh every hour. Arnold was employed as a clerk at headquarters and Spangler as a carpenter, and both at times were compelled to work very hard.

After their release they left the Tortugas in a government sailing vessel and went over to Key West, where they remained several days, awaiting the arrival of the Cuba, and were treated in the kindest manner by the citizens.

On the terrible ordeal of the trial, under the circumstances by which they were surrounded, it is not to be supposed they would delight to dwell. Spangler says that from the torture he endured he was mostly unconscious of the proceedings in the case, and often knew nothing of what was going on around him.

When the padded hood was placed upon his head in prison, covering over his eyes and tightened about his neck and chest, with manacles already on both hands and feet, he was told it was by order of Secretary Stanton, the subordinate thus excusing himself for his action. After arriving at the fort, and up to the time of his release, Spangler avers that the sense of his entire innocence only made his chains more galling, whilst at the same time it often kept him from utter despair. Both Arnold and Spangler speak of the kindness and attention they received on board the Cuba from Capt.

Dukehart, his officers and passengers, who generally were disposed to make them comfortable.

Home again, Arnold lived quietly out of the public eye for more than 30 years. In 1902, Arnold wrote a series of newspaper articles for the *Baltimore American* describing his imprisonment at Fort Jefferson. Arnold died four years later on September 21, 1906. He is buried at Green Mount Cemetery in Baltimore, Maryland.

Michael O'Laughlen, who died of yellow fever at Fort Jefferson, is also buried at Green Mount Cemetery.

With Arnold's death in 1906, the only main figure in the Lincoln assassination story still alive was John H. Surratt. He died 10 years later, April 21, 1916, at the age of 72. Surratt is buried in the New Cathedral Cemetery in Baltimore, Maryland.

~

THE FINAL YEARS

When Dr. Mudd returned home, well-wishing friends and strangers and inquiring newspaper reporters besieged him. Dr. Mudd was very reluctant to talk to the press because he felt they had misquoted him in the past. He gave one interview to a *New York Herald* reporter, but immediately regretted it. The reporter's story contained several factual errors, and Dr. Mudd complained that it misrepresented his work at Fort Jefferson during the yellow fever epidemic.

On the whole though, he must have been gratified to find that he continued to enjoy the respect and friendship of his friends and neighbors. Dr. Mudd resumed his medical practice, slowly brought the family farm back to productivity, and became active once again in the life of his community.

In 1874, he was elected Master (chief officer) of the local farmers association, Bryantown Grange 47. In 1876, seven years after he returned home, he was elected vice president of the local Democratic Tilden-Hendricks presidential election committee. Tilden lost that year to Republican Rutherford B. Hayes in a hotly disputed election.

The next year Dr. Mudd ran as a Democratic candidate for the

Maryland House of Delegates, but was defeated by the popular Republican William D. Mitchell.

Before he went to prison, Dr. and Mrs. Mudd had four children – Andrew, Lillian, Thomas, and Samuel. After prison, they had five more – Henry, Stella, Edward, Rose de Lima, and Mary Eleanor, known as "*Nettie.*"

Andrew Jerome Mudd (1858-1882)

Lillian Augusta Mudd (1860-1940)

Thomas Dyer Mudd (1861-1929)

Samuel Alexander Mudd II (1864-1930)

Henry Mudd (1870-died after 8 months)

Stella Marie Mudd (1871-1952)

Edward Joseph Mudd (1873-1946)

Rose de Lima Mudd (1875-1943)

Mary Eleanor "Nettie" Mudd (1878-1943)

THE 1870 CENSUS showed 20 people living at the Mudd farm. This included Dr. Mudd (35), Mrs. Mudd (34), their children Andrew (11), Lillian (10), Thomas (8), Samuel (6), and infant Henry, Mary G. Simons (49), Mrs. Mudd's sister Betty Dyer (42), their long-time farm worker John Best (70), two domestic servants, Lettie Hall (17) and Louisa Cristie (14), farm laborer William Moore (18), and the Washington family, Frank Washington (32), wife Betty (30), and their children, Edward (13), J.R. (9), Sidney (7), Catherine (5), and William (2).

Frank Washington had been a slave on Dr. Mudd's farm before emancipation, and remained there afterwards as a paid farm hand. His wife Betty, who had been a slave to Mrs. Adelaide Middleton, joined her husband on the Mudd farm after emancipation, working as the family cook. Frank and Betty Washington both testified in Dr. Mudd's defense at the conspiracy trial. Betty testified: "*Dr. Mudd treated me very well. I have no fault to find with him.*"

Dr. Mudd continued to study and write about yellow fever after his pardon. An article he wrote on yellow fever was printed in the Baltimore Sun newspaper on June 25, 1873. In the article, Dr. Mudd points out that there is *a wonderful diversity of opinion*" about the cause and treatment of yellow fever. It would be almost two decades after he died in 1883 that researchers would discover that yellow fever was transmitted by infected mosquitoes. After that, yellow fever was controllable by mosquito eradication programs, and eventually by a yellow fever vaccine.

Edman Spangler

When Edman Spangler left Fort Jefferson, he went to work at the Holliday Street Theatre in Baltimore for his old boss John T. Ford, the former owner of Ford's Theatre where Lincoln was shot. When the Holliday Street Theatre burned down in 1873, Spangler traveled to the Mudd farm, where Dr. Mudd and his wife welcomed him as the friend whom Dr. Mudd credited with saving his life while suffering with yellow fever. Spangler lived with the Mudd family for about 18 months, earning his keep by doing carpentry, gardening, and other farm chores.

Edman Spangler died in the Mudd farmhouse on February 7, 1875, in the upstairs bedroom next to the one in which John Wilkes Booth had stayed 10 years earlier. He was baptized into the Catholic faith just before he died by Father Henry Volz from St. Mary's Church in Bryantown. He was buried in the nearby St. Peter's Church cemetery, now known as St. Peter's Old Cemetery, on February 9, 1875.

Nettie Mudd, in her book on the life of her father, said of Ned Spangler:

> He was a quiet, genial man, greatly respected by the members of our family and the people of the neighborhood. His greatest pleasure seemed to be found in extending kindnesses to others, and particularly children, of whom he was very fond.

The furniture and children's toys Spangler made while staying with the Mudd family may be seen today in the Dr. Samuel A. Mudd House Museum in Waldorf, Maryland.

Not long after Spangler's death, Dr. Mudd found a handwritten manuscript in Spangler's toolbox, containing Spangler's account of what he saw at Ford's Theatre when Lincoln was assassinated. Spangler's statement said:

I was born in York County, Pennsylvania, and am about forty-three years of age, I am a house carpenter by trade, and became acquainted with J. Wilkes Booth when a boy. I worked for his father in building a cottage in Harford County, Maryland, in 1854.

Since A. D. 1853, I have done carpenter work for the different theaters in the cities of Baltimore and Washington, to wit: The Holliday Street Theater and the Front Street Theater of Baltimore, and Ford's Theater in the City of Washington. I have acted also as scene shifter in all the above named theaters, and had a favorable opportunity to become acquainted with the different actors. I have acted as scene shifter in Ford's Theater, ever since it was first opened up, to the night of the assassination of President Lincoln.

During the winter of A.D. 1862 and 1863, J. Wilkes Booth played a star engagement at Ford's Theater for two weeks. At that time I saw him and conversed with him quite frequently. After completing his engagement he left Washington and I did not see him again until the winters of A.D. 1864 and 1865. I then saw him at various times in and about Ford's Theater.

Booth had free access to the theater at all times, and made himself very familiar with all persons connected with it. He had a stable in the rear of the theater where he kept his horses. A boy, Joseph Burroughs, commonly called 'Peanut John,' took care of them whenever Booth was absent from the city. I looked after his horses, which I did at his request, and saw that they were properly cared for. Booth promised to pay me for my trouble, but he never did. I frequently had the horses exercised, during Booth's absence from the city, by 'Peanut John,' walking them up and down the alley. 'Peanut John' kept the key to the stable in the theater, hanging upon a nail behind the small door, which opened into the alley at the rear of the theater.

Booth usually rode out on horseback every afternoon and evening, but seldom remained out later than eight or nine o'clock. He always went and returned alone. I never knew of his riding out on horseback and staying out all night, or of any person coming to the stable with him, or calling there for him. He had two horses at the stable, only a short time. He brought them there some time in the month of December. A man called George and myself repaired and fixed the stable for him. I usually saddled the horse for him when 'Peanut John' was absent. About the first of March Booth brought another horse and a buggy and harness to the stable, but in what manner I do not know; after that he used to ride out with his horse and buggy, and I frequently harnessed them up for him. I never saw any person ride out with him or return with him from these rides.

On the Monday evening previous to the assassination, Booth requested me to sell the horse, harness, and buggy, as he said he should leave the city soon. I took them the next morning to the horse market, and had them put up at auction, with the instruction not to sell unless they would net two hundred and sixty dollars; this was in accordance with Booth's orders to me. As no person bid sufficient to make them net that amount, they were not sold, and I took them back to the stable. I informed Booth of the result that same evening in front of the theater. He replied that he must then try and have them sold at private sale, and asked me if I would help him. I replied, 'Yes.' This was about six o'clock in the evening, and the conversation took place in the presence of John F. Sleichman and others. The next day I sold them for two hundred and sixty dollars. The purchaser accompanied me to the theater. Booth was not in, and the money was paid to James J. Gifford, who receipted for it. I did not see Booth to speak to him, after the sale, until the evening of the assassination.

Upon the afternoon of April 14 I was told by 'Peanut John' that the president and General Grant were coming to the theater that night, and that I must take out the partition in the president's box. It was my business to do all such work. I was assisted in doing it by Rittespaugh and 'Peanut John.'

In the evening, between five and six o'clock, Booth came into the theater and asked me for a halter. I was very busy at work at the time on the stage preparatory to the evening performance, and Rittespaugh went upstairs and brought one down. I went out to the stable with Booth and put the halter upon the horse. I commenced to take off the saddle when Booth said,

'Never mind, I do not want it off, but let it and the bridle remain.' He afterward took the saddle off himself, locked the stable, and went back to the theater.

Booth, Maddox, 'Peanut John,' and myself immediately went out of the theater to the adjoining restaurant next door, and took a drink at Booth's expense. I then went immediately back to the theatre, and Rittespaugh and myself went to supper. I did not see Booth again until between nine and ten o'clock. About that time Deboney called to me, and said Booth wanted me to hold his horse as soon as I could be spared. I went to the back door and Booth was standing in the alley holding a horse by the bridle rein, and requested me to hold it. I took the rein, but told him I could not remain, as Gifford was gone, and that all of the responsibility rested on me. Booth then passed into the theater. I called to Deboney to send "Peanut John" to hold the horse. He came, and took the horse, and I went back to my proper place.

In about a half hour afterward I heard a shot fired, and immediately saw a man run across the stage. I saw him as he passed by the center door of the scenery, behind which I then stood; this door is usually termed the center chamber door. I did not recognize the man as he crossed the stage as being Booth. I then heard some one say that the president was shot. Immediately all was confusion. I shoved the scenes back as quickly as possible in order to clear the stage, as many were rushing upon it. I was very much frightened, as I heard persons halloo, "Burn the theater!" I did not see Booth pass out; my situation was such that I could not see any person pass out of the back door. The back door has a spring attached to it, and would not shut of its own accord. I usually slept in the theater, but I did not upon the night of the assassination; I was fearful the theater would be burned, and I slept in a carpenter's shop adjoining.

I never heard Booth express himself in favor of the rebellion, or opposed to the government, or converse upon political subjects; and I have no recollection of his mentioning the name of President Lincoln in any connection whatever. I know nothing of the mortise hole said to be in the wall behind the door of the president's box, or of any wooden bar to fasten or hold the door being there, or of the lock being out of order. I did not notice any hole in the door. Gifford usually attended to the carpentering in the front part of *the theater, while I did the work about the stage. Mr. Gifford was the boss carpenter, and I was under him.*

Edman Spangler is buried just two miles from Dr. Mudd's farm, at Old St. Peter's Cemetery, Waldorf, Maryland.

THE FIVE-YEAR PERIOD from 1873 to 1878 encompassed the third longest economic depression in U.S. history. Bankruptcies and insolvencies were widespread. In rural areas, the downward pressure on prices reduced farm income and created great hardship. Dr. Mudd and his family were not exempt from this hardship.

In 1878, despite their own hardships. Dr. and Mrs. Mudd temporarily took in a 7-year-old orphan named John Burke. He was one of 300 abandoned children sent to Maryland families from the New York City Foundling Asylum run by the Catholic Sisters of Charity. A large number of orphans and abandoned children was one of the legacies of the Civil War. Other local families also took in children. The Burke boy was permanently settled with farmer Ben Jenkins.

Although the rural economy began to recover as the depression of 1873 - 1878 ended, Dr. Mudd's financial problems continued. On April 28, 1880, the *Port Tobacco Times and Charles County Advertiser* reported that Dr. Mudd's barn and its contents, including his tobacco crop, were destroyed by fire. The paper reported:

Heavy Loss by Fire
*   On Saturday last, a barn belonging to Dr. S.A. Mudd, near Bryantown, was entirely destroyed by fire, together with its contents, between 6000 and 8000 pounds of tobacco, two horses, a wagon and a lot of farm implements. It seems that some hands had been engaged in clearing a piece of new land on the doctor's farm about a quarter of a mile from the barn, fire being used for the purpose of burning the brush and other growth. The fire it appears was neglected and communicated to the barn, which was totally*

destroyed in a very few minutes. We understand that there was no insur-
ance upon the barn or any portion of its contents. Thus we have been called
upon to chronicle two very heavy losses from fire by citizens of our county
within the last few weeks.

NETTIE MUDD TOLD the story of her father's trial, imprisonment, and
return home in her 1906 book The Life of Dr. Samuel A. Mudd. Nettie
was just five years when her father died, so she relied on her mother
for details of her father's life. Dr. Mudd died on Nettie's fifth birthday,
January 10, 1883. This is Nettie's account of her father's pardon and
life after returning home:

My father regained his liberty on the 8th day of March, 1869, having
endured imprisonment for a period of four years, lacking about six weeks.
Two days prior to the issue of the above order from the War Department,
on the 13th of February, President Johnson wrote a note to my mother and
sent it to her home by a special messenger, requesting her to come to Wash-
ington and receive my father's pardon. She left for Washington immedi-
ately, but being detained on the way, did not reach the city till the
following morning.

Once there, she repaired, in company with Dr. J. H. Blanford, my
father's brother-in-law, to the White House. In a few moments President
Johnson sent for my mother to come into the executive office. There he
delivered to her the papers for the release of my father. My mother asked
him if the papers would go safely through the mails. His reply, before he
had signed the papers, was: "Mrs. Mudd, I will put the president's seal on
them. I have complied with my promise to release your husband before I
left the White House. I no longer hold myself responsible. Should these
papers go amiss you may never hear from them again, as they may be put
away in some pigeon-hole or corner. I guess, Mrs. Mudd, you think this is
tardy justice in carrying out my promise made to you two years ago. The
situation was such, however, that I could not act as I wanted to do."

After he had signed and sealed the papers, he handed them to my

*mother, who took them, thanked him and left. She had intended going to
the Dry Tortugas and delivering in person the release to her long-afflicted
husband. This, however, she was not permitted to do, as when she reached
Baltimore, intending to take the steamer from that port for the Dry Tortugas, she found that the boat had departed a few hours before her arrival,
and that another would not sail for two or three weeks. She therefore sent
the papers by express to her brother in New Orleans, Thomas O. Dyer,
who paid a Mr. Loutrel three hundred dollars to deliver them to my father
at Fort Jefferson.*

*On the 20th day of March, 1869, sixteen days after President Johnson's
term of office had expired, my father arrived home, frail, weak and sick,
never again to be strong during the thirteen years he survived. It is needless
for me to try to picture the feelings and incidents of his home-coming. Pleasure and pain were intermingled - pleasure to him to be once more in his
old home surrounded by his loved ones, and pleasure to them to have him
back once more; pain to them to see him so broken in health and strength,
and pain to him to find his savings all gone and his family almost destitute.*

*Again we find him, after a brief period for rest, engaged in the struggle
to regain in a measure his lost means and position. This he never accomplished. He found himself surrounded by exacting duties, yet handicapped
by innumerable disadvantages. There were no laborers to cultivate the
farm; the fences had fallen down or been destroyed by the Federal soldiery,
and the fields were unprotected against intrusive cattle; buildings were out
of repair, and money almost unobtainable. His hardships in prison,
however, had in a measure taught him to be patient. Gradually things
became brighter. When the warm glow of summer passed into harvest
time, he was encouraged by the fact that a generous yield of earth's products rewarded him for his labor. He only partially regained his practice.
While he was confined in prison many of the families he had attended
employed other physicians. Many of these families sought my father's
services on his return, but some did not. Apart from this, the people of the
neighborhood had become comparatively poor by reason of their losses
occasioned by the war. A great deal of his attention and skill was therefore
given gratuitously.*

During the four years they were together in prison Edward Spangler became very much attached to my father. As a consequence, a short time after Spangler's release, he came to our home early one morning, and his greeting to my mother, after my father had introduced him, was: "Mrs. Mudd, I came down last night, and asked some one to tell me the way here. I followed the road, but when I arrived I was afraid of your dogs, and I roosted in a tree." He had come to stay.

He occupied himself chiefly in helping our old gardener, Mr. Best, and in doing small jobs of carpenter's work in the neighborhood. My father gave him five acres of land in a wood containing a bubbling spring, about five hundred yards from our dwelling. Here Spangler contemplated erecting a building and establishing for himself a home. This purpose, however, was never to be realized. About eighteen months after he came he contracted a severe illness, the result of having been caught in a heavy rain, which thoroughly saturated his clothing. His sickness resulted in his death - rheumatism of the heart being the immediate cause.

He was a quiet, genial man, greatly respected by the members of our family and the people of the neighborhood. His greatest pleasure seemed to be found in extending kindnesses to others, and particularly to children, of whom he was very fond. Not long after his death my father, in searching for a tool in Spangler's tool chest, found a manuscript, in Spangler's own handwriting, and presumably written while he was in prison. This manuscript contained Spangler's statement of his connection with the great 'conspiracy.'

My father died from pneumonia, January 10, 1883, after an illness of nine days. He contracted the disease while visiting the sick in the neighborhood in the nighttime and in inclement weather. He was buried in Saint Mary's cemetery, attached to the Bryantown church, where he had first met Booth. He was in the fiftieth year of his age at the time of his death.

Nettie's sister Stella was 11 when their father died, and remembered more details of her father's death. In a 1950 letter to a nephew, an elderly Stella (now Sister Rosamunda) wrote:

About a year before his death, he was not well and I was left to keep him company. While busy elsewhere he walked the floor. I thought he was

saying 'misery me' - it was the Misererie. New Year's Day he went to Mass,
visited a very sick patient after Mass - had pneumonia - died Jan. 10th. The
day before his death he said to my mother 'Don't wait till it is too late, send
for the priest, I know I am going to die.' The priest came, did not think need
urgent and had to meet train, so did administer sacraments. The priest of
Bryantown parish paid father a visit that day, heard his confession. Tom,
your father, went for Father Southgate that night in snow and bitter cold.
Father S. came, gave last rites - said prayers for dying and he was gone to
God. I was present at death bed. Father said to my Mother - "It is not hard
to die. I am just waiting for call of the Old Master." Mother said to him
"How can you talk like that and leave me with a house full of children?" He
replied "God knows best" (his last words) and died.

Dr. Mudd is buried in the cemetery at St. Mary's Catholic Church
in Bryantown, the same church where he first met John Wilkes
Booth. The Port Tobacco Times and Charles County Advertiser ran
the following obituary for Dr. Mudd on January 19, 1883:

Dr. Samuel A. Mudd died at his residence near Bryantown in this county
on Wednesday of last week after a short illness of pneumonia. So short had
been his illness that no information of it had been received here, and being,
as he was, in the prime of manly vigor, the sudden intelligence of his death
received here on Friday was as great a surprise as it was an unfeigned and
universal regret.

In the death of Dr. Mudd, Charles County has lost one of its most
honored citizens, the profession a learned and useful member, while his
family must endure the loss of a kind, loving and painstaking husband and
father. He was ever ready to lend his aid and assistance to the poor and
needy, and around the bed of pain and suffering his generous nature was
ever ready to extend comfort and solace, with his means and the talents
with which God had endowed him.

In the death of Dr. Mudd has passed from earth the last of those who
were associated in the assassination of the lamented President Lincoln. As
free from any guilty connection with conspirators in this crime, which will
ever darken the pages of history, as an unborn babe, he nevertheless, upon

bare suspicion was made to suffer from the brutal treatment of an enraged and ungovernable people. Awed by the circumstances of finding the assassin of the president in his house, he having imposed upon his generous nature by false statements as to the origin of his accident, his crime was simply not admitting the service rendered to Booth in setting his leg.

Under the excitement prevailing at the time, Dr. Mudd denied any knowledge of Booth, or that he had been at his house. He was afraid to admit service rendered even under the misapprehension that the accident occurred by a fall from his horse while traveling through the county, as he had been told by Booth, would certainly secure his arrest and incarceration, his courage forsook him and he denied his having been with him, when upon search of his house the boot leg was found which had been cut from the broken limb with "J. Wilkes" written within it.

To then tell the whole truth availed him nothing. He was tried for conspiracy in the assassination, convicted and sentenced to the Dry Tortugas for life, when after some three years he was pardoned by President Johnson. It is an injustice to the memory of a generous, warmhearted man to associate him with the guilty Booth. His only crime being rendering medical aid to Booth in his suffering, he not knowing Booth to be guilty of any crime, but laboring under the false impression he had sustained his accident in an innocent fall from his horse.

He was in his 48th year at the time of his death. He leaves a widow and six children to mourn his great loss.

Whatever Dr. Mudd's faults may have been, many people at Fort Jefferson owed their lives to him for his heroic and selfless work there during the horrific 1867 yellow fever epidemic when he risked and almost lost his own life to save others.

Dr. Mudd is buried in the cemetery at St. Mary's Church in Bryantown, the same church where he first met John Wilkes Booth. Sarah passed away on November 29, 1911 at the home of her daughter Rose De Lima Mudd Gardiner. She is buried with Dr. Mudd at the St. Mary's Church cemetery.

~

THE MUDD FAMILY

Dr. Samuel A. Mudd

Sarah Frances Dyer Mudd

The Children

Andrew Jerome Mudd

A ndrew Jerome Mudd was born on September 28, 1858, the first of Sam and Sarah Mudd's nine children. Dr. Mudd mentions Andrew in two of his letters from prison, one concerning an accident, and the other a sickness:

June 2, 1866 - Andrew was 7 years old: "*I received yours of the 7th today, and beyond the fact that Andrew has recovered from his accident, and that you are all well, etc.*"

April 3, 1868 - Andrew was 9 years old: "*I am in hopes Andrew's sickness will not assume anything grave.*"

Andrew was only 24 when he died on November 25, 1882, just a month and a half before his father died.

Lillian Augusta Mudd

Lillian Augusta "Sissie" Mudd was born June 2, 1860, the second of Sam and Sarah Mudd's nine children.

In 1873, Sissie left home in 1873 to attend the same boarding school Sarah had attended, Visitation Academy in Frederick, Maryland. She didn't like it. She transferred to the new Mt. Saint Agnes Academy high school in Baltimore for her remaining three years of high school. She graduated in 1877.

Lillian married Francis Xavier Gardiner on January 24, 1882 at St. Ann's Church in Baltimore. They lived in Baltimore and had ten children there:

Mary Melita Gardiner (1882-1942)
Henry Elmer Gardiner (1884-1945)
Joseph Merton Gardiner (1885-1958)
Joseph Clement Gardiner (1888-1966)
Charles Leroy Gardiner (1889-unknown)
Stanislaus Kostka Gardiner (1891-1959)
Sophia Althea Gardiner (1893-1974)

William Leo Gardiner (1894-1964)

William Russell Gardiner (1898-1977)

Lillian Augusta Gardiner (1900-1965)

The 1921 Baltimore City Directory lists Lillian's occupation as Nurse. The 1910 Federal Census lists Francis' occupation as Solicitor.

Francis died on February 28, 1918. Lillian passed away on January 16, 1940. Both were interred in Baltimore's New Cathedral Cemetery. Both interments were preceded by a Requiem High Mass at St. Ann's Church where they had been active congregants for many years.

Thomas Dyer Mudd

Thomas Dyer Mudd, born June 6, 1861, was the third of Sam and Sarah Mudd's nine children. He was 22 years old when his father passed away in 1883. As the oldest son, Tom ran the Mudd farm with his brothers and sisters for a few years, but eventually left for city life, first in Philadelphia, and then in Baltimore.

Deciding to follow in his father's medical footsteps, he studied medicine at Baltimore's College of Physicians and Surgeons, graduating in 1894. After obtaining his medical degree, Tom set up his medical practice in the Anacostia section of Washington, D.C.

In 1898, Tom married Mary Elizabeth Hartigan. They had four children before Mary passed away in 1917. They were:

Stella Maria Mudd (1899-2000)

Richard Dyer Mudd (1901-2002)

Thomas Paul Mudd (1904-1981)

Robert Leo Mudd (1906-1955)

Tom married again, in 1922, to Amelia Baker (1887-1957). He died on February 11, 1929 in Washington, D.C., and is interred at Mount Olivet Cemetery, Washington, D.C.

Samuel Alexander Mudd II

Sam and Sara's fourth child, Samuel Alexander Mudd II, was born on January 30, 1864.

Over the years, Sam's brothers and sisters left the farm one by one to build their lives elsewhere. In the end, it was only Sam who stayed, married, and kept the farm in the Mudd family.

Sam married Claudine Louise Burch, known by family and friends as Loulie, on November 26, 1897. He was 33. She was 22. They had nine children:

Mary Phyllis Mudd (1898-1984)
Lucille Augusta Mudd (1900-1946)
Christine Eveline Mudd (1902-2004)
Samuel Alexander Mudd III (1905-1929)
Emily Theresa Mudd (1906-1999)
Joseph Burch Mudd (1909-1991)
Marie Carmelite Mudd (1911-2012)
Cecilia Drey Mudd (1914-2003)
Claudine Louise Mudd (1917-2002)

Sam died on June 21, 1930. Loulie passed away on February 3, 1961.

Henry Mudd

Henry Mudd, Sam and Sarah's fifth child, was born a year after Sam returned from Fort Jefferson, in January 1870, but sadly died as an infant.

Stella Marie Mudd

Stella Maria Mudd was the sixth of the nine Mudd children. She was born on the Mudd family farm near Bryantown on July 4, 1871.

When a young woman, Stella left home to attend college at St. Catherine's Normal Institute in Baltimore, graduating in 1888. St. Catherine's was a teacher training school established in 1875 by the Sisters of the Holy Cross. Her experience there changed her life. Shortly after turning twenty in 1891, Stella entered the Congregation of the Sisters of the Holy Cross, taking the religious name Sister Mary Rosamunda.

Stella taught high school at the Sacred Heart Academy in Fort

Wayne, Indiana from 1892 to 1893, the St. Joseph's Academy in South Bend, Indiana from 1893 to 1894, and the Sacred Heart Academy in Ogden, Utah from 1894 to 1938. From 1938 to1952 she was a retired resident at the Western Provincial House in Ogden.

Stella died on December 13, 1952, and is interred at the Mount Calvary Cemetery in Salt Lake City, Utah. It was the end of an era. She was the last of Dr. and Mrs. Mudd's children to pass away.

Edward Joseph Mudd

Edward Joseph Mudd, the seventh of Dr. and Mrs. Mudd's nine children, was born July 27, 1873 on the Mudd family farm. When he was 24, Edward left the farm to join the Washington, D.C. police department. He married Gertrude Veronica Casey three years later.

Edward served with the police department as a policeman and detective for twenty-five years, retiring on disability in 1922.

For the last 12 years of his life, he and his wife lived in Shadyside, Maryland. Edward Joseph Mudd passed away on December 22, 1946.

Rose DeLima Mudd

Rose DeLima "Emie" Mudd, born on October 8, 1875, was the eighth of Sam and Sarah Mudd's nine children. She married Albert J. Gardiner on February 13, 1901. She was 25. He was 53.

Emie and Albert had six children:

Samuel Jerome Gardiner (1901-1967)

Albert Joseph Gardiner (1903-1978)

Sarah Frances Gardiner (1907-1992)

James Rudolph Gardiner (1911-1986)

Mary Marjorie Gardiner (1914-1992)

Joseph Bernard Gardiner (1916-1992)

Albert died on May 13, 1934 at age 86. Rose passed away on March 15, 1943 at age 67.

Mary Eleanor Mudd

Mary Eleanor Mudd, known as Nettie, was Dr. Mudd's ninth and youngest child. The day she celebrated her 5th birthday, January 10, 1883, was the day Dr. Mudd died. Like many educated young women of her day, Nettie became a school teacher, teaching at the Gallant Green elementary school just a short distance from where she lived with her family on the Mudd farm.

Nettie published The Life of Dr. Samuel A. Mudd in 1906 when she was 28 years old. Her mother, who passed away in 1911, was undoubtedly a valuable resource for information on Dr. Mudd's life, including access to all of Dr. and Mrs. Mudd's correspondence over the years.

The Preface to Nettie's book was written by Daniel Eldridge Monroe, a 61 year-old Baltimore lawyer whose wife had died in 1869, leaving him to raise their five daughters and two sons. Nettie married Eldridge on December 8, 1906 and moved to Baltimore where Eldridge had his law practice. A year later, September 27, 1907, Nettie gave birth to twins, William Eldridge Monroe and Sarah Frances Monroe. Unfortunately, the twins died soon after birth. Nettie and Eldridge had two more children, James Victor Monroe, born November 7, 1908, and Frances Dyer Monroe, born October 12, 1910.

When Eldridge Monroe died in 1914, Nettie remained in Baltimore, raised her two children there, and earned her living as a bookkeeper. She and her children often visited her extended family back at the Mudd farm.

Samuel Arnold, one of those in prison with Dr. Mudd, was still alive when Nettie was writing her book. She wrote to him, saying:

Dear Sir:

I have edited a "Life" of my father, the late Dr. Samuel A. Mudd, who suffered imprisonment with you at the Dry Tortugas for a crime of which you were wholly innocent. I have endeavored in this book to vindicate the memory of my father, and incidentally have shown I think the innocence of the other Dry Tortugas prisoners.

My book is now in the hands of the publishers, but before it can be put to press I must obtain 500 bona fide subscribers. I have thought, that as you were a fellow sufferer with my father, you might be willing to help me secure these preliminary subscriptions. I therefore have taken the liberty of sending you copies of the prospectus and subscription blank, and will be greatly obligated to you if you will kindly obtain all the subscribers possible. Please send to me and not to the publishers. Of course, the book is not to be paid for until delivered.

I understand that you have some valuable photographs of scenes at the Dry Tortugas. Would it be convenient for you to let me have some of these photographs to be reproduced in my book.

Kindly answer, and oblige,

Very respectfully yours,

Nettie Mudd

Nettie apparently didn't receive any photographs from Arnold, as none are reproduced in her book.

Nettie died at 65 years of age on December 31, 1943.

~

PHOTO GALLERY

John Wilkes Booth

Mary Surratt

John Surratt

David Herold

George Atzerodt

Lewis Powell

Edman Spangler

Samuel Arnold

Michael O'Laughlen

Dr. Mudd's Attorney Thomas Ewing

Dr. Mudd's Attorney Frederick Stone

State of Maine

The State of Maine transported Dr. Mudd, Edman Spangler, Samuel Arnold, and Michael O'Laughlen from Washington to Fort Monroe. Credit National Archives.

U.S.S. Florida

THE U.S.S. FLORIDA transported Dr. Mudd, Edman Spangler, Samuel Arnold, and Michael O'Laughlen from Fort Monroe to Fort Jefferson. Credit National Archives.

Fort Jefferson Entrance

THIS IS the Sally Port entrance to Fort Jefferson. The casemate cell behind the three vertical rifle embrasure openings above the Sally Port is where Dr. Mudd and his companions lived most of their time at Fort Jefferson.

Fort Jefferson Dungeon Door

THIS IS the door to the dungeon where Dr. Mudd and his companions were placed after Dr. Mudd's failed escape attempt.

Inside the Dungeon

THIS IS the inside of the dungeon where Dr. Mudd and his companions were placed after Dr. Mudd's failed escape attempt.

Dr. Mudd's Cell

THIS PHOTO SHOWS the second tier of casemate cells where prisoners lived. Dr. Mudd and his companions lived in the casemate in the middle of the row, above the slanted roof shading the Sally Port entrance. The lighthouse keeper and his family lived in the cottage at the left of the photo.

Inside Dr. Mudd's Cell

THIS IS the inside of the casemate cell where Dr. Mudd and his companions lived most of their time at Fort Jefferson. It sits directly above the Sally Port.

Inside Fort Jefferson

THIS IS the interior of Fort Jefferson. The officers' barracks are at the left, and the soldiers' barracks are at the right. The central area is the parade ground. The small garden in the center was probably the vegetable garden Dr. Mudd and Grenfell tended. Credit National Archives.

The Matchless Schooner

AFTER BEING PARDONED, the Matchless carried Dr. Mudd from Fort Jefferson to Key West where he boarded the steamship Liberty that took him to Baltimore. Credit National Archives.

The Liberty Steamship

THE STEAMSHIP LIBERTY transported Dr. Mudd from Fort Jefferson to Baltimore.

10-17-1852: EXPULSION FROM GEORGETOWN COLLEGE

S ource: Letter from Fr. Callaghan to Fr. George, Georgetown University Lauinger Library, Special Collections Division, Washington, D.C.

~

Georgetown College, Oct. 31st, 1852

Rev. & Dear Father George,

... The most exciting thing that we have had lately was a disturbance among the boys. It is entirely settled now, so that I can give you a full account of it...

Last Friday week a boy a refused a punishment which Mr. Tehan had given him for going out of studies without permission. Fr. Maguire therefore gave him his choice to submit to the punishment or leave the College. He chose the latter. When the boys heard of the affair, they murmured about it, and complained of the regulation that prefects have about going out of studies. They held a sort of indignation meeting, and decided that the boy ought to be excused from his punishment, and the rule abolished.

They tried an appeal to Fr. Maguire and to Mr. Tehan, but to no purpose. When the bell rang for free studies at 12 ¾ (this was Friday noon) none of them went. Mr. Clark, who kept those studies, went up to the study room, and finding no one there, walked down as cooly and naturally as he does everything else. At the time for regular studies, he rang the bell, but none of the boys moved. Their resolution held for about five minutes, and at length one started, and another, and finally they all went. The middle studies were undisturbed.

All was quiet from that time till the recreation after school which was spent in indignation, like the one after dinner. In night studies there was a good deal of stamping in the beginning. Mr. Brady kept these studies. He bore with the noise for a little while, and then said a few calm words to them which had the effect of producing quiet for the rest of the studies. The next day some of the larger ones apologized in the name of all to Mr. Brady, explaining to him that the indignation was only against Mr. Tehan. He answered them bluntly that he required no special regard from them, he entirely approved Mr. Tehan's course, and would do the same thing himself if he were in Mr. Tehan's place.

The next morning Mr. Tehan kept studies, and then the grand row took place. At the beginning of studies they saluted him with a hip, and when he said the prayers, they answered with a howl. He did nothing but 'keep cool' which was all that he could do, and was not a very easy task, for during the whole studies they kept up a regular beating on their desks to a tune prepared for the occasion.

During both of the studies the prefects were on the watch and secured the names of many and especially of six who took a principal part in the meetings and the noise. A great many in the house thought the best plan would be to expel those six immediately and publicly, but Fr. Maguire judged it more prudent to wait a little. It is probable that if the ring leaders had been expelled immediately, a great many of the others would have followed them.

When they came down to breakfast after studies, they were all in the humors of uproar. Fr. Maguire met them in the refrectory, and addressed them in a quiet but decided manner. He mentioned to them that six of their leaders had been noted, and that he would deal with them as he thought they deserved. The effect of his words was that the noisy doings were stopped, and those who were conscious of having been notable, were put on their good behavior, hoping to save themselves.

Fr. Maguire wrote immediately to the parents of the six, and requested them to come and take their children home. This was on Saturday. The next Tuesday five of the parents or guardians came, and the boys were despatched at very short notice. The way of proceeding was this. The parent or guardian came. The whole matter was explained to them, the prefects were called in to testify, the boys clothes were packed, and he went away in the carriage that had brought his father or guardian.

Those sent the first day were **Samuel Mudd from Maryland,** Coleman from Cincinnati (the boy who came to Holy Cross with Fr. Blox 4 summers ago), Rogers from Baltimore, Ned Campbell and Mooney from N. York.

The boys were pretty well sobered down by these dismissals and those who had done anything were quaking, for fear their turn should come next. Tuesday night, one of them went to Fr. Maguire, and asked to go of his own accord. He was allowed to go of course. The next day the sixth one, Miller of N. York went. His father is a lawyer in New York with whom John Devlin is in partnership. Devlin came for the boy, with a message from his father, that before leaving the College, his son should apologize to Fr. Maguire for his conduct.

The next day, Thursday, the boys were made perfectly quiet by being told that those who were to be dismissed had all been dealt with, that if any remaining in the college were dissatisfied, they might apply to the president and he would permit them to go home, that if they made any further trouble, they were watched, and would be immediately sent home. Now that their fears are removed, they are quite orderly.

The whole affair has been advantageous to the College. Some of those who would have been most troublesome during the year have been got rid of (the prefects say the selection could not have been better made). The parents are satisfied, and the disorderly fellows that remain know that they are watched, and know what they may expect if they commit themselves...

Truly yours in Christ,

J.G. Callaghan, S.J.

04-22-1865: STATEMENT TO COLONEL HENRY WELLS

S ource: Investigation And Trial Papers Relating To The Assassination Of President Lincoln, 1865. (NARA microfilm publication M-599). National Archives, Washington, D.C. The statement was drafted on April 21st and signed on April 22nd.

~

FOLLOWING his arrest by Lieutenant Alexander Lovett, Dr. Mudd provided the following signed and sworn statement to Colonel Henry H. Wells in Bryantown. Note the sentence that says Dr. Mudd did not see Booth again between the time Booth stayed overnight at his home, and the time Booth appeared with his broken leg. This was not true. He met Booth, John Surratt, and Louis Weichmann in Washington, D.C. just a few weeks after Booth had stayed overnight at his home. When Secretary of War Edwin Stanton learned of this undisclosed meeting from Louis Weichmann, Dr. Mudd's status changed from witness to alleged conspirator.

~

Bryantown, Md
  April 21, 1865

Dr. S.A. Mudd, residing four miles north of Bryantown, Maryland, being duly sworn deposes and says:

Last Saturday morning, April 15th, about four o'clock, two men called at my house and knocked very loudly. I was aroused by the noise, and as it was such an unusual thing for persons to knock so loudly, I took the precaution of asking who were there before opening the door. After they had knocked twice more, I opened the door, but before doing so they told me they were two strangers on their way to Washington, that one of their horses had fallen by which one of the men had broken his leg. On opening the door, I found two men, one on a horse led by the other man, who had tied his horse to a tree near by. I aided the man in getting off of his horse and into the house, and laid him on a sofa in my parlor. After getting a light, I assisted him in getting upstairs where there were two beds, one of which he took. He seemed to be very much injured in the back, and complained very much of it. I did not see his face at all. He seemed to be tremulous and not inclined to talk, and had his cloak thrown around his head and seemed inclined to sleep, as I thought in order to ease himself, and every now and then he would groan pretty heavily.

I had no proper paste-board for making splints, and went and got an old band-box and made one of it; and as he wanted it done hastily, I hurried more than I otherwise would. He wanted me to fix it up any way, as he said he wanted to get back, or get home and have it done by a regular physician. I then took a piece of the band-box and split it in half, doubled it at right angles, and took some paste and pasted it into a splint. On examination, I found there was a straight fracture of the tibia about two inches above the ankle. My examination was quite short, and I did not find the adjoining bone fractured in any way. I do not regard it a peculiarly painful or dangerous wound; there was nothing resembling a compound fracture. I do not suppose I was more than three-quarters of an hour in making the examination of the wound and applying the splint. He continued still to suffer, and complained of severe pain in the back, especially when being moved. In my opinion, pain in the back may originate from riding; I judge that in this case it originated from the fall and also from riding, as he seemed to be prostrated. He sometimes breathed very shortly and as if exhausted.

He was a man, I should suppose about five feet ten inches high, and appeared to be pretty well made, but he had a heavy shawl on all the time. I suppose he would weigh 150 or 160 pounds. His hair was black, and seemed to be somewhat inclined to curl; it was worn long. He had a pretty full forehead and his skin was fair. He was very pale when I saw him, and appeared as if accustomed to in-door rather than out-door life. I do not know how to describe his skin exactly but I should think he might be classed as dark, and his paleness might be attributed to receiving this injury. I did not observe his hand to see whether it was small or large. I have been shown the photograph of J. Wilkes Booth and I should not think that this was the man from any resemblance to the photograph, but from other causes I have every reason to believe that he is the man whose leg I dressed as above stated.

In order to examine and operate upon his leg, I had occasion to cut his boot longitudinally in front of the instep. It seems that when he left my house, this boot was left behind. Yesterday morning my attention was called to this boot, which is a long top-boot. On making an examination of it, I find written on the inside in apparently a German hand, what I take to be *"Henry Luz, Maker. 445 Broadway, J. Wilkes."* I did not notice the writing in this boot until my attention was called to it by Lieutenant Lovett. [Boot produced and identified by deponent as the one taken from the leg of the wounded man.]

I have seen J. Wilkes Booth. I was introduced to him by Mr. J.C. Thompson, a son-in-law of Dr. William Queen, in November or December last. Mr. Thompson resides with his father-in-law, and his place is about five miles southwesterly from Bryantown, near the lower edge of what is known as Zechiah Swamp. Mr. Thompson told me at the time that Booth was looking out for lands in this neighborhood or in this county, he said he was not very particular where, if he could get such a lot as he wanted, whether it was in Charles, Prince Georges, or Saint Mary's county; and Booth inquired if I knew any parties in this neighborhood who had any fine horses for sale. I told him there was a neighbor of mine who had some very fine traveling horses, and he said he thought if he could purchase one reasonable he would do so, and would ride up to Washington on him instead of riding in the stage. The next evening he rode to my house and staid with me that night, and the next morning he purchased a rather old horse, but a very fine mover, of Mr. George Gardiner, Sr., who resides but a short distance from my house. I would know the horse if I should see him again. He is a darkish bay horse, not bright bay, with tolerably large head, and had a defect in one eye. Booth gave eighty dollars for the horse. **I have never seen Booth since that time to my knowledge until last Saturday morning.**

When I assisted the wounded man into my house on Saturday morning last, the other party with him, who appeared to be very youthful, took charge of the horse and said he would keep it and the other one until they could be put in the stable. As soon as I could I woke my colored man Frank Washington, and sent him out to put the horses in the stable, and the young man came into the house. After setting the wounded man's leg the best I could for the time, I think I walked around to my farm-yard and gave some directions, and when I returned breakfast was ready; and as this young man was up and knocking about, I asked him to come to breakfast. He did so, but the other man remained upstairs in bed. I did not know who this young man was, but he remarked that he had seen me. He appeared to be a very fast young man and was very talkative. He was about five feet two or three inches high. I would not be positive as to his height. He had a smooth face and appeared as if he had never shaved; his hair was black, and I should consider his complexion dark. I did not notice his eyes very particularly. He wore a dark-colored business coat. I have seen the photograph of Harold, but I do not recognize it as that of the young man. He seemed to be well acquainted throughout the whole country, and I asked his name; he gave it as

Henson, and that of the wounded man as Tyser or Tyson. I did not hear either of them address the other by the first name.

The only thing that excited my suspicion, on reflecting upon these circumstances, was that after breakfast, when I was about to leave for my farm-work, this young man asked me if I had a razor about the house that his friend desired to take a shave, as perhaps he would feel better. I had noticed that the wounded man had whiskers and a moustache when he came into the house. After dinner, I went to see the patient and although he kept his face partly turned away from me I noticed that he had lost his moustache, but still retained his whiskers. I did not pay sufficient attention to his beard to determine whether it was false or natural.

This young man asked me if I could fix up clumsily some crutches for his friend to hobble along with, and I went down to the old Englishman I had there who had a saw and auger, and he and I made a rude pair of crutches out of a piece of plank and sent them to him. This young man mentioned the names of several parties in this neighborhood whom we knew; among others, several here in Bryantown. He mentioned being in the store of William Moore; he did not say when. I think he said he knew Bean, who kept store here; and he knew very well Len Roby, Rufus Roby, & Major James Thomas, Sr. He inquired the way from my house to Bryantown, although he represented in the morning that they had come from Bryantown. He said he knew parson Wilmer, who lives at a place called Piney Church; he said also that they had met two persons, a lady and a gentleman, walking somewhere near Bryantown that morning, and inquired of them the way to my house, and that they also met a negro, but did not state where; & that they also inquired of him the way to my place.

I saw only one of the horses which these men rode to my house. She was a bay mare, moderately long tail, dark mane and tail. I won't be certain whether she had a star in the forehead or not; she appeared to be a mettlesome, high-spirited animal. I saw her after dinner, between twelve and one o'clock, when this young man and I rode over to my father's place in order to see if we could get a carriage for the wounded man; but I found that the carriages were all out of

repair except one and we could not get that one. He then concluded
to go to Bryantown for a conveyance to get his friend over as far as his
friend's Mr. Wilmer's. I then went down to Mr. Hardy's, and was in
conversation fully an hour when I returned home leisurely, and
found the two men were just in the act of leaving. The young man
inquired of me the nearest way to Mr. Wilmer's. I told them there
were two ways; one was by the public road leading by Beantown; the
other led across the swamp directly across from me, by which they
could save a mile; both are easterly. This road from my house is
directly across in a strait line; it is not a public way, but by taking
down a fence you can get through. They concluded to take this latter
route, and I gave them the necessary directions. I did not see them
leave my house. The man on crutches had left the house when I got
back, and he was some fifty to seventy yards from me when this
young man came to me and began to inquire of me the direction. I do
not know how or where Booth got a conveyance away from my
house; he did not go in a carriage; but he undoubtedly went on
horseback.

When they came there in the morning this young man said that
one of the horses would not stand without tying and asked that both
of them should be put in the stable. He held one of the horses until I
returned into the house with the wounded man, when I called a
colored boy named Frank Washington and sent him round to take
the horses to the stable. I have also a white man named Thomas
Davis, who has charge of my horses, and I judge that he saw the
horses which were in the stable during Saturday.

I judge that between four and five o'clock on Saturday afternoon
they left my house. I do not know where they went; I have not been
spoken to by any one for professional advice in their behalf since
that time, and have not seen either of them since.

It is about four miles across from my house to Parson Wilmer's,
and by the public road it is about five miles. I suppose they could go
in about an hour or an hour and a half by walking their horses.

I suppose in a day or two swelling would take place in the
wounded man's leg; there was very little tumefaction in the wound,

and I could discover crepitation very distinctly. It would be necessary to dress it again in two or three days if it were left in a recumbent posture, but if moved at a moderate rate, I do not know as it would aggravate it very much unless it was struck by something. I do not know much about wounds of that sort; a military surgeon would know more about those things.

    Saml A Mudd

Subscribed and sworn before me this 22nd day of April 1865
    H H Wells
    Col. & P.M. Genl Def. S of P

04-23-1865: COLONEL WILLIAM P. WOOD'S REPORTS

S ource: U.S. National Archives Microfilm M599, Reel 7.

~

COLONEL WILLIAM P. Wood was the Superintendent of the Old Capitol Prison in Washington, D.C. Secretary of War Stanton sent him to Bryantown, Maryland to assist in the hunt for Booth. Colonel Wood filed two reports on April 23, 1865:

~

Bryantown, Chas. Co. Md.
    April 23, 1865 (1st report)
    Maj. L.C. Turner
    Dear Sir,

After receiving my orders from the Hon. Sec. of War, I started from Washington, having in my company (or employ) Matthew Kirby, Aquilla Allen & Bernard Adamson, having received permission from Hon. Ed. M. Stanton, that I might release Zadock Jenkin's daughter.

I had sent Allen to get a correct description from the hostler of the horse (mare) which was hired by Booth, & after certain other little preliminaries started in pursuit of the murderers. Arriving at the Anacostia bridge (Navy Yard) about 9½ pm we learned that two persons had crossed the bridge on the night of the murder, who answered the description of Booth and David Herold, and the identification of the horses they rode. They (the murderers) passed the bridge at an interval of about 10 or fifteen minutes between them, J. Wilkes Booth crossing first. We stopped at the house of Zadock Jenkins. Jenkins was not at home - learned he was under arrest at the Post Office store kept by Robey. Jenkin's daughter was left at the house of her father and we proceeded to Surratt's Store, learned that the proprietor, a Mr. Lloyd, was under arrest at Robey's place; we proceeded to Robey's store (post office) and I saw Jenkins. He informed me that if I would call on Gabriel Thompson I would learn something of the murderers' passing up the road. I would find a Dr. Mudd who resided near Bryantown who could give me further particulars.

Receiving these reports, I left Jenkins at Robey's, 3½ am, April 22 (yesterday) & returned - had our horses fed & took breakfast - before sunrise we were at Gabriel Thompson's house. His son George Thompson (a boy of about 14 or 16 years) informed me that the parties, supposed to be Booth and Herold, passed him on the night of the murder, that his father's cart or conveyance had broken down in the road and he was there waiting for his father's return with another conveyance, that there was a black man now in the employ of Dr. Blankford (or Blanchard) named Henry Butler who was with him at the time the two men passed and that he had conversation with them, to the effect that if any person should make any inquiry for them to say they had taken the Marlborough road.

We left Thompson's house, and proceeded to Dr. Blanford's farm. Allen and myself proceeded to the house and after a hunt all over the farm we found Henry Butler. He fully corroborated the boy Thompson's statement. Neither one of these parties had been interrogated by any person previous to our interview with them, and I was thus fully satisfied we were on the track of the villains - proceeded then to Bryantown (the place where I am now working). Here I learned Col. Wells was stationed. After some conversation with him we left for Dr. Mudd's house, taking the Dr. in my buggy. He informed me that Booth had been introduced to him and had been at his home in the fall of 1864 and he had known him then as Booth - that he now believed since his examination that he had set the leg of Booth who was at his house on Saturday morning, about 4 o'clock am.

Visited Dr. Mudd's house and made an examination of the premises. The Dr. tells a tale not to be believed about their departure from his house, stated that he had cut the boot off Booth's leg as it was much swollen, and gave him a shoe or slipper. Crutches were made for Booth by the Dr. and an Englishman in the Dr.'s employ. Learning these and other matters, I returned with the Dr. and returned him to the custody of Col. Wells as promised. Col. Wells had arrived here the day previous to my arrival, and Dr. Mudd's action in the matter was patent to any one in the village who took any interest in the matter; I received every assistance & kindness at the hands of Col. Wells, who is taking every step in the prosecution of the business at hand.

As I could get no lead of the horses any distance from Dr. Mudd's house, I was determined to go out again (distance some 3 or 5 miles from this place). On arriving at the place I thought there were suspicious transactions and movements and Allen, Kirby, & Adamson were left at the Dr.'s house (last night) and I returned to Bryantown. Met Dr. Mudd on his return to his house unaccompanied by any one, just at the edge of the village. Conversed with Col. Wells (he had paroled Dr. Mudd). The Col. had sent down to Robey's after the prisoner Lloyd; and in the evening was in at his confession. He stated that Mrs. Surratt's visit there on the day - Friday, was in relation to giving Booth & David Herold arms (carbines) which were left in his house by John Surratt. Booth told Lloyd (the prisoner) who resides in Mrs. Surratt's house (on the road) near Robey's that they (we) had murdered the president & Sec. Seward.

You can take all precautions necessary now with Mrs. Surratt for she was beyond the question of a doubt in the conspiracy. Lloyd knew David Herold personally and fully recognized him as being with Booth, and on being shown the likeness of Booth this morning fully identifies it as the man who had his leg broken and was in company with Herold, and who was the person who said we murdered the president. We have rumors that they have made their way to the Potomac & have crossed. We have lost all tracks of the horses from the time they were at Dr. Mudd's, where they remained nearly all the day on Saturday last. I have concluded to remain here (in the vicinity of Dr. Mudd's) until I can learn the trail of the horses. Should I receive any information of the murderers crossing the Potomac, I shall cross and follow them. It is impossible to form correct conclusions as to their whereabouts from the time they were at Dr. Mudd's house. There is no doubt but that Booth broke one of the bones in his leg in the jump on the stage of the theatre immediately after the murder. Col. Wells & myself are now going to Dr. Mudd's house. Will write again if I remain here another day. I send this for your information. Your good judgement will prevent any improper use thereof.

Hoping for success, I remain respectfully,

Your Obt. Servant,
    William P. Wood,
    Supt. OCP

April 23rd 1865 (2nd report)

Have been out to the residence of Dr. Mudd, accompanied by Col. Wells. The Col., A. Allen, Dr. Mudd and myself have made a personal examination of the premises and matters relating to the murderers. We traced both their horses and know they left Dr. Mudd's house on horseback. About dusk they were lost. Herold dismounted and went up the road to enquire for directions, and there is no doubt they have left for the Potomac via Port Tobacco, & going by way of Mathias Point in Va.

Dr. Mudd's statement I now believe to be true.

The assassins changed horses. Herold was riding the bay mare obtained from Pumphrey's Stable, and it may be possible that she fell or threw off Booth and broke his leg. However, I believe as I have written this morning. I will start for Port Tobacco this evening. My men Kirby & Allen slept last night in the bed used by Booth when his leg was bandaged.

All the tales about Booth being in Washington, Pennsylvania, or upper Maryland are a hoax. We are on his tracks, rely on it. We are all well.

Resp.,
William P. Wood, Supt.

～

05-01-1865: GEORGE ATZERODT'S STATEMENT

S ource: Statement of George A. Atzerodt to Provost Marshal McPhail in the presence of John L. Smith on the night of May 1, 1865, from 8 p.m. to 10 p.m.

～

ON MAY 1, 1865, George Atzerodt was questioned for two hours, from 8 p.m. to 10 p.m., by Maryland's Provost Marshal, James L. McPhail, at the Washington Arsenal where Atzerodt was being held. McPhail's deputy, John L. Smith, who also happened to be Atzerodt's brother-in-law, summarized Atzerodt's comments in the statement below.

Speaking of the kidnap plot, Atzerodt said in his statement that:

I am certain Dr. Mudd knew all about it, as Booth sent (as he told me) liquor & provisions for the trip with the president to Richmond, about two weeks before the murder to Dr. Mudd's.

Booth may have told this to Atzerodt, but it is unlikely that Booth actually sent supplies to Dr. Mudd about two weeks before the April 14th assassination. Booth would have known there was no way he could secretly carry a kidnapped president through the ranks of the entire Union army assaulting Richmond without being discovered. The fighting was so fierce there that Jefferson Davis' civilian government and General Lee's army both abandoned Richmond on April 2nd.

If Booth did send liquor and provisions to Dr. Mudd, he didn't give any to Booth. When Booth and Herold left the Mudd farm, they asked the first person they met for liquor and food.

∾

Atzerodt's Statement

James Wood sometimes called Mosby boarded with Mrs. Murray an Irish woman on the corner of 9 & F St. in a three story house, front on the upper end of the P.O. and South End of Patent Office - with basement entrance on the left side going up 9th St. from Avenue. He was a little over six feet, black hair, smooth round face, gray coat black pants, & spring coat mixed with white & gray. Saw him last time on Friday evening about 5 o'ck with Booth. He sent for letters to the post office for James Hall. He was brought from New York. Surratt told me so. He said he had been a prisoner in Balte, near the depot. He was arrested for whipping a negro woman. Mosby was Wood's nick name - did not know him by any other name than mentioned. Gust. Powell now arrested in Old Capitol was one of the party. He went also by name of Gustavus Spencer, Surratt and Spencer came from Richmond, together just after it had fallen.

James Donaldson, a low chunky man about 23 or 24 years of age, small-potted, dark complexion (not very) deep plain black suit; only saw him one time & this was Wednesday previous to the murder, he was having an interview with Booth and told him to meet him on Friday eve & he replied he would and left and went up Penn. Avenue towards the Treasury building. I was under the impression he came on with Booth.

Arnold, O'Laughlin, Surratt, Harold, Booth, and myself met once at a saloon or restaurant on the Aven. bet 13 & 14 St.

The Saml. Thomas registered on the morning of the 15th April at Penn Hotel, I met on my way to hotel, he was an entire Stranger to me. I left the Hotel alone on the morning of 15th of April. A Lieut. in room No. 51 will prove this. Surratt bought a boat from Dick Smoot & James Brawner living about Port Tobacco, for which they paid $300.00 and was to give one hundred Dolls. extra for taking care of it till wanted. Booth told me that Mrs. Surratt went to Surrattsville to get out the guns (Two Carbines) which had been taken to that place by Herold. This was Friday. The carriage was hired at Howard's.

I saw a man named Weightman who boarded at Surratt's at Post Office. he told me he had to go down the Country with Mrs. Surratt. This was on Friday, Also.

I am certain Dr. Mudd knew all about it, as Booth sent (as he told me) liquor & provisions for the trip with the president to Richmond, about two weeks before the murder to Dr. Mudd's.

Booth never said until the last night (Friday) that he intended to kill the president.

Herold came to the Kirkwood House, same evening for me to go to see Booth. I went with Herold & saw Booth. He then said he was going to kill the president and Wood, the Secy. of State. I did not believe him. This occurred in the evening about 7½ o'clock. It was dark. I took a room at Kirkwood's. Both Herold & I went to the room left Herold's coat, knife, & pistol in room and never again returned to it. Booth said during the day that the thing had failed and proposed to go to Richmond & open the theatre. I am not certain but I think I stayed one night at Kirkwood's (Thursday) we were to try and get papers to Richmond from Mr. Johnson.

Booth spoke of getting the papers. He would get them out of the Theatre. Wood & Booth were apparently confidential with one another. Plenty of parties in Charles County knew of the kidnapping affair.

One of the men named Charles Yates, knew all about it, he went to Richmond during the winter he was to row the Presdt & party over.

Thos. Holborn was to meet us on the road and help in the kidnapping. Bailey & Barnes knew nothing of the affair unless Booth told Bailey & he told Barnes. Booth had met Bailey on "C" St. with me. I did not meet Booth or any other of the party in Baltimore on or about the 31 of March.

Boyle also killed Capt. Watkins near Annapolis last month, was one of the party, in the conspiracy.

I repeat I never knew anything about the murder.

I was intended to give assistance to the kidnapping. They come to Port Tobacco (Surratt & Booth) several times and brought me to Washington. The pistol given me I sold or received a loan on it Saturday morning after the murder from John Caldwick at Matthews & Wells, Store, High St. Georgetown. The knife I threw away just above Mrs. Canby's boarding house the night of the murder about 11 o'clock when I took my horse to stable. I had the horse out to help to take the president. I did not believe he was going to be killed, although he Booth had said so. After I heard of the murder I run about the city like a crazy man.

I have not seen Arnold for some time, but saw O'Laughlin on Thursday evening, on the Avenue at Saloon near U.S. Hotel. He told me he was going to see Booth.

Wood did not go on the street in day time for fear of arrest. When he first came to Washington he boarded at Surratt's. This was in Feby. He (Wood) went with Booth last of February to N. Y. Booth we understood paid the way. I know nothing about Canada. Wood told me he had horses in Virginia. Saml. Arnold and Mike O'Laughlin ought to know where the horses and pistols were bought. Sam and Mike have a buggy and horse kept at stable in rear of Theatre. Booth had several horses at same place. I think the horses owner was in Surratt's name. I sold one of the horses & paid part of the money to Booth and part to Herold, who said he would see Booth about it. The saddle and bridle belonging to Booth is at Penn House, where I left it. I overheard Booth when in conversation with Wood say, that he visited a chambermaid at Seward's House & that she was pretty. He said he had a great mind to give her his diamond pin. Herold talked about powders & medicines on Friday night at Mrs. Condby's. Wood, Herold, Booth, and myself were present. This was a meeting place because Wood could not go out for fear of arrest.

Kate Thompson or Kate Brown, as she was known by both names, put up at National & was well known at Penn House. She knew all about the affair. Surratt went to Richd. with her last March and April. Howell made a trip with her to same place. This woman is about twenty yrs of age, good looking and well dressed. Black hair & eyes, round face from South Carolina & a widow.

I did not see Surratt for seven or eight days before the murder nor have I seen him since.

Miss Thompson or Brown had two large light trunks, one much larger than the other. Young Weightman at Surratt's ought to know about this woman.

The remark made by me in Baltimore on the 31 of March alluded to blockade running & privateering altogether & Booth said he had money to buy a steamer & wanted me to go in it.

I was to be one of them. In this way I was going to make a pile of money.

Booth said he had met a party in N. York who would get the Prest. certain. They were going to mine the end of Pres. House, next to War Dept. They knew an entrance to accomplish it through. Spoke about getting friends of the Presdt. to get up an entertainment & they would mix in it, have a serenade & thus get at the Presdt. & party.

These were understood to be projects.

Booth said if he did not get him quick the N. York crowd would. Booth knew the New York party apparently by a sign. He saw Booth give some kind of sign to two parties on the Avenue who he said were from New York. My Uncle Mr. Richter and family in Monty. Co. Md. knew nothing about the affair either before or after the occurrence & never suspected me of any thing wrong as I was in the habit of visiting and working in the neighborhood & staying with him. My father formerly owned part of the property now owned by Richter.

Finis.

05-09-1865: MRS. MUDD'S LOYALTY OATH

Sarah Mudd's Loyalty Oath

Mrs. Mudd signed this loyalty oath on the first day of the trial. Credit National Archives.

05-13-1865: TESTIMONY OF LOUIS J. WEICHMANN

Source: Benn Pitman, The Assassination of President Lincoln and the Trial of the Conspirators. New York, N.Y.. Moore, Wilstach, and Baldwin. 1865.

∼

LOUIS WEICHMANN WAS a long-time friend of John Surratt, who remained in hiding in Canada during the conspiracy trial. He had gone to school with Surratt, lived at the Surratt boarding house where Booth and his fellow conspirators often met, and was considered by his fellow workers at the War Department to be a Southern sympathizer. John Surratt later said the only reason Weichmann never became an active member of Booth's gang was because Weichmann couldn't ride and shoot. Nevertheless, Weichmann came across as a believable witness at the trial.

Part of Weichmann's testimony was about a meeting in Washington, D.C. in December 1864 with himself, Dr. Mudd, Booth, and John Surratt. The testimony was quite favorable to Dr. Mudd. Weichmann said that Dr. Mudd *"spoke like a Union man"* and *"there was nothing in the conversation between Dr. Mudd, Booth, and Surratt, at the National*

Hotel, that led me to think there was anything like a conspiracy going on between them."

The problem for Dr. Mudd was that he had sworn in writing that he didn't see Booth between the time he first met Booth in November 1864 and the morning after the assassination in April 1865. Weichmann's testimony showed this was not true, raising a question about why Dr. Mudd would want to hide his meeting with Booth.

Dr. Mudd went to Washington on December 23, 1864 to do some last minute Christmas shopping with his cousin Jeremiah Mudd. After checking in at the Pennsylvania House hotel, they had something to eat and then wandered over to the National Hotel, where the two men became separated in the crowd.

Dr. Mudd stepped outside to Pennsylvania Avenue, and was spotted by Booth, who was staying at the National. Booth said he was just on his way to meet a man named John Surratt to inquire about Southern Maryland real estate. Dr. Mudd was acquainted with the Surratt family since they had run the Surrattsville post office and tavern not far from Mudd's farm. Booth told Dr. Mudd that the Surratts now lived in a boarding house about five blocks away. He asked Dr. Mudd to accompany him and introduce him to Surratt. Dr. Mudd agreed. Weichmann's testimony described what happened next:

> About the 15th of January [note: actually December 23, 1864] last I was passing down Seventh Street, in company with John H. Surratt, and when opposite Odd Fellows' Hall, some one called "Surratt, Surratt;" and turning round, he recognized an old acquaintance of his, Dr. Samuel A. Mudd of Charles County, Md.; the gentleman there [pointing to the accused, Samuel A. Mudd] He and John Wilkes Booth were walking together. Surratt introduced Dr. Mudd to me, and Dr. Mudd introduced Booth to both of us. They were coming down Seventh Street, and we were going up. Booth invited us to his room at the National Hotel.
>
> When we arrived there, he told us to be seated, and ordered

cigars and wines for four. Dr. Mudd then went out into a passage and called Booth out, and had a private conversation with him. When they returned, Booth called Surratt, and all three went out together and had a private conversation, leaving me alone. I did not hear the conversation; I was seated on a lounge near the window. On returning to the room the last time, Dr. Mudd apologized to me for his private conversation, and stated that Booth and he had some private business; that Booth wished to purchase his farm, but that he did not care about selling it, as Booth was not willing to give him enough. Booth also apologized and stated to me that he wished to purchase Dr. Mudd's farm. Afterward they were seated round the center-table, when Booth took out an envelope, and on the back of it made marks with a pencil. I should not consider it writing, but from the motion of the pencil it was more like roads or lines.

... After their return to the room, we remained probably twenty minutes; then left the National Hotel and went to the Pennsylvania House, where Dr. Mudd had rooms. We all went into the sitting-room, and Dr. Mudd came and sat down by me; and we talked about the war. He expressed the opinion that the war would soon come to an end, and spoke like a Union man. Booth was speaking to Surratt. At about half-past 10, Booth bade us good night, and went out. Surratt and I then bade Dr. Mudd good night. He said he was going to leave next morning.

... There was nothing in the conversation between Dr. Mudd, Booth, and Surratt, at the National Hotel, that led me to believe there was anything like a conspiracy going on between them.

05-16-1865: TESTIMONY OF
LIEUTENANT LOVETT

S ource: Benn Pitman, The Assassination of President Lincoln
and the Trial of the Conspirators. New York, N.Y.. Moore,
Wilstach, and Baldwin. 1865.

~

Lieutenant Alexander Lovett
  For the prosecution - May 16

On the day after the assassination of the president, I went with
others in pursuit of the murderers. We went by way of Surrattsville to
the house of Dr. Samuel A. Mudd, which is about thirty miles from
Washington, and about one-quarter of a mile or so off the road that
runs from Bryantown, arriving there on Tuesday, the 18th of April.
Dr. Mudd, whom I recognize among the accused, did not at first
seemed inclined to give us any satisfaction; afterward he went on to
state that on Saturday morning, at daybreak, two strangers had come
to his place; one of them rapped at the door, the other remained on
his horse. Mudd went down and opened the door, and with the aid of
the young man who had knocked at the door helped the other, who

had his leg broken, off his horse, took him into the house and set his leg.

On asking him who the man with the broken leg was, he said he did not know; he was a stranger to him. The other, he said, was a young man, about seventeen or eighteen years of age. Mudd said that one of them called for a razor, which he furnished, together with soap and water, and the wounded man shaved off his moustache. One of our men remarked that this was suspicious, and Dr. Mudd said it did look suspicious. I last him if he had any other beard. He said, "*Yes, he had a long pair of whiskers.*" He said the men remained there but for a short time, and I understood him that they left in the course of the morning. He said that the wounded man went off on crutches that he (Mudd) had had made for him. He said the other led the horse of the injured man, and he (Mudd) showed them the way across the swamp. He told me that he had heard, at church, on Sunday morning, that the president had been assassinated, but did not mention by whom. We were at his house probably an hour, and to the last he represented that those men were entire strangers to him.

It was generally understood at this time that Booth was the man who assassinated the president; even the darkeys knew it; and I was told by them that Booth had been there, and that he had his leg broken.

On Friday, the 21st of April, I went to Dr. Mudd's again, for the purpose of arresting him. When he found we were going to search the house, he said something to his wife, and she went up stairs and brought down a boot. Mudd said he had cut it off the man's leg, in order to set the leg. I turned down the top of the boot and saw the name "*J. Wilkes*" written in it.

I called Mudd's attention to it, and he said he had not taken notice of it before. Some of the men said the name of Booth was scratched out, but I said that the name of Booth had never been written.

[A long riding boot, for the left foot, slit up in front for about eight inches, was exhibited to the witness.]

That is the boot.

[The boot was offered in evidence.]

At the second interview, he still insisted that the men were strangers to him. I made the remark to him that his wife said she has seen the whiskers detached from the face, and I suppose he was satisfied then, for he subsequently said it was Booth. After we left his house, one of the men showed him Booth's photograph, and Mudd remarked that it did not look like Booth, except a little across the eyes. Shortly after that, he said he had an introduction to Booth in November or December last, at church, from a man named Johnson or Thompson. On being questioned, he said he had been along with Booth in the country, looking up some land, and was with him when he bought a horse of Esquire Gardiner, last fall.

Although I was in citizen's clothes at the time, and addressed no threats to him, Dr. Mudd appeared to be much frightened and anxious. When asked what arms the men had, Dr. Mudd stated that the injured man had a pair of revolvers, but he said nothing about the other having a carbine, or either of them having a knife; his manner was very reserved and evasive.

Cross-examined by Mr. Ewing

At the time that Dr. Mudd was describing to me the *"two strangers"* that had been to his house, I did not tell him of my tracking Booth from Washington; I did not mentioned Booth's name at all; it was not my business to tell him whom I was after.

On my second visit, Dr. Mudd was out, and his wife sent after him; I walked down and met him. I was accompanied by special officers Simon Gavacan, Joshua Lloyd, and William Williams. After we entered the house, I demanded the razor that the man had used. It was not until after we had been in the house some minutes, and one of the men said we should have to search the house, that Dr. Mudd told us the boot had been found, and his wife brought it to us.

I asked him if that might not be a false whisker; he said he did not know. I asked this because Mrs. Mudd has said that the whisker became detached when he got to the foot of the stairs. The Doctor never told me that he had Booth up stairs; he told me he was on the sofa or lounge.

Mudd stated, at our first interview, that the men remained but a short time; afterward his wife told me that they had staid to about 3 or 4 o'clock, on Saturday afternoon. I asked Mudd if the men had much money about them. He said they had considerable greenbacks; and, in this connection, although I did not ask him if he had been paid for setting the man's leg, he said it was customary to make a charge to strangers in such a case. When Dr. Mudd said he had shown the men the way across the swamps, I understood him to refer to the swamps a thousand yards in the rear of his own house. He told us that the men went to the Rev. Dr. Wilmer's, or inquired for Parson Wilmer's; that he took them to the swamps; that they were on their way to Allen's Fresh; but I paid no attention to this at the time, as I considered it was a blind to throw us off the track. We, however, afterward searched Mr. Wilmer's, a thing I did not like to do, as I knew the man by reputation, and was satisfied it was unnecessary. We tracked the men as far we could. We went into the swamp and scoured it all over; I went through a half a dozen times; it was not a very nice job though. I first heard from Lieutenant Dana that two men had been at Mudd's house. I afterward heard from Dr. George Mudd that a party of two had been at Dr. Samuel Mudd's.

Cross-examined by Mr. Stone

When we first went to Dr. Samuel Mudd's house, we were accompanied by Dr. George Mudd, whom we had taken from Bryantown along with us. Our first conversation was with the Doctor's wife. When we asked Dr. Mudd whether two strangers had been there, he seemed very much excited, and got as pale as a sheet of paper, and blue about the lips, like a man that was frightened at something he had done. Dr. George Mudd was present when I asked if two strangers had been there. He had spoken to Dr. Samuel Mudd previous to that. He admitted that two strangers had been there, and gave a description of them.

In my first interview with Mudd on the Tuesday, I did not mention the name of Booth at all; and it was not till I had arrested him, when on horseback, that he told me he was introduced to Booth last fall, by a man named Johnson or Thompson.

07-10-1865: GENERAL EWING'S LETTER TO PRES. JOHNSON

S ource: Samuel A. Mudd Pardon File B-596, RG 204, U.S. National Archives, College Park, Md.

~

AFTER THE TRIAL, General Ewing had Mrs. Mudd prepare an affidavit describing Booth's visit to the Mudd farm, and sent it to President Johnson as an attachment to a transmittal letter requesting that Dr. Mudd's sentence be set aside.

Mrs. Mudd's affidavit

I, Sarah F. Mudd, wife of Dr. Mudd, on oath do say,

That I saw John Wilkes Booth when he was in Charles County last fall. He came Sunday evening after supper, staid all night, and next day my husband went with him to Gardiner's where Booth bought the horse - Booth did not return from Gardiner's with my husband - and was never at my husband's house, or so far as I know in the neighborhood before or after until the 15th of April - nor did I ever hear of my husband having met him elsewhere, or being in any way directly or indirectly in communication with him.

The two men came to the house on the 15th of April just before daybreak. After my husband had set the leg he went to bed again, and slept till about 9 o'clock when he breakfasted and went to the field where the hands were working. He returned between 11 and 12 and went to the crippled man's room for a few minutes and then went back to the field to get a pair of crutches made. He returned at dinner, when Herold (who called himself Hanson, or Harrison) asked if he could not get a carriage or buggy to take his friend (who was called Tyson) away. The Doctor said his father had a carriage which might be got, and he would go with him and see about it. I then told the Doctor that I wanted some calico, soda, needles, and matches, and asked him to go on to Bryantown to get them. He said he would, and I am sure that is all he went to Bryantown for.

The Doctor and Herold had not been gone over a half an hour, when Herold returned and said he could not get father's carriage and that Doctor had gone into Bryantown and he was going to take his friend off horseback. While Herold was gone, I went to the room where the crippled man was. He had heavy whiskers on - and looked pale, thin and haggard. I staid about five minutes and talked with him. He said his leg was broken a mile and a half from our house by the fall of his horse, and that he had been thrown against a stone which injured his back.

About an hour after Herold got back, they left. As Booth came down to go I was in the hall and saw his whiskers become detached and he pushed them back. Herold came down with him, and went to the front gate where his horse had been standing after his return from Bryantown, and rode him around the house to the stable. Booth went on his crutches through the back yard towards the stable, and just as he was getting to the stable the Doctor rode up from Bryantown to the front gate. The stable is 300 yards from the house. The Doctor dismounted at the front gate and came into the house. He did not see either Booth or Herold on his return near enough to speak to either of them. He came into the house, and went to the fire, and took a book and commenced reading. He did not leave the room until supper time - an hour and a half after they had gone.

Before supper he told me of the report in Bryantown that the president was killed and Mr. Seward and his son. After supper I was speaking of the two men and told him of the crippled man's whiskers becoming detached. He said that that looked suspicious; and that he had also shaved off his moustache and seemed more excited than the mere fracture of the limb would cause him to be. He then sent for his horse to go to Bryantown and tell the military authorities about these two men. I begged him not to go himself - but to wait till Church next day and tell Dr. George Mudd or some one else living in Bryantown all the circumstances, and have him tell the officers at Bryantown about it. He was very unwilling to delay and warned me of the danger from failure to tell of these men at once. I told him that if he went himself Boyle who was reported to be one of the assassins and who killed Capt. Watkins last fall in that country might have him assassinated for it, and that it would be just as well for the authorities to hear it next day because the crippled man could not escape.

Up to this time I had not the least suspicion that the crippled man was Booth - and I am sure no one would have recognized him as being the same man who was at our house last fall - for he was very much thinner, and looked so pale and haggard, and changed with his heavy whiskers, as to alter entirely his appearance. I am certain that my husband did not recognize him, or suspect him to be Booth even after I told him of the false whiskers. I am sure too that Herold was a total stranger to the Doctor, as he was to me.

Something was said at the trial about the boot, but it was not shown when it was found. I found it on Thursday under the bed, when I was cleaning the room. And next day my husband told Lt. Lovett about it as soon as he saw him and before a word had been said between them as Mr. Hardy testifies.

On Tuesday when the officers came to the house I sent for the Doctor to the field and before he came told the officers everything in presence of Dr. George Mudd. They said from my description the smaller man was certainly Herold. When my husband came to the house and before he saw the officers I told him that I had given them a full statement. He said *"That was right."* Then Dr. George Mudd before he introduced my husband told him that he had bought the officers there in compliance with his request on Sunday, for further information about the two suspected men who had been at our house.

The description given by my husband to Herold of the short route to Parson Wilmer's was given before they started to Bryantown. I saw my husband point out the route to him - they both were then standing in the yard from which the by road could be seen. This was in the early part of the day, while the young man was talking of taking his friend off horseback. The carriage was not spoken of until dinner. I do further certify that Dr. Mudd was not from home but three nights from the 23rd of December until the 21st of April, one of which was in January when he went with me to a party at Mr. George Gardiner's. On the 23rd of March he came up to Washington with Mr. Lewellyn Gardiner to attend a sale of government horses and mistook the day. On the third occasion, which was the 10th of April, he came up to Dr. Blanford's with his brother Henry, remained all night, went to Giesborough the next day in company with Dr. Blanford and his brother Henry and did not come into Washington. If my husband knows John Surratt at all, it is nothing more than a passing acquaintance - having seen him at his hotel at Surrattsville. I saw John Surratt once at Surrattsville. I have never seen him at our house and never know of his having stopped there.

It was said in the Argument of the Judge Advocate that Booth and Herold were secreted in the woods near our house after they left. If they were secreted there, neither I nor my husband knew it. My husband was not out of the yard that evening or the next day until he went to church, and we both supposed the men had gone to Parson Wilmer's.

As to my husband having recognized Booth while he was at our house, I repeat that he did not recognize or suspect the stranger to be Booth; had he done so he certainly would have mentioned it to me, but he did not. Moreover, he did not notice the crippled man specially, nor seem to be interested in learning where he came from or where he was going.

Sarah F. Mudd

Sworn and Subscribed before me this 6th day of July 1865 B.W. Ferguson J.P.

General Ewings transmittal letter

Washington, D.C.
   No. 12 North "A" Street
   July 10th 1865
   His Excellency Andrew Johnson
   President of the United States

Sir,

I enclose herewith the affidavit of Sarah F. Mudd, wife of Dr. Samuel A. Mudd who has recently been tried before a Military Commission on the charge of conspiracy to assassinate the president and other Chief Officers of the government, and also the affidavits of Dr. J. H. Blanford, Mrs. Elizabeth A. Dyer and Sylvester Mudd in corroboration of her statements - to all of which I ask your Excellency's most earnest attention, in connection with the record in that case.

Mrs. Mudd's affidavit, if accepted as truthful, shows:

1st That the testimony of Norton as to the accused having entered his room at the National on the 3rd of March enquiring for Booth is false - and that Evans' statement in corroboration of Norton that Mudd came to Washington on either the 1st, 2nd or 3rd of March is also false.

Her statement would not have been taken to refute the evidence of these witnesses (because it was fully and overwhelmingly refuted on the trial by the evidence of Thomas Davis, J. H. Blanford, Frank Washington, Betty Washington, Mary, Fannie, Emily and Henry L. Mudd, and John Davis) were it not for the fact that the Special Judge

Advocate insisted on the truth of the statements of Evans and Norton, who were strangers to Mudd, against the flatly contradictory evidence of these nine witnesses, who all knew him intimately. And it is not unfair to presume that the Court were greatly influenced by its legal advices all on questions of the weight of evidence, as they were controlled by them on all other questions arising in the trial.

2d Mrs. Mudd's affidavit also shows that her husband was not here between the 23rd of December and the 23rd of March - and therefore the statement of Weichmann as to the interview between Booth, Surratt and Mudd at the National, which that witness swears occurred about the middle of January, is not entitled to credence. On this point she corroborates the evidence of Betty Washington, Thomas Davis, Henry L. Mudd Jr., Mary Mudd and Frank Washington - whose evidence the Special Judge Advocate also declared in his argument could not outweigh the statements of the one witness Weichmann, who was a stranger to the accused - while the five witnesses contradicting him knew the accused intimately.

3d Her affidavit also shows that on Tuesday after the assassination her husband could not have denied to Williams and Gavacan (the detectives) that the two strangers had been at his house, as they swear he did. In this she is corroborated by Dr. George Mudd - and also by Lieut. Lovett who was quoted by the Special Judge Advocate in his argument as having sworn to the denial, whereas in fact he swears to the opposite.

4th Her affidavit also shows that on Friday after the assassination the accused spoke of Booth's boot having been found, voluntarily, and not as claimed only after a threat was made to search the house. In this she is corroborated by Hardy.

5th Her affidavit also shows that the boot was not discovered until Thursday - so that her husband practiced no concealment in not producing it Tuesday.

6th It also shows that she saw and conversed with Booth when he was at her husband's house last fall - and again saw and talked with them while her husband was gone to Bryantown on Saturday the 15th April - and that he was then so thin, pale and haggard, and so thoroughly disguised by his false whiskers, that she did not expect at all that he was the same man she met and talked with last fall.

This point is of great importance because the Special Judge Advocate assumed it was proved beyond all question that the accused recognized the crippled man as Booth - while there is no evidence to show that he did, except the bare fact that he had met him in the fall or winter before; added to Colonel Wells' statement which is only of an indistinct impression as to what he inferred from Mudd's statements, while all other witnesses say the accused denied having recognized Booth while at his house. Mrs. Mudd says also that she is certain her husband did not recognize or suspect the crippled man to be Booth at any time that day.

On this point of recognition the accused was not able to offer any direct evidence of a single witness - because none whose saw him last fall saw him that Saturday again.

This was, perhaps, a controlling point with the Court against the accused - and therefor Mrs. Mudd's statement as to her own failure to recognize or suspect the crippled man to be Booth is of vital importance.

7th Mrs. Mudd's affidavit also shows that Herald could not have gone to Bryantown with her husband, as the Judge Advocate claims, (8 miles) as he was gone not over half an hour. In this she is corroborated by Primus Johnson and others (see page 25 of argument).

8th It also shows that he pointed out the short route through the swamp (to Parson Wilmer's) to Herold before going to Bryantown and before he learned of the assassination. And that when he returned home, Booth and Herold had left the house and he never spoke to them after he heard of the assassination. In this she is corroborated by her husband's admissions in evidence, and by Betty Washington. See Col. Wells statement also; and pages 35 & 36 of argument, and evidence of there cited.

The Special Judge Advocate claimed that the evidence showed that after the accused returned from Bryantown, where he heard of the assassination, and that a man named Booth was one of the assassins, he aided the escape and concealment of Booth and Herald. The

Court doubtless accepted that fact as proved on the Judge Advocate's assertion and on the statement of the detective Gavacan as to Mudd's statement on the subject to him. (See page 27 of argument.) Gavacan's statement as to Mudd's denial on Tuesday that the two men had been at his house at all was clearly shown false (see pages 29 & 30 argument). And I think that evidence on this point as to Mudd's having gone with Booth and Herold part of the way was also fairly overthrown (pages 27 & 28 argument). But the Special Judge Advocate had the ear of the Court, and was with it throughout its deliberations on this case, I am informed - and I have no doubt the Court therefore accepted as true the falsehood that Mudd said he helped the men off after he returned from Bryantown. That act of pointing the route to Wilmer's was the only act shown to have been done by Mudd which could have implicated him had he from the first known the crime and the criminal. Mrs. Mudd's affidavit shows that that act was done before her husband knew of the assassination, or suspected the crippled man to be Booth. And that after he knew of the assassination he did not see Booth or Herold. (See pages 35 & 36 argument)

9th Her affidavit also shows that her husband's suspicions towards those men were not aroused until she told him, an hour after they had gone, that the whiskers of the crippled man were false. And that he then ordered his horse to go to Bryantown to tell the authorities about them, and was only prevented doing so by her fears and entreaties. And that in consequence of her advice only he delayed until next day and sent the information through Dr. George Mudd. This delay was dwelt on by the Special Judge Advocate as proof of his complicity with the assassins, and had, I think, great weight with the Court.

10th The Special Judge Advocate asserted that it was shown that he accused secreted Booth and Herold in the woods Saturday night. There is not a word of evidence justifying that assertion - and Mrs. Mudd's affidavit shows it to be utterly erroneous.

11th Some evidence was offered by the Prosecution (Mary and Milo Simms) going to show that John H. Surratt frequented the house of the accused last year and year before, which, though fully disproved, (see argument pages 14, 15 & 16) was yet insisted on by the Assistant Judge Advocate as true. Mrs. Mudd says she had seen John H. Surratt at his mother's house, at Surrattsville Hotel, before the war - but that she never saw him at the house of the accused or heard of his having been there.

In connection with this letter and its enclosures I ask the attention of your Excellency to my letter to you of the 3rd instant, in which I pointed out in the argument of the Special Judge Advocate eleven material errors in his statement of the evidence against Dr. Mudd, which errors I was not permitted by the Court to call to its attention. In addition to these errors in statements of fact his argument was full of erroneous inferences and inconsequent deductions.

As one of the legal advisers of the Court in its discussions and deliberations on the evidence he was in position to give effect to his conclusions in the finding and sentence which followed, and doubtless did much to lead them into the errors, into which he himself had fallen. I venture to say that the recorded evidence, aside from the affidavits herewith offered, does not support the finding of the Court - and that not only was there not sufficient proof to exclude reasonable doubt of guilt, but that there was not such proof as made guilt more probable that innocence.

But by these affidavits, if they be accepted as true, all doubt is removed, and the innocence of Dr. Mudd is established beyond question. For, if the interview described by Weichmann did occur, it was on the 23rd of December, and was followed by no further intercourse between the accused and Booth or Surratt either written or oral. If can not be claimed that the conspiracy was entered into then, at Booth's first introduction to Surratt and in presence of Weichmann, who was a stranger to Mudd and Booth, and known to Surratt as an employee of the War Department. Besides, the evidence shows that the conspiracy to capture the president - as Booth first professed its object to his accomplices - was got up late in January or in February. If Dr. Mudd had on the 23rd of December had such a scheme proposed to him, and if he had assented to it, no one can doubt that he would have subsequently met the conspirators or some of them.

But it is shown he did not see Booth or Surratt after the 23rd of December, and did not even call on either when he was here on the 23rd of March, and at Giesboro on the 11th of April. Admit, what I think the recorded evidence and Mrs. Mudd's statement clearly show, that Dr. Mudd did not have any intercourse whatever with Booth or Surratt after the 23rd of December - before the assassination - and it follows beyond dispute that he was not informed of or assenting to the conspiracy.

If this be so, his entire innocence then follows from the evidence, and these affidavits.

For even though he recognized Booth while at his house, which he constantly asserted and still asserts he did not, and which Mrs. Mudd's failure to recognize him makes most probable, yet no one can suppose that Booth on reaching his house disclosed his horrid crime. In fact the open manner of Mudd in going out with Herold to get his father's carriage, and keeping the men without the slightest effort at concealment, or appearance of concern, at his house, makes it to my mind certain that he did not suspect their guilt before he got to Bryantown. When he got back to his house the men had gone, and he saw them no more - they taking the route he has shown Herold in the forenoon. When his wife told him of the false whiskers of the crippled man, his suspicions were aroused, and his first impulse was that of an innocent man and a good citizen - to go at once to Bryantown and tell of these men to the authorities. Her fears and and entreaties led him to delay sending word to them until next day, when he did it fully and truthfully.

I feel confident that the recorded evidence on an examination will not be found to sustain the finding and sentence of the Court in whole or in part - and that had the case been tried in a Civil Court no jury would have hesitated to rendered a verdict of acquittal. And I feel safe in appealing to the Judge Advocate General, who was probably present at the deliberations of the Court, to sustain me in the assertion that but for the evidence, 1st: as to Mudd's seeking Booth at the National Hotel on the 3rd of March; and 2nd: as to his having seen and assisted Booth and Herold after his return from Bryantown on the 15th of April; and 3rd: as to his unexplained delay until the 16th to communicate his information to the authorities, the Commission itself would have entirely acquitted him. On these three vital points Mrs. Mudd's testimony, if it could have been received by the Court, would have wholly relieved her husband of suspicion; and procured his acquittal. I appeal to your Excellency to receive it now, and give at the weight and effect it would probably have had if received by the Court. It would be not unworthy of Executive consideration if the prisoner had been tried and convicted by a Civil Tribunal with the benefit of every safeguard of liberty provided by law. But as he was tried before the tribunal where many of these safeguards were relaxed, inapplicable or ineffective - and especially as he was borne down by more false testimony than ever took the life of an innocent man in a Court of Justice - I can not be mistaken in believing that you will hear and give effect to the sworn statements of her, who (though she be the wife of the prisoner) knows more of the vital issues of the cause that all other witnesses together; and of whose perfect truth no one, who knows or talks with her, can doubt.

On this corroborated testimony of Mrs. Mudd, I respectfully ask on behalf of the prisoner, his wife, and children, a remission of his sentence.

I am, Sir, Very Respectfully,
Your Obedient Servant

Thomas Ewing Jr.
Atty

P.S.

Since writing the foregoing, I have seen an alleged confession by Atzerodt, in which he is reported as saying that two weeks before the assassination Booth told him that "he had sent provisions and liquors to Dr. Mudd's to be used by the conspirators on the route to Richmond with the president, and that he was acquainted with him, and had letters to him." If such a statement was in fact made by Atze-rodt, the statement by Booth as to his having sent anything to the house of the prisoner we can show was utterly false. The statement on its face shows that Mudd was not then a conspirator; for if he were, why should Booth mention the letters? Would he not have told Atzerodt that he was a conspirator with them? I am informed by Mr. Stone, who was counsel for Herold, that he said he tried to dissuade Booth from going so far out of his route - but that Booth said he must get his leg set and dressed. And that they did not while there inti-mate to Mudd what had been done. If Herold's confession is in the hands of the Judge Advocate, I ask that it be considered with this application for remission of sentence.

Thomas Ewing Jr.
    Attorney

08-03-1865: WASHINGTON EVENING STAR ARTICLE

S ource: Washington Evening Star, August 3, 1865

THE FOLLOWING Washington Evening Star article reports on the trip of Dr. Samuel Mudd, Samuel Arnold, Edman Spangler, and Michael O'Laughlen to Fort Jefferson in the Dry Tortugas aboard the U.S.S. Florida:

> The United States steamer Florida, Lieut. Commander Budd, which conveyed Dr. Mudd, Spangler, O'Laughlin, and Arnold to the Dry Tortugas, in charge of Gen. Dodd, arrived at New York on Tuesday, having left the prisoners at their destination on the 25th; and some of the officers who accompanied them have returned to the city.
>
> The prisoners, as we have stated before, left their quarters at the penitentiary (where they were tried) at two o'clock on the morning of July 18th, in the steamer State of Maine, and carried to Fortress Monroe, where they were transferred to the U. S. steamer Florida, Capt. Budd, on the afternoon of the same day, and proceeded to sea.

They were in charge of Gen. Levi A. Dodd, who had been on duty at the penitentiary during the whole of their confinement, who was accompanied by Col. Turner, Assistant Judge Advocate General, who went out to examine into the mode of keeping and treating prisoners there, Brevet Capt. Potter, Surgeon U.S.A. who had medical supervision of the prisoners during their incarceration here, and Capt. Dutton, of the Veteran Reserve Corps, with a guard of 28 men.

The prisoners, all of whom with the exception of Spangler, were sentenced to imprisonment and hard labor for life, and he for six years, had no idea of their destination, unless it was to Albany, until they reached Fortress Monroe, and then seeing the large quantity of rations placed on board, they began to suspect that they were bound to a more distant place than Albany. They were allowed to be together at times during the trip, and frequently engaged in a game of draughts, &c., during the day, but at night they were placed in separate state-rooms, closely guarded. The weather during the whole trip was pleasant, and but one on board (Mudd) was sea sick, and he on the first day at sea only. They were considerably depressed in spirits soon after starting, and when informed of their destination by Gen. Dodd after leaving Port Royal on the 21st, they became quite gloomy; but on reaching the Tortugas, and finding it an island of about 13 acres, enjoying a fine sea breeze and comparatively healthy, they expressed themselves as agreeably surprised, and became more buoyant in spirits. On landing and seeing comfortable quarters inside the fort, and a clump of coconut trees and other vegetation growing, and noticing the other prisoners confined there in good spirits, they soon became quite cheerful.

There are about 550 prisoners confined at the Dry Tortugas at this time, who are well treated, and seemingly enjoy life as well as they could in confinement anywhere. At present there are but nine persons on the sick list, a fact which speaks well for the treatment of the prisoners. The 110th New York Volunteers, Col. Hamilton, has been on duty here for the past sixteen months.

The Florida reached the Tortugas (about sixty miles from Key West) at noon on the 25th of July, and Gen. Dodd with his charge, immediately landed. Sam Arnold was immediately assigned to a desk as clerk in the engineers department, he being familiar with such work. Spangler at once noticed workmen shingling some of the buildings, and expressing a wish to take hand in his old business, was permitted to resume the hatchet and saw. Doctor S. A. Mudd arrived just in the nick of time, the Surgeon of the Post who has been there for six years past, stating that he wished an assistant, Dr. Mudd was notified that he would in future be expected to follow the practice of medicine among the prisoners. O'Laughlin had not, when the Florida left on the morning of the 26th, had his work allotted to him, but would no doubt be assigned some suitable occupation.

On the trip Dr. Mudd acknowledged to Capt. Budd, Gen. Dodd and others, that he knew Booth when he came to his house with Herold on the morning after the assassination, but that he was afraid to tell of his having been there, fearing the life of himself and family would be endangered thereby. He knew that Booth would never be taken alive. He also acknowledged that he had been acquainted with Booth for some time, and that he was with Booth at the National Hotel on the evening referred to by Weichman; that he met Booth in the street and Booth said he wanted him (Mudd) to introduce him to John Surratt; that they started up 7th street on their way to Mrs. Surratts house, and on the way they met John Surratt and Weichman, and returned to Booth's room at the National, where he and John Surratt had some conversation of a private character. He said that the Military commission in his case had done their duty, and as far as they were concerned the sentence in his case was just; but some of the witnesses had sworn falsely and maliciously.

O'Laughlin acknowledged that the Court had done its duty, and said that he was in the plot to capture the president, but that after the ineffectual attempt in March, when the party hoped to have captured the coach containing the president, he thought that the entire project was given up, and it was as far as he was concerned. He denies positively that he had part or knowledge in the plot to assassinate the president, Gen. Grant, or anyone else.

Sam Arnold made about the same statement as he did before the trial, that he was in the plot to capture, but not to assassinate; that that had failed and he considered himself out of it, and never knew anything about the assassination, which he thought was gotten up by Booth only a few hours before executing it. He thought the Court could not have done otherwise than it did. He expressed his sorrow that he had been led into the plot to capture by Booth and others, and expressed himself thankful that the punishment was no worse.

Spangler talked considerably during the trip, but like the others, was despondent at times, in the uncertainty about their place of destination. While on the voyage he expressed some impatience at his own stupidity in not having recollected while on trial a circumstance in connection with Booth's escape from the stage, that would have told materially to his (Spangler's) advantage. Some of the testimony went to show that Spangler has slammed the door to after Booth's exit, in a way to hinder immediate pursuit. Spangler says it quite escaped his recollection that some time previous to the assassination a patent spring had been put on the door for the purpose of closing it when left carelessly open. He says, however, that he supposes the Court had done right, and if they gave them plenty of work and plenty to eat he was satisfied; although he was not guilty, and knew nothing of Booth's intentions. He says he did say to Booth *"I would do all I can for you"* but that was in reference to selling his (Booth's) horse and buggy, and that it was three days before the assassination. He says that some of the witnesses lied in their testimony, especially about his slapping anyone in the mouth and telling him to keep his mouth shut.

The officers in charge of the prisoners carried out their instructions fully, and before leaving they received the thanks of each of the prisoners for the kind treatment to them.

08-17-1865: LETTER FROM PROVOST MARSHAL L.C. BAKER

S ource: The Life of Dr. Samuel A. Mudd, 1906, by Nettie Mudd.

~

LOUISVILLE, Ky., August 17, 1865, 9 A. M.
  Hon. T. T. Echert, Actg. Asst. Sec. of War:

I HAVE IMPORTANT PAPERS. I think the commanding officer at the Dry Tortugas should be put on his guard against an attempt to rescue the State prisoners in his charge. A company is organizing in New Orleans for that purpose. I have all the facts from a reliable source.

(SIGNED) L. C. BAKER, Br. Gen'l Pro. Mar. War Dept.

A TRUE COPY:

A. G. Office, Aug. 17, 1865.
E. D. TOWNSEND, Asst. Adj.-Gen.

08-22-1865: THE DUTTON REPORT

S ource: Dutton Report: Pitman, Benn, The Assassination of
President Lincoln and the Trial of the Conspirators. New
York, N.Y.. Moore, Wilstach, and Baldwin. 1865.

NEWSPAPER REPORTERS WERE NOT ALLOWED on the U.S.S. Florida when
it transported Dr. Mudd and the others to Fort Jefferson. However,
when the Florida returned to New York, reporters talked to the Army
officers who had gone on the trip. A *Washington Evening Star* article
said:

> *On the trip, Dr. Mudd acknowledged to Capt. Budd, Gen. Dodd and others,*
> *that he knew Booth when he came to his house with Herold on the morning*
> *after the assassination, but that he was afraid to tell of his having been*
> *there, fearing the life of himself and family would be endangered thereby.*
> *He knew that Booth would never be taken alive.*

Judge Advocate General Joseph Holt was the lead prosecutor in
the Lincoln assassination trial. When he read the newspaper story, he

asked Captain George W. Dutton, who had been in charge of the guards aboard the Florida, to tell him if Dr. Mudd had actually said what the article claimed he said. Captain Dutton submitted the following affidavit confirming the accuracy of the *Washington Evening Star* article. His report was the last document added to Benn Pitman's official record of the assassination trial, The Assassination of President Lincoln and the Trial of the Conspirators. Captain Dutton's report said:

Camp Fry, Washington, D.C.
    August 22,1865.

Brig. Gen. Joseph Holt,
    Judge Advocate General, U. S. A.:

Sir - I am in receipt of your communication of this date, in which you request information as regards the truthfulness of certain statements and confessions reported to have been made by Dr. Mudd while under my charge, en route to the Dry Tortugas.

In reply, I have the honor to state that my duties required me to be constantly with the prisoners, and during a conversation with Dr. Mudd, on the 22nd of July, he confessed that he knew Booth when he came to his house with Herold, on the morning after the assassination of the president; that he had known Booth for some time but was afraid to tell of his having been at his house on the 15th of April fearing that his own and the lives of his family would be endangered thereby. He also confessed that he was with Booth at the National Hotel on the evening referred to by Weichmann in his testimony; and that he came to Washington on that occasion to meet Booth by appointment, who wished to be introduced to John Surratt; that when he and Booth were going to Mrs. Surratt's house to see John Surratt, they met, on Seventh street, John Surratt, who was introduced to Booth, and they had a conversation of a private nature. I will here add that Dr. Mudd had with him a printed copy of the testimony pertaining to his trial, and I had, upon a number of occasions, referred to the same. I will also state that this confession was voluntary, and made without solicitation, threat or promise, and was made after the destination of the prisoners was communicated to them, which communication affected Dr. Mudd more than the rest; and he frequently exclaimed, *'Oh, there is now no hope for me.' 'Oh, I can not live in such a place.'*

Please acknowledge receipt of this letter.

I am General, very respectfully, your obedient servant,
George W. Dutton
Capt. Co. C, 10th Reg't. V. R. C., com'dg. Guard.

WHEN DR. MUDD learned of Captain Dutton's report, he wrote a heated rebuttal, which included an admission of his December 23, 1864 meeting with Booth in Washington, but also included his continued denial that he recognized Booth at his farmhouse. The official report on the Lincoln conspiracy trail included a copy of Captain Dutton's report, but not Dr. Mudd's rebuttal, so Dr. Mudd sent it to his wife, who then made it public, saying:

The following is a sworn statement written by my husband while he was a prisoner in Fort Jefferson and which he was not permitted by the authorities to have published. He sent it to me in a letter about the 1st of October, 1865. This statement was made to correct erroneous statements, which had appeared in the public press, allegedly quoting my husband.

August 28, 1865

1st. That I confessed to having known Booth while in my house; was afraid to give information of the fact, fearing to endanger my life, or made use of any language in that connection - I positively and emphatically declare to be notoriously false.

2nd. That I was satisfied and willingly acquiesced in the wisdom and decision of the Military Commission who tried me, is again notoriously erroneous and false. On the contrary I charged it (the Commission) with irregularity, injustice, usurpation, and illegality. I confess to being animated at the time but have no recollection of having apologized.

3rd. I did confess to a casual or accidental meeting with Booth in front of one of the hotels on Pennsylvania Avenue, Washington, D. C. on the 23d of December 1864, and not on the 15th of January, 1865, as testified to by Weichman. Booth, on that occasion desired me to give him an introduction to Surratt, from whom he said he wished to obtain a knowledge of the country around Washington, in order to be able to select a good locality for a country residence. He had the number, street, and name of John Surratt, written on a card, saying, to comply with his request would not detain me over five minutes. (At the time I was not aware that Surratt was a resident of Washington.) I declined at first, stating I was with a relative and friend from the country and was expecting some friends over from Baltimore, who intended going down with me to spend Christmas, and was by appointment expected to be at the Pennsylvania House by a certain hour - eight o'clock. We started down one street, and then up another, and had not gone far before we met Surratt and Weichman.

Introductions took place, and we turned back in the direction of the hotel. Arriving there, Booth insisted on our going to his room and taking something to drink with him, which I declined for reasons above mentioned; but finding that Weichman and Surratt were disposed to accept - I yielded, remarking, I could not remain many minutes. After arriving in the room, I took the first opportunity presented to apologize to Surratt for having introduced to him Booth - a man I knew so little concerning. This conversation took place in the passage in front of the room and was not over three minutes in duration. Whilst Surratt and myself were in the hall, Booth and Weichman were sitting on the sofa in a corner of the room looking over some Congressional documents. Surratt and myself returned and resumed our former seats (after taking drinks ordered), around a center table, which stood midway the room and distant seven or eight feet from Booth and Weichman. Booth remarked that he had been down in the country a few days before, and said he had not yet recovered from the fatigue.

Afterward he said he had been down in Charles County and had made me an offer for the purchase of my land, which I confirmed by an affirmative answer; and he further remarked that on his way up he lost his way and rode several miles off the track. When he said this he left his seat and came over and took a seat immediately by Surratt; taking from his pocket an old letter, he began to draw lines, in order to ascertain from Surratt the location and description of the roads. I was a mere looker on. The conversation that took place could be distinctly heard to any part of the room by any one paying attention. There was nothing secret to my knowledge that took place, with the exception of the conversation of Surratt and myself, which I have before mentioned. I had no secret conversation with Booth, nor with Booth and Surratt together, as testified to by Weichman. I never volunteered any statement of Booth having made me an offer for the purchase of my land, but made an affirmative response only to what Booth said in that connection.

Booth's visit in November 1864, to Charles County was for the purpose, as expressed by himself, to purchase land and horses; he was inquisitive concerning the political sentiments of the people, inquiring about the contraband trade that existed between the North and South, and wished to be informed about the roads bordering on the Potomac, which I declined doing. He spoke of his being an actor and having two other brothers, who also were actors. He spoke of Junius Brutus as being a good Republican. He said they were largely engaged in the oil business, and gave me a lengthy description of the theory of oil and the process of boring, etc. He said he had a younger brother in California. These and many minor matters spoken of caused me to suspect him to be a government detective and to advise Surratt regarding him.

We were together in Booth's room about fifteen minutes, after which, at my invitation, they walked up to the Pennsylvania House, where the conversation that ensued between Weichman and myself as testified to by him is in the main correct - only that he, of the two, appeared the better Southern man, and undertook to give me facts from his office to substantiate his statements and opinions. This was but a short time after the defeat of Hood in Tennessee. The papers stated that over nine thousand prisoners had been taken, and that the whole of Hood's army was demoralized and falling back, and there was every prospect of his whole army being either captured or destroyed. To this Weichman replied that only four thousand prisoners had been ordered to be provided for by the Commissary-General, and that he was far from believing the defeat of Hood so disastrous. I spoke with sincerity, and said it was a blow from which the South never would be able to recover; and that the whole South then laid at the mercy of Sherman. Weichman seemed, whilst on the stand, to be disposed to give what he believed a truthful statement. I am in hopes the above will refresh his memory, and he will do me the justice, though late, to correct his erroneous testimony.

To recapitulate - I made use of no such statement as reported by the *"Washington Correspondent of the New York Times,"* only in the sense and meaning as testified to by Dr. George D. Mudd, and as either misunderstood or misrepresented by Colonel Wells and others before the Commission.

I never saw Mrs. Surratt in my life to my knowledge previous to the assassination, and then only through her veil. I never saw Arnold, O'Loughlin, Atzerodt, Payne alias Powel, or Spangler - or ever heard their names mentioned previous to the assassination of the president. I never saw or heard of Booth after the 23d of December 1864, until after the assassination, and then he was in disguise. I did not know Booth whilst in my house, nor did I know Herold; neither of whom made himself known to me. And I further declare they did not make known to me their true destination before I left the house. They inquired the way to many places and desired particularly to go to the Rev. Mr. Wilmer's. I gave a full description of the two parties (whom I represented as suspicious) to Lieutenant Lovett and three other officers, on the Tuesday after the assassination.

I gave a description of one horse - the other I never took any notice of, and do not know to this day the color or appearance. Neither Booth's nor Herold's name was mentioned in connection with the assassination, nor was there any name mentioned on the Tuesday after the assassination, nor was there any name mentioned in connection with the assassination, nor was there any photograph exhibited of any one implicated in the infamous deed. I was merely called upon to give a description of the men and horses and the places they inquired. The evidence of the four detectives - Lovett, Gavacan, Lloyd, and Williams - conflict (unintentionally) vitally on this point; they evidently prove and disprove the fact as they have done in every instance affecting my interest, or upon points in which my welfare was at issue. Some swore that the photograph of Booth was exhibited on Tuesday, which was false. I do not advert to the false testimony; it is evident to the reader, and bears the impress of foul play and persecution somewhere - it may be owing to the thirst after the enormous reward offered by the government, or a false idea for notoriety. Evans and Norton evidently swore falsely and perjured themselves. Daniel I. Thomas was bought by the detectives - likewise the negroes who swore against me. The court certainly must have seen that a great deal of the testimony was false and incompetent - upon this I charge them with injustice, etc.

Reverend Evans and Norton - I never saw nor heard their names in my life. I never knew, nor have I any knowledge whatsoever, of John Surratt ever visiting Richmond. I had not seen him previous to the 23d of December, 1864, for more than nine months. He was no visitor to my house.

The detectives, Lovett, Gavacan, Lloyd, and Williams, having failed to search my house or to make any inquiries whether the parties left anything behind on the Tuesday after the assassination, I myself did not think - consequently did not remind them. A day or two after their leaving, the boot that was cut from the injured man's leg by myself, was brought to our attention, and I resolved on sending it to the military authorities, but it escaped my memory and I was not reminded of its presence until the Friday after the assassination, when Lieutenant Lovett and the above parties, with a squad of cavalry, came again and asked for the razor the party shaved with. I was then reminded immediately of the boot and, without hesitation, I told them of it and the circumstances. I had never examined the inside of boot leg, consequently knew nothing about a name which was there contained. As soon as I handed the boot to Lieutenant Lovett, they examined and discovered the name "J. Wilkes"; they then handed me his photograph, and asked whether it bore any resemblance to the party, to which I said I would not be able to recognize that as the man (injured), but remarked that there was a resemblance about the eyes and hair. Herold's likeness was also handed me, and I could not see any resemblance, but I had described the horse upon which he rode, which, one of the detectives said, answered exactly to the one taken from one of the stables in Washington.

From the above facts and circumstances I was enabled to form a judgment, which I expressed without hesitation, and I said that I was convinced that the injured man was Booth, the same man who visited my house in November, 1864, and purchased a horse from my neighbor, George Gardiner. I said this because I thought my judgment in the matter was necessary to secure pursuit promptly of the assassins.

09-16-1865: LIEUTENANT CARPENTER
TO GEN. TOWNSEND

Source: Provost Marshal, Fort Jefferson, Florida. Records Relating to Prisoners 1865-1870. Record Group 393, Entry 56, Volume 5. U.S. National Archives. Washington, D.C.

∽

Washington, September 16th 1865
   Brvt. Brig. Gen. E.D. Townsend
   Assistant Adjutant General

General,

I have the honor to submit the following report of matters at Fort Jefferson which came to my knowledge from personal observation or from conversations with the commanding officer at that Post during my late visit there as the bearer of despatches. I deem it my duty to submit this although not called for by your letter of instructions of the 16th inst.

Captain W.R. Prentiss, 161st N. Y. Vols. cmd'g his regiment relieved Colonel Hamilton, 110th New York of the command of the Post

August 16th. Major Willis E. Craig of the same regiment at the same time relieved Colonel Hamilton of the command of the Sub Dist. of Key West and Tortugas, Headquarters at Key West. The Garrison at Key West numbers about 300 men while the prisoners number 495. The quarters of the prisoners are in the second tier of casemates commencing to the left of the Sally Port and occupying through the second face of the work from it while the quarters of the soldiery are next in this order, thus throwing the prisoners between the main guard at the Sally Port and the rest of the Garrison and in case of an emute giving the prisoners the chance to overpower the guard before the other troops could get under arms and come to their aid.

In a small room built with rough boards on the floor of casemates occupied by the prisoners having two lightly laticed windows looking on a passage way for prisoners between it and the rear wall are placed in the racks about 40 muskets, with the locks removed, not under guard, which it would be but the work of a moment for the prisoners to seize unopposed. Drawn through a broken or uncompleted passage in the breakwater and near the Sally Port are moored in the moat three small barges nearly under the embrasures to casemates of prisoners. These I should judge by their situation would at least afford a temptation to prisoners giving access for an attack on the guard without the Sally Port.

From 6 a.m. to 6 p.m. several squads of prisoners, each under charge of a single soldier may be and are continually employed outside the work on the wharfs or bar discharging vessels, shifting materials, ordinance stores and alike. The passing promiscuously of these parties, or individually without a guard, the employees of the Engineering Department (of whom there are about one hundred) and others through the Sally Port was so illy regulated that it was easy for a prisoner unauthorized to slip out to the shipping, lurk among the piles of material or buildings, seize one of the numerous sail or row boats about, and be off, under cover of night at least unobserved.

There being no practiced artillerists in the Garrison, merely a squad of men drilled at odd hours by a non-commissioned officer in the manual of the piece; the fact that a vessel can by a skillful pilot be put clear around the fort very near the breakwater; and the absence of any steam vessel to give immediate notice in case of mutiny or rescue are considerations in favor of any concerted plan to release the prisoners by aid from without.

I could not learn that there were any regular hours for roll-call of prisoners, only that each soldier in charge of a squad of laborers was responsible for any absentee from his squad. The numbers that were in quarters lounging, card playing and the like at 10 a.m. and the appearance of a few rowing and fishing not under guard about the harbor gave evidence of an exceeding lax discipline over these convicts. Many prisoners were not in the dress I was told was prescribed for them. No surveillance whatever was exercised over their mail; the same facilities for communicating by letter was open to them as to any in the garrison.

Of the four state prisoners Mudd and Arnold have of late not been locked up at night. Mudd is on duty as nurse in the Hospital situate midway nearly of the parade. Arnold is on duty as clerk to the Provost Marshal where he must have every facility for learning all regulations touching the guards, and the two others are employed as laborers and are locked in cells at night.

The commanding officer informed me that about the 20th inst. eight prisoners were missing whom it was supposed escaped by concealing themselves on the steamer T. A. Scott which left Fort Jefferson the evening before for New York under charge of Lieutenant Flood, 2nd Infty., statement of the case had been made to Major Craig, Commanding Sub District of Key West.

There were no permanent books of record for the Post, not even a morning-report-book, save at the Provost Marshal's office there was a descriptive book of prisoners. There however the papers pertaining to the case of each prisoner were separately filed with a numerical designation to which there was an index book for convenience of reference. The Post order book it was said had been taken away by the former commanding officer when he left the Post. No Post funds were turned over to Captain Prentice by his predecessor, nor were there any records pertaining to any such funds or of any Council of administration.

About one hundred prisoners were under orders to be discharged but owing to the fact that there were no blanks on hand it was the commanding officer's intention to send these men to New Orleans to be discharged there as soon as transportation could be obtained. Complaints were made of the difficulty of obtaining supplies - that the Commissary stores on hand were of bad quality - that there was then no fresh beef and several cases of scurvy in the Hospital.

On the 5th inst. Major W.E. Craig, 161st New York was relieved of the command of the Sub. District by Colonel B. Townsend, 2nd U.S. Colored Infantry and left Key West that day for Fort Jefferson to assume the command of that Post. He, in conversation with reference to matters of Fort Jefferson, assured me that he was aware of the loose discipline there and should endeavor to remedy this and should see to it that the four state prisoners there were under strict surveillance.

I have the honor to be,

Very Respectfully
    Your Obt, Servant

(S) G.S. Carpenter
    1st Lieut. 18th U.S. Infty.

09-17-1865: EWING'S PRINTING BILL

7 oo copies of the arguments of General Ewing and the evidence in support of Dr. Mudd at the trial were printed and given to the military judges and others. General Ewing apparently paid the printing bill, and has asked Sarah for reimbursement.

∽

ROCK HILL, Nov. 17th, 1865
    Gen'l Ewing

DEAR SIR,

Your letter of the 14th has just been received. It grieves me much to know you have been annoyed and mortified by our delay in paying you the printing bill. I did not know you were responsible for the amount. I wrote to you some time ago that I would take the responsibility on myself and try and pay the amount. I will be up one day next week, probably Monday, and pay the bill.

I hope you will not think unkindly of Doctor's father. He is a very old man and has grown somewhat irritable by his many misfortunes. Besides he has been advised by a lawyer not to pay the bills.

General Ewing, Doctor nor I did not consider your fee large for the services rendered. I do not wish you to give up the $200 still due you, true you may have to wait some time, but the last dime shall be paid.

When I tell you that everything on our farm for man and beast was destroyed by the soldiers who were in pursuit of Booth and that nothing has been made on the farm this year owing to the destruction of fencing and farming utensils and by putting the farm hands in prison and keeping them there until it was too late to plant a crop. And that I have been obliged to buy everything I have used since that time and will be obliged to buy all of next year's provisions, you can form some idea of my circumstances.

I dread my fate. I have never known poverty from childhood. I have been gratified in every wish. But a few months ago (which now seems a lifetime) I thought my life was to be one of continual sunshine. Now I cannot see one ray of light in my future existence. I hope dear Sir the annoyance you have been subjected to will not cause you to think less of Dr. and prevent you using your influence for his release.

Could Doctor have been home to attend to his own affairs these things never would have happened. I have been so bowed down by my weight of woe and misery I have thought of no outside affairs. I must blame myself somewhat for the annoyance you have undergone and beg that by circumstances be a palliative.

Most Truly Yours,
S.F. Mudd

09-27-1865: REPORT OF DR. MUDD'S ESCAPE ATTEMPT

S ource: The Life of Dr. Samuel A. Mudd, 1906, by Nettie Mudd

∾

HEADQUARTERS FORT JEFFERSON, Fla., September 27th, 1865.
  Captain E. C. Woodruff, Actg. Ass't. Adj't Gen'l.
  Dep't. of Florida.

SIR, I have the honor to report, that, on the 25th ins't Dr. Samuel A. Mudd, one of the Conspirators, sentenced to this place for life, made an attempt to escape.

Since he has been in confinement here, he has been employed in the Prison Hospital, as Nurse and Acting Steward. When he came here, it was noticed that he immediately adopted the same clothing as worn by other prisoners, although he had good clothes of his own. On the day he attempted to escape he put on one of the suits he brought with him and in some way got outside the Fort to the Wharf, where the U.S. Transport, Thos. A. Scott, was lying. He went on board that boat and, (with the assistance rendered him by one of the Crew, Henry Kelly), secreted himself under some plank in the lower hold. After a short search he was found and I put him in irons, into one of the dungeons. I also ordered the arrest of the man Kelly, and put him in close confinement.

Dr. Mudd`s statement is that Kelly promised to assist him but had not done so, while Kelly denies knowing him or ever having seen him. Enclosed I forward the deposition of Jas. Healy, Coal Passer on the steamer, which clearly proves that Kelly has told a falsehood. He has the appearance of being a hard case, and his reputation on the boat was bad.

I AM VERY RESPECTFULLY,

YOUR OBEDIENT SERV'T.,
    GEO. E. WENTWORTH,
    Major 82nd U. S. C. Inf'ty., Commanding Post.

~

08-26-1867: TOO HOT FOR BASE BALL

S ource: U.S. National Archives, Record Group 393, Part 5, Entry 3, Endorsements Sent, Fort Jefferson, Florida.

~

"BASE BALL" was commonly two words instead of one in the early days of the sport. It was spreading in popularity in the mid-1800's, including among the soldiers at Fort Jefferson, where the large grassy parade ground inside the fort made an ideal playing field. But four days after Private James Forsythe became the first death in the fort's 1867 yellow fever epidemic, Major Valentine H. Stone, the Post Commander, issued the following order:

~

Fort Jefferson, Fla
  August 26, 1867

The Post Surgeon having recommended that as the sickly season of the year is now approaching, that the Enlisted Men of the Command should go in the sunshine as seldom as practicable, all drill will therefore for the present be suspended. Base ball playing will cease and everyone is enjoined to keep in the shade as much as possible.

By order of Brev. Maj. Val H. Stone

PAUL Roemer
1st Lt., 5th NY Artillery
Post Adjutant

~

09-04-1867: MAJOR SMITH'S LETTER TO DR. MILHAU

Source: Record Group 94. Records of the Adjutant General's Office, 1780's - 1917, Medical Records: 1814-1919. Reports on Diseases and Individual Cases, 1841-93, Papers Relating to Cholera, Smallpox, & Yellow Fever Epidemics, 1849-1893. U.S. National Archives, Washington, D.C.

∾

DR. J. Sim Smith, Fort Jefferson's physician, wrote the following letter. A day later, he was stricken with yellow fever, and died. He wrote:

Fort Jefferson
   Sept 4th 1867

Genl,

Since my last report up to the present about twenty five more cases have occurred - of these, two have died making three deaths in all. Among those taken since my last report is Lt. Paul Roemer,

Commanding Co. K and Acting Sr Asst & C.S. He was taken during the night of the 30th but did not notify or send for me until between three and four o'clock in the morning. He was very ill and is still quite so but improving I think.

The day after my last report to you the wind died out and since that time until yesterday we had little or no breeze and the average temperature has been a little more than eighty nine (89°) degrees. The result of this condition was very manifest yesterday in the fact that six cases recurred with an aggravation of all the symptoms. But during the day a strong breeze from the north east sprang up and has been blowing with occasional squalls ever since and today or rather since last evening no additional cases have occurred. I have established a Quarantine Hospital upon Sand Key consisting of two hospital tents, two wall tents and a temporary frame building thirty five by twelve feet. This last is the remains of the Hospital originally on the Key, built there during the war at a cost of fourth thousand dollars and complete I understand in all its appointments. This when I arrived at the Post had been torn down and the lumber used to build a theatre at the fort. Sand Key is a little island about an acre in extent a mile and a half North East of this Post.

There are now fourteen cases of yellow fever in Hospital about half of whom are convalescent. This morning by my advices the Commanding Officer detached Co. L and ordered it into encampment upon Bird Key which is a mile and a half to the South West of the Fort and if the other Keys were approached in rough weather I would advise him to detach another company.

The casemates in which three of the Companies are quartered are quite damp but airy and cool. A curious fact connected with the appearance of the disease at this place is that the only case last year at the Post occurred in the person of a Private of M Company who died but so far this year not a single case has occurred in that Company but has been confined to K, I, and L. My hospital at Sand Key is under the charge of Acting Steward James T. Moses, Prvt. Co. L 5th Arty, who has proved so far a valuable and efficient man but if the number of cases should increase I shall send there Hospital Steward

W.W. Wathes U.S.A. on duty at this Post - whose conduct during the epidemic is worthy of the highest commendation.

In the three cases in which death has occurred a very distressing hiccough has appeared about twelve hours preceding death. I would again call attention to the very unsatisfactory manner that this Post is supplied with commissary stores and must protest against it in the most earnest manner. Our supplies are received by a steamer which arrives at this point once a month and the supplies she brings are limited in quantity and indifferent in quality. Our supplies should be derived direct from the Northern markets with which we have direct communication every ten days. In this way our stores would reach us in a direct manner of good quality and in such quantities as are needed. Now as the perishable articles are first shipped from the North to New Orleans and thence back to this place, the loss is I should judge at least one third especially in the articles of flour. In point of economy of transportation I am quite sure that the expenses of transporting commissary stores from New York or Baltimore to Key West would not be as great as sending them by a special steamer from New Orleans.

I am Sir
    Very Respectfully
    Your Obdt Svt
    J. Sim Smith
    Asst Surg & Brvt Maj USA

J.J. Milhau USA
    Med. Dir. 3rd Mil. Dist.

10-31-1867: HOW THEY TREATED
YELLOW FEVER

S ource: Surgeon General's Office Papers Referring to Cholera
and Yellow Fever in the Army, 1867-69, Call Number: MS C 18,
History of Medicine Division, National Library of Medicine,
National Institutes of Health

~

WHEN DR. EDWARD THOMAS arrived at Fort Jefferson after the yellow
fever epidemic had subsided, he wrote a brief report entitled Treatment Remarks to describe how patients had been treated before his
arrival, and the changes he instituted. Although Dr. Thomas notes in
the report that no one died after his arrival, the yellow fever epidemic
was essentially over by the time he arrived.

Dr. Mudd was credited with using a procedure called blanketing
during the epidemic. Fort Jefferson's commander, Major George P.
Andrews, wrote to Dr. Mudd that:

> Your changing the mode of treatment and 'blanketing' patients so as to
> bring the period of fever under your full control, was regarded by the

medical gentlemen with whom I conversed as a bold and valuable alteration, and seems to have produced the very best results.

Blanketing was a technique used to break a fever by raising a patient's body temperature. The patient was first submerged to his chin in a hot bath until he sweated profusely, and then put into bed between blankets.

Although standard at the time, none of the techniques or medicines used during the epidemic such as powdered opium (Dover's Powder) or powdered mercury (Calomel), would be used to treat yellow fever today. Following is the October 31, 1861 report prepared by Dr. Thomas:

Treatment Remarks

The treatment pursued here before my arrival, as I am informed, consisted in the administration of 10 gr. Calomel & 10 gr. Dover's Powder when the patient was first taken with the fever. Afterward, the sick were allowed to drink freely of warm teas, such as Boneset, fever plant, & hyson. Cold water & ice was peremptorily and uniformly denied them. During the progress of the fever in cases of great restlessness and hot, dry skin, spirit of nitre ether & Dover's Powder were occasionally administered. In convalescence, ale, porter & other stimulants were used.

My treatment has been substantially as follows: At the outset, a brisk cathartic, composed of ten grains of calomel, ten of jalap, and one of podophyllin. Sometimes the podophyllin was omitted, as the case seemed to require. After the bowels had been thoroughly cleansed out, the following was given: Chlorate of potassa, a drachm and a half to the ounce of water; dose, a tablespoonful, in half a tumbler of water, every four hours.

The patients have been allowed all the ice and cold water that they wanted. Limeade and lemonade also has been given them ad libitum, whenever they desired it. In cases of a marked typhoid character, even in the height of the fever, ale and porter has been freely used until sweating was induced. The principal aim in the treatment has been to keep the skin moist and the kidneys active. So soon as convalescence set in, ale, porter, and milk punch were administered two, three, or four times a day, as the case required.

The underclothing of the patients has been changed twice a week; they have also, occasionally, been changed from bed to bed. Their quarters have been thoroughly cleansed, with a thin solution of chloride of lime, from time to time. The chambers, after being used, had chloride of lime sprinkled in them. In cases of delirium ice poultices to the head and mustard plasters to the stomach were used.

This has been, substantially, the treatment which I have pursued, and not a single death has occurred since its adoption.

From all that I can learn the disease was brought here from Key West on the schooner Matchless, one of the little vessels used by the Quartermaster's Dept. here.

Edward Thomas

AA Surgeon, USA in charge

12-03-1867: STATEMENT OF DR. SAMUEL MUDD

S ource: Library of Congress Manuscripts Division, Benjamin F. Butler File, Manuscripts of Testimony Before Committee on Assassination of President A. Lincoln 1867-68.

~

BENJAMIN F. BUTLER was a Union General during the Civil War, and after the war was elected to the U.S. House of Representatives where he chaired a congressional committee to investigate the assassination of Abraham Lincoln. Butler sent William H. Gleason to Fort Jefferson to obtain statements from Dr. Mudd, Spangler, and Arnold. O'Laughlen had died in the yellow fever epidemic.

Mr. Wm. H. Gleason
    Sir,
    Considering my present situation, I doubt the propriety of making a detailed statement, but in answer to your request and by the advice of Major Andrews our kind Commandant, I submit to the Committee, whom you have the honor to represent, the following

brief declaration, which I believe covers every point of your inquiry, viz:

1st. I never heard at any time during the war or since a desire expressed favorable to the assassination of the President.

2nd. I never had the least knowledge or suspicion that the murder of the President was contemplated by any individual or band of men previous to the commission of the horrid deed.

3rd. I was not acquainted with Mrs. Surratt, and to the best of my knowledge, never in her company'

4th. I knew Booth and Surratt, but not intimately.

5th. I did not know either Arnold, O'Laughlen, Spangler, Payne alias Powell, Herold, or Atzerodt, and never heard their names mentioned in any connection whatsoever, previous to the assassination.

Saml. A. Mudd

~

DR. MUDD'S statement above was attached to a cover note by Fort Jefferson's Post Commander, George P. Andrews. The note said:

Fort Jefferson, Florida
December 3rd, 1867

The annexed affidavit (ex parte) of Dr. Samuel Mudd, a prisoner under my charge requires that I should say a few words. I advised Dr. Mudd, first, to answer and make a full statement; next, to make his own statement and be cross-examined upon it. He, after much discussion, finally declined to make a detailed statement and be cross-examined, and made the one on the annexed page of this sheet. He had no other advice from me than that the reception of his evidence would be considered in his favor if reasons for commutation of his sentence were educed by his own examination and that of the other prisoners or other witnesses.

George P. Andrews
  Major, 5th Artillery
  Comdg Post

~

12-03-1867: STATEMENT OF EDMAN SPANGLER

S ource: Library of Congress Manuscripts Division, Benjamin F. Butler File, Manuscripts of Testimony Before Committee on Assassination of President A. Lincoln 1867-68.

∼

BENJAMIN F. BUTLER was a Union General during the Civil War, and after the war was elected to the U.S. House of Representatives where he chaired a congressional committee to investigate the assassination of Abraham Lincoln. Butler sent William H. Gleason to Fort Jefferson to obtain statements from Dr. Mudd, Spangler, and Arnold. O'Laughlen had died in the yellow fever epidemic. This is Spangler's statement:

> I was born in York County, Pennsylvania, and am about forty-three years of age, and am a house carpenter by trade, and became acquainted with J. Wilkes Booth when a boy. I worked for his father in building a cottage in Harford County, Md. AD 1854, and have since about 1853 done carpenter work for the different theatres in the city

of Baltimore, and Washington, to wit the Holliday Street Theatre, Charles Street Theatre, and the Front Street Theatre of Baltimore, and Ford's Theatre in the city of Washington.

I have also acted as scene shifter in all of the above named theatres, and had an opportunity to become acquainted with the different actors. I have acted as scene shifter in Ford's Theatre ever since it was first opened up to the night of the assassination of President Lincoln.

During the winter of AD 1862 & AD 1863 J. Wilkes Booth played a star engagement at Ford's Theatre for two weeks, at which time I saw and conversed with him frequently. He then left Washington and I did not see him again until the winter of 1864 & 1865. I then saw him at various times in and about Ford's Theatre. Booth had free access to the theatre at all times, and made himself very familiar with all persons connected with it.

He had a stable in the rear of the theatre where he kept his horses. A boy Joseph Borrows, commonly called Peanut John, took care of them. When Booth was absent from and away from the city, I looked after his horses which I did at his request, and saw that they were properly cared for. Booth promised to pay me for my trouble, but he never did.

I frequently had the horses exercised during Booth's absence from the city by Peanut John walking them up and down the alley. Peanut John kept the key of the stable in the theatre hanging upon a nail behind a small door which opened into the alley at the rear of the theatre.

Booth occasionally rode out on horseback afternoons and evenings, but seldom remained out later than 8 or 9 o'clock. He sometimes rode out in the morning. He always went and returned alone. I never knew of his riding out on horseback and remaining out all night, or of any persons coming to the stable with him, or calling there for him.

He had two horses at the stable only a short time. He brought them there sometime in the month of December. A man by the name of George and myself repaired and fixed the stable for him. I usually saddled the horse for him when Peanut John was absent.

About the first of March Booth bought another horse and a buggy to the stable. He had previously disposed of the other two horses and taken them away from the stable, but in what manner I do not know. After that he used to ride out in his horse and buggy, and I frequently harnessed them up for him. I never saw any person ride out with Booth or return with him from these rides.

On the Monday evening previous to the assassination, Booth requested me to sell the horse, harness, and buggy, as he said he should leave the city soon. I took them the next morning to the horse market, and had them put up at auction with instructions not to sell unless they would bring two hundred and sixty dollars. This was in accordance with Booth's order to me. As no person bid sufficient to make them net that amount, they were not sold, and I took them back to the stable.

I informed Booth of the result that same evening in front of the theatre. He replied he must try and have them sold at private sale, and asked me if I would "keep him." I replied "Yes". This was about six o'clock in the evening, and the conversation took place in the presence of others. The next day I sold them for two hundred and fifty dollars. The purchaser accompanied me to the theatre. Booth was not in, and the money was paid to James J. Gifford, who receipted for it. I did not see Booth to speak to him after the sale until the evening of the assassination.

Upon the afternoon of April 14th I was told by Peanut John that the president and General Grant were coming to the theatre that night, and that I must take the partition out in the president's box. It was my business to do all such work. I was assisted in doing it by Ritterspaugh and Peanut John.

In the evening between 5 and 6 o'clock Booth came into the theatre and asked me for a halter. I was very busy at the time on the stage preparatory to the evening performance, and Ritterspaugh went upstairs and brought one down. I went out to the stable with Booth, and put the halter upon the horse & commenced to take off the saddle when Booth said never mind, I do not want it off, but let it and the bridle remain. He afterwards took the saddle off himself, locked the stable, and went back to the theatre.

Booth, Maddox, Peanut John, and myself immediately went out of the theatre to the adjoining restaurant next door, and took a drink at Booth's expense. I then went immediately back to the theatre, and Ritterspaugh and myself went to supper. I did not see Booth again until between nine and ten o'clock. About that time someone called to me and said that Booth wanted me to hold his horse. As soon as I could be spared, I went to the back door, and Booth was standing in the alley holding a horse by the bridle rein and requested me to hold it. I took the rein, but told him I could not stay, as Gifford was gone, and that all of the responsibility was on me. Booth then passed into the theatre. I called to send Peanut John to hold the horse. He came, took the horse, and I went back to my proper place. I did not hold the horse to exceed three minutes.

In about a half hour afterwards, I heard a shot fired and immediately saw a man run across the stage. I saw him as he passed the center door of the scenery behind which I then stood. I did not recognize the man as he crossed the stage as being Booth. I then heard someone say that the president was shot. Immediately all was confusion. I shoved the scene back as quickly as possible in order to clear the stage, as many were rushing upon it.

I was very much frightened. I did not see Booth pass out. My situation was such that I could not see any person pass out of the back door. The back door had a spring attached to it, and would shut of its own accord. I usually slept in the theatre, but I did not upon the night of the assassination. I was fearful the theatre would be burned, and slept in a carpenter shop adjoining.

I never heard Booth express himself in favor of the rebellion, or opposed to the Government, or converse upon political subjects, and I have no recollection of his mentioning the name of President Lincoln in any connection whatever. I know nothing of the mortice hole said to be in the wall behind the door of the president's box, or of their being any wooden bar to fasten or hold the door, or of the lock being out of order. I did not notice any hole in the door. Gifford usually attended to the carpentering in the front part of the theatre, while I did the work about the stage. Mr. Gifford was the top carpenter and I worked under him.

Edman Spangler

12-03-1867: STATEMENT OF SAMUEL ARNOLD

S ource: Library of Congress Manuscripts Division, Benjamin F. Butler File, Manuscripts of Testimony Before Committee on Assassination of President A. Lincoln 1867-68.

∽

BENJAMIN F. BUTLER was a Union General during the Civil War, and after the war was elected to the U.S. House of Representatives where he chaired a congressional committee to investigate the assassination of Abraham Lincoln. Butler sent William H. Gleason to Fort Jefferson to obtain statements from Dr. Mudd, Spangler, and Arnold. O'Laughlen had died in the yellow fever epidemic. This is Arnold's statement:

It was in the latter part of August, or about the first of September AD 1864, that J. Wilkes Booth, hearing I was in town, sent word to me that he would like to see me at Barnum's Hotel in the city of Baltimore, at which place he was then stopping. I had not seen Booth since the year 1862, at which time we were fellow students at St. Timothy's

Hall, Catonsville, Md., the Rev. L. Van Bokkelen being then president of said institute.

I called upon him and was kindly received as an old schoolmate and invited to his room. We conversed together, seated by a table smoking a cigar, of past hours of youth and the present war. He said he heard I had been South, when a tap at the door was given, and O'Laughlen was ushered into the room. O'Laughlen was a former acquaintance of Booth's from boyhood up, so he informed me. I was introduced to him, and this was my first acquaintance with O'Laughlen.

In a short time wine was called for by Booth and we drank and freely conversed together about the war, the present condition of the South, and in regard to the non-exchange of prisoners. Booth then spoke of the abduction or kidnapping of the president, saying if such could be accomplished, and the president taken to Richmond and held as a hostage, he thought it would bring about an exchange of prisoners. He said the president frequently went to the Soldiers Home alone and unguarded, that he could be easily captured on one of these visits, and carried to the Potomac, boated across the river, and conveyed to Richmond.

These were the ideas advanced by Booth, and he alone was the moving spirit. After a debate of some time and his pointing out the feasibility, and being under the effects of some little of wine, we consented to join him in the enterprise. We alone comprised the entire party to this scheme at that time as far as my knowledge extends.

We separated that afternoon and I returned to my brother's near Hookstown, Baltimore County, Maryland, Booth stating he would leave for New York the next day to wind up his affairs and make over his property to different members of his family, reserving enough to carry out his projected scheme and would soon return.

Booth said he would furnish all the necessary materials to carry out the project. He showed me the different entries in his diary of what his engagements paid him in his profession, and I judge from what I have heard his income therefrom to be $20,000 to $30,000. He also informed me he owned property in the oil regions of Pennsylvania.

He was taken sick while at home and upon his recovery he arranged his business and went to the oil regions from which place he wrote me enclosing twenty dollars for expenses, requesting me to look around and pick out a horse for him. This is all the money I ever received from Booth or any other person in connection with this undertaking.

He went from the oil regions to Canada and shipped his wardrobe there as he afterwards informed me. Booth returned to Baltimore some time in November or December 1864. He had purchased whilst North some arms to defend himself in case of pursuit, viz: 3 carbines, 3 revolvers, 3 knives, and 2 pairs of handcuffs. Fearful that the weight of his trunk might attract attention, he asked me to take part of them, which I did and sent them to him by express to Washington.

A short time after his return from Canada to Baltimore, he went to the lower counties of Maryland bordering on the Potomac as he said for the purpose of purchasing horses and boats. I met him in Baltimore in January I think, at which time he purchased the horse I had selected for him. He also purchased a buggy and harness and now said that all was completed and ready to go to work.

I informed my parents I was in the oil business with Booth to prevent them from knowing the true cause of my association with Booth. O'Laughlen and myself drove the buggy to Washington; this was some time in the latter part of December 1864. We left the horse at Taylor's Livery Stable on the avenue near 13th Street and we went to Rullman's Hotel on Pennsylvania Avenue. We remained there a few days and then went to Mitchell's Hotel near Grover's Theatre and remained a few days. We went from there and rented rooms from Mrs. Van Pyne, 420 D Street and obtained our meals at Franklin Hotel at the corner of D and 8th Streets and there remained off and on until the 20th day of March 1865, during which time I frequently went to Baltimore nearly every Saturday.

O'Laughlen as a general thing always went and returned with me on these visits. When in Baltimore, I remained at my father's. When in Washington, I spent most of my time at Rullman's Hotel on Pennsylvania Avenue, at which place O'Laughlen and myself had acquaintances. The president having ceased visiting the Soldiers Home, Booth proposed a plan to abduct him from the theatre by carrying him off the stage by the back entrance, place him in a buggy which he was to have in attendance, and during the confusion which would be produced by turning off the gas, make good our escape.

I objected to any such arrangement and plainly pointed out its utter impossibility, and told Booth it could not be accomplished. He would listen to no argument I could bring forth and seemed resolved in carrying out this mad scheme. He endeavored to obtain a man from New York to turn off the gas. In this he failed, so he informed me.

This was in the latter part of January 1865, or the early part of February 1865. Booth at this time was stopping at the National Hotel. About this time I called at his room, accompanied by O'Laughlen, and upon entering was introduced to Surratt, under the name I think of Cole. This was about 10 or 11 o'clock AM, and Booth was still in bed. This was the first time I ever met Surratt. Surratt left a few moments after we came in, and Booth informed us he was one of the parties engaged in the abduction, and his name was Surratt.

About this time, Booth told me he had received a letter from his mother in which she stated she had fearful dreams about him. She sent his brother Junius Brutus to Washington to persuade him to come home, so Booth told me. Booth told me he did not wish his brother to know how many horses he had, as he knew his brother would ask an explanation why he kept so many. He asked me then to go down to Cleaver's Stable and I did so. He told Mr. Cleaver I had purchased the horse, and he was turned over to me.

About a week afterwards, I went to the stable, paid the livery on the horse, and rode him up to the corner of D and 8th Streets, and turned him over either to O'Laughlen or Booth and I never saw the horse afterwards. Booth afterwards repaid me for the board of the horse.

Booth was absent from the city of Washington the best part of the month of February. On his return, he stated he had been to New York. On the night of the 15th of March 1865 about 12 or 12:30 at night, as O'Laughlen and myself were about leaving Rullman's Hotel on our way to our room, Booth sent a messenger (Herold), who at that time was unknown to me requesting us to accompany Herold to Golier's Eating Saloon. Herold, I learned from O'Laughlen, had been introduced to him that day by Booth during their buggy ride.

We accordingly went up and were ushered into the room where seated around a table were Booth, Surratt, Atzerodt alias Port Tobacco, and Payne alias Mosby, all of whom with the exception of Booth and Surratt, we had never seen or heard of before. We were then formally introduced. Oysters, liquors, and cigars were obtained. Booth then remarked these were the parties engaged to assist in the abduction of the president. Whereupon the plan of abducting him from the theatre was introduced and discussed upon, Booth saying if it could not be done from the lower box, it could from the upper one.

He set forth the part he wished each one to perform. He and Payne alias Mosby were to seize him in the box. O'Laughlen and Arnold to put out the gas. I was to jump upon the stage and assist them as he was lowered down from the box. Surratt and Atzerodt alias Port Tobacco were to be on the other side of the Eastern Branch Bridge to act as pilots, and to assist in conveying him to the boats which had been purchased by Booth. Booth said everything was in readiness.

The gist of the conversation during the meeting was whether it could or could not be accomplished in the manner as proposed. After listening to Booth and the other's comments, I firmly protested and objected to the whole scheme, and told them of its utter impracticability. I stated that prisoners were now being exchanged, and the object to be obtained by the abduction had been accomplished, that patriotism was the motive that prompted me in joining in the scheme, not ambition, that I wanted a shadow of a chance for my life, and I intended on having it.

Then an angry discussion arose between Booth and myself in

which he threatened to shoot me. I told him two could play at that game, and before them all expressed my firm determination to have nothing more to do with it after that week. About 5 o'clock in the morning the meeting broke up and O'Laughlen and myself went to our room.

The next day as I was standing in front of Rullman's Hotel in company with O'Laughlen, Booth was riding by on horseback and called O'Laughlen. He conversed with him a short time and returned saying Booth wanted to see me. I went to the curb and met him. Booth apologized for the words he had used at the meeting, remarking he thought I must have been drunk in making the objections I did at the meeting in reference to his proposed plan of carrying out the abduction. I told him No! Drunkenness was on his and his party's part, that I was never more sober in my life, and what I said last night I meant, and that this week should end my connection in the affair.

On the 17th day of March 1865 about 2 o'clock, Booth and Herold met O'Laughlen and myself. Booth stated he was told the president was going to attend a theatrical performance out on 7th Street at a soldiers' encampment or hospital at the outer edge of the city. Booth had previously sent a small black box containing 2 carbines, a monkey wrench, ammunition and a piece of rope by the Porter of the National Hotel to our room. Not wishing it to remain in our room, O'Laughlen sent the box to an acquaintance of his in Washington. This box was sent to our room in the early part of March I think, and was removed in about a week or 10 days.

After Booth and Herold met O'Laughlen and myself and made an arrangement to go out to the performance on 7th Street, Booth, Herold, and O'Laughlen went for the box containing the 3 carbines etc. The understanding was that Herold was to take the box with Booth's horse and buggy to either Surrattsville or T.B. And there meet us in case the abduction was successful. This was the last time I saw Herold until our trial. O'Laughlen returned and we took our dinner at the hotel as usual.

After dinner we met Booth and accompanied him to a livery stable near the Patent Office at which place Booth obtained horses for us. O'Laughlen and myself rode to our room on D Street and made all our necessary arrangements, each arming himself. O'Laughlen and myself rode out to where the performance was to take place. We stopped at a restaurant at the foot of the hill to await the arrival of the other parties, they not arriving as soon as we expected. We remounted our horses and rode out the road about a mile. We then returned and stopped at the same restaurant.

Whilst in there, Atzerodt came in who had just arrived with Payne. A short time after Booth and Surratt came in and we drank together. Booth made inquiries at the encampment at which place the performance was to be held, and learned the president was not there. After telling us this, we separated, O'Laughlen, Payne, and myself riding back to the city together. Surratt and Booth rode out the road towards the country. O'Laughlen and myself left our horses back of the National Hotel at a livery stable. About 5 o'clock I met Booth and Surratt near the stable. This was the last time I ever saw Surratt, and I never saw Payne after we parted in our ride to the city until the day of our trial.

O'Laughlen and myself left Washington on the 20th of March and went to Baltimore. Booth went to New York, and thus I thought the whole affair abandoned. I then told my family I had ceased business in Washington and severed my connections with Booth. Father told me if I would apply to J.H. Wharton for employment I might obtain it as Wharton was looking for a clerk the last time he came up from Old Point Comfort to Baltimore. I went out to my brother's at Hookstown, Baltimore County and I returned March the 25th to Baltimore.

I was informed at my father's that Booth had called to see me and left a card requesting me to call upon him at Barnum's Hotel. I found a letter there also from him for me in which he stated he desired to give it another trial the week following, and if unsuccessful to abandon it forever. The letter found in Booth's trunk was in answer to this letter which I innocently wrote to prevent his undertaking it.

On the same day, March 27, 1865 I applied to J.H. Wharton at Old Point Comfort for employment and received a favorable answer to my application on the 31st of March 1865.

O'Laughlen came to my father's to which place I had returned from my brother's and requested me to accompany him to Washington to see Booth for the purpose of obtaining $500 which Booth had borrowed of him. I went with him that morning and returned with him in the early afternoon of the same day.

At the Depot at Washington, we accidentally met Atzerodt. We drank and parted with him. I never saw him from the 17th of March until then, and never afterwards until our trial. We saw Booth. During our conversation he told us the president was not in Washington. He also said that Surratt had gone to Richmond, as he had understood through Weichman that a Mrs. Slater had arrived from Canada with dispatches and that the party who had been in the habit of ferrying persons across the river had been arrested by the Government in consequence of which Surratt offered his services to accompany her to Richmond.

I asked him if he had received my letter of the 27th. He replied he had not. I asked him when the letter was received to destroy it. He told me he would. This interview on the 31st March took place in his room at the National Hotel (O'Laughlen, Booth, and myself). He in the conversation stated that the enterprise was abandoned. He also stated he intended to return to his profession. It was at this interview and time I asked Booth what I should do with the arms I had. He told me to keep them, to sell them, or do anything I chose with them.

We left him at his room at the hotel about 2 o'clock, and after that time I never received either a letter from him, or any other communication, nor he from me, neither have I seen him since. We returned to Baltimore on the afternoon train. I parted with O'Laughlen and went to my father's. I there found a letter from Wharton in which he gave me employment. This was in reply to my letter to him dated 27th March 1865 applying for a situation.

The next morning I went to my brother's at Hookstown, packed up my valise preparatory to go to Wharton's. I then gave my brother a revolver and the knife. One revolver I carried with me. My brother drove me to the city and I took the boat that evening for Old Point and commenced clerking for Mr. Wharton on my arrival there, which was April 2nd, 1865. This ended my connection with Booth.

Samuel Arnold

12-19-1867: STATEMENT OF WILLIAM H. GLEASON

S ource: Library of Congress Manuscripts Division, Benjamin F. Butler File, Manuscripts of Testimony Before Committee on Assassination of President A. Lincoln 1867-68.

∾

Statement of Wm. H. Gleason of Biscayne Bay, Florida, given at Washington City, District of Columbia, Dec. 19th, 1867.

Under the direction of Hon. Benj. F. Butler, Chairman of the Committee appointed by Congress to investigate the facts and circumstances attending the assassination of President Lincoln I proceeded to Fort Jefferson, Dry Tortugas, Florida, there to examine and to take statements to be voluntarily given by the several persons there confined for complicity in the assassination of President Lincoln.

I left the City of Washington on the 21st day of September 1867 and went to Atlanta, Georgia, the headquarters of Maj. Genl. Pope, commanding the 3rd military district in whose jurisdiction the prisoners were held. From him I received the necessary orders giving me permission to visit Fort Jefferson and access the prisoners. I then proceeded to St. Marks, Florida and was there detained a number of days waiting for the steamer which makes monthly trips between St. Marks, Key West, and Fort Jefferson.

I left St. Marks on the 5th day of October 1867 and arrived at Key West October 11th, 1867, there learning that the yellow fever was raging at Fort Jefferson to an alarming extent, and had assumed an epidemic fever. I here learned of the death of O'Laughlin, one of the prisoners convicted of being a party to the assassination of President Lincoln.

In consequence of the serious aspect of the fever, I went to Fort Dallas and there remained until the fever abated. I left Fort Dallas on the 5th day of November and proceeded direct to Fort Jefferson, Dry Tortugas, where after presenting my credentials and Genl. Pope's order, I was at once admitted to the Fort and put in communication with the prisoners, viz. Dr. Samuel A. Mudd, Samuel Arnold, and Edward Spangler.

My first conversation was with Dr. Saml. Mudd, to whom I read the resolution of the Congress of the United States organizing the Committee, and my authority to receive any statements he or the other prisoners might wish to make in relation to their connection or any knowledge they might possess of facts, circumstances, or persons connected with the assassination of President Lincoln.

Doctor Saml. Mudd refused to make any statement whatsoever. He (Mudd) said he did not see how he could be benefitted by so doing, and was fearful if he did make a statement it might be used against him hereafter. I explained to him I thought the language of the resolution contemplated that no such use should be made of any statement any person might make against themselves.

He stated that efforts were being made by his friends to obtain from the president his pardon and release and he was fearful that if he made any statement it might delay and prevent the pardon he expected. I told him I should remain a number of days on the island and he could think it over. He (Mudd) said he would consult with his friends and be advised by them.

I remained on the island two weeks and saw Mudd every day and quite often had conversation with him about the assassination of President Lincoln. At one of those conversations, he (Mudd) said he would not object to make a statement if he could be taken before the Committee at Washington, it being his idea that once there he could be released on a writ of Habeas Corpus. He (Mudd) seemed to think and so stated that he considered his release certain, and only a matter of time. He thought the late elections north denoted the downfall of the Republican Party and the success of the Democratic.

He (Mudd) considered himself a political prisoner and not as having been convicted of any crime, and that the success of the Democratic Party would result in his own release and that of his comrades. I said to him (Mudd) that he need not hope for aid from that quarter as the Democratic Party would not sanction murder and assassination any more than any other party. He (Mudd) thought otherwise and contended that their triumph was his release.

He (Mudd) stated that he became acquainted with J. Wilkes Booth through a Mr. Thompson, a son-in-law of Dr. Queen's of Maryland. He (Mudd) said at the first interview he had with Booth he (Booth) stated that he wished to buy some horses and also asked if a party of three or four actors could not cross the river in a small boat to go South and not be caught. Booth said he intended to play South and had sent his wardrobe there. Mudd said this first conversation took place at his (Mudd's) house in the month of Nov. 1864. He (Mudd) told Booth that he would have no trouble to effect a crossing of the river at any time, as parties were constantly coming and going.

He (Mudd) said that in December 1864 he met Booth in the City of Washington near the National Hotel and that Booth took a card from his pocket that appeared to have some address written on it and asked him (Mudd) if he would take him (Booth) to Mrs. Surratt's house and introduce him to John H. Surratt. He (Mudd) said he made some excuses as he did not wish to introduce Booth to Surratt. Booth appeared very anxious and insisted on an introduction.

While we (Booth & Mudd) were conversing on the sidewalk John H. Surratt and Lewis Weichman came down the street on the opposite side. I spoke to Surratt, calling to him. He came across the street and I (Mudd) introduced him (Booth) to Surratt. Booth invited us all up to his room in the National Hotel. After we got to the room Booth commenced conversation with Weichman, and I (Mudd) stepping out into the hall called John H. Surratt out and cautioned him in relation to Booth, I (Mudd), thinking Booth to be a spy for the North.

After cautioning Surratt we returned to the room and conversed in regard to the war news as to the number of prisoners captured, and that he (Weichman) occupied a position in the Office of the Commissary General of Prisoners, which gave him an opportunity to know the exact numbers. Weichman expressed himself as favorable to the South and hostile to the Government of the United States.

Mudd said he never met Booth but three times. The first being in November 1864 when he came to his (Mudd's) house to buy horses, and making inquiries about the river. The second was in December 1864 at Washington when he (Mudd) introduced him (Booth) to John H. Surratt. The third and last time was on the morning of April 15th 1865 at about 4 o'clock a.m. When he (Booth) and Herold came to his (Mudd's) house, Booth having a broken leg a little above the foot joint which he (Mudd) set for him.

Mudd avoided saying anything about what took place between himself, Booth, and Herold while they were at his (Mudd's) house. Mudd said he went to Bryantown in the morning, leaving Booth and Herold at his house. While at Bryantown he heard of the assassination of President Lincoln and that a man named Boyd was said to be the assassin, and afterwards that it was Edwin Booth the actor. He (Mudd) said that there was a body of soldiers in town preventing people from leaving, but he (Mudd) evaded them and went back to his house. When he got home, Herold had the horse he brought with him at the gate and was preparing to go.

Mudd came to me before I came away from Fort Jefferson and gave me the annexed statement marked (A) and requested me to deliver it to the Committee at Washington.

He formerly refused to answer any questions under oath, or swear to any statements he had made. It is my opinion that Doctor

Mudd has knowledge of important information, and in his conversations with me desired to present only such remarks as would tend to be favorable to himself.

In my interview with Samuel Arnold he expressed himself as being willing to give a statement and to answer any questions that might be proposed to him, provided he be assured that if any of it should be published it all should be as he stated. He had made a statement to detectives and others and that they had been used against him, and he had been misrepresented. I assured him that the objects of the Committee were only to get the facts. He then gave me the annexed statement (B).

Saml. Arnold's health is very bad, and part of the time in which he was engaged in making the statement he was confined to his bed. He seemed to be very careful and anxious to give a clear, complete, and full statement, and I have no doubt of its truth, and think it should receive full confidence.

Edward Spangler at first objected to give me any statement because a former statement he had made had been used against him, but after showing him the resolution of Congress and explaining the objects of the investigation he consented and made a statement which is hereunto annexed and marked (C).

While on the island I had a number of interviews and conversations with St. Leger Grenfell who was formerly Adjutant General to the rebel Genl. Morgan, and is confined on the Tortugas for being connected with the Chicago conspiracy to release the rebel prisoners who were there confined. He stated that while he was with General Morgan a letter was received from Jefferson Davis signed by Adj. Genl. Cooper in relation to an officer in Morgan's by the name of Crozier.

It seemed by the contents of the letter that Crozier had proposed to the president of the Confederate States, Davis, to abduct President Lincoln from Washington and take him to Richmond, and asked that he might be detailed with 15 men of Morgan's command to proceed to Washington for that special purpose. At the time the letter was received, Crozier was out of camp and was killed and never returned.

Grenfell was hopeful of receiving a pardon and considers himself purely a political prisoner, and as soon as the Democrats came into power he would be released, if not sooner. Grenfell is still a rebel and does not care to say much about his own affidavit.

Having completed the business on which I was sent, I started on the 5th day of December for Washington, which city I reached on the 13th day of December 1867, and now under oath submit the foregoing as a true report.

12-31-1867: DR. WHITEHURST'S LETTER TO DR. CRANE

S ource: Samuel A. Mudd Pardon File B-596, RG 204, U.S. National Archives, College Park, Md.

∾

Dr. C.H. Crane
  Asst. Surgeon General
  U.S. Army
  Washington

Sir.

I have the honor of acknowledging receipt of copy of a petition, signed by soldiers of the 5th U.S. Artillery at Fort Jefferson, Fl. in behalf of Dr. Mudd, a state prisoner thereat, and referred to me by order of the Surgeon General for remark incident thereto.

On the morning of 7th August last, at 2 o'clock, I was called on by 2nd Master Thorpe & Dr. Cornick, and was informed that there was much apprehension felt at Fort Jefferson, in consequence of fever existing there; and I was asked if I could not go down; to which I replied, if the situation of my sick of Engineer Hospital, as well as private patients, would admit of leaving that I would cheerfully do so.

At daylight I commenced visiting my patients, and received at the same time, a note from Major Stone, importuning me to come over, as Dr. Smith was extremely ill, and they were all in great affliction. An appeal of this character could not pass unheeded, and turning my sick over to the care of another, I left for Fort Jefferson, arriving there at 10 o'clock that night, and immediately visited Dr. Smith, whom I found in the wildest phrensy. As soon as Major Stone entered, he sprang at him, and demanded that he should be allowed to see his wife, then laying ill in the next room.

I had iced water poured over the head, and in a short time, he fell off into a gentle slumber - awakening at 12, with returning cerebral disturbance, and at 2 of the morning of the 8th I closed his eyes - dying without a struggle.

Dr. Mudd was and had been in attendance on Dr. Smith, as well as Mrs. Smith. Dr. Mudd, at 6 o'clock called on me, and remarked *"that he had been doing medical service, from the emergency of events, and as I had come down, he would now retire."* Favorably impressed with his services, I asked him to continue them, which he did, visiting the sick with me, taking down prescriptions, putting them up, and attending to the various duties which the increasing sick required at his hands.

The Hospital Steward, Wythe, was convalescing, with a sick wife and child, and altho' as efficient as he could be, under such circumstances, he had continued claims upon his attention, in supplying cooks and nurses; for those of one day were patients the next, and thus his duties were exacting in the extreme. Incidentally, I would remark that I found Grenfell a volunteer nurse with Dr. Smith; and after his death in the hospital; and I must say that his attention and kindness was most continuous - to many a sick soldier, their return to health was the result I have no doubt of his continued devotion.

On my arrival, I found a hospital at Sand Key, and that the island was used as a burial place of the dead. The island was small, and had been used during the war for a similar purpose, leaving really but little room for new interments. The hospital tents were located over, and surrounded by graves, and the small wood building, tho' not so much, was still subject to the same objections. As the communication which I made daily with the island was liable to interruption, and as the sick continued to improve, I thought it best to discontinue the use of the island for that purpose and on the 15th Sept. it was abandoned. From the first development of fever (Aug 18th) there were 27 cases treated, and 6 deaths on Sand Key. In removing the convalescents, and ceasing to make a further use of Sand Key, the most important consideration was that the weather was boisterous, and a hurricane might occur at any moment, a contingency which would have been fatal to all the occupants thereon.

The companies at Sand Key were removed to Loggerhead, and the depressing influences of burials was thus removed from among the soldiers stationed there.

Major Stone and Lieuts Orr & Gordon frequently spoke to me in relation to Dr. Mudd, and they expressed themselves, warmly commendations in his favor, as well also in favor of Grenfell, and that they desired reporting to the government their excellent conduct, and asking its benignant recognition in their behalf.

These gentlemen were all victims of the disease and it seems but just to their memories that opinions so formed and expressed should be made a matter of record.

I believe that these remarks will explain all sought for by the Surgeon General in relation to Dr. Mudd; and in conclusion, I feel that I should be unfaithful to a common humanity did I fail to recognize his useful, unwearying and continued service in a period of sorrow and deep distress.

I have the honor to be
    Very Respectfully,
    D.W. Whitehurst M.D.

04-13-1868: LIZZIE SMITH'S LETTER TO PRES. JOHNSON

S ource: Samuel A. Mudd Pardon File B-596, RG 204, U.S. National Archives, College Park, Md.

◇

MANY LETTERS WERE WRITTEN to President Johnson asking him to pardon Dr. Mudd for his work during the 1867 yellow fever epidemic at Fort Jefferson. This letter was written by the widow of Dr. Joseph Sim Smith, Fort Jefferson's physician, and one of the first casualties of the epidemic.

When Dr. Smith died, Dr. Mudd stepped in and began ministering to the sick and dying. Smith's wife and son also contracted yellow fever. His son died, but his wife survived to write this letter.

To His Excellency Andrew Johnson
    President of the United States

Sir

I have the honor to address a few words to you in behalf of Dr. Mudd, prisoner at Ft. Jefferson, Dry Tortugas Florida.

Feelings of deep gratitude to him for his great kindness and attention to my late husband and only son, both of whom were victims to the yellow fever which raged so fearfully at the Fort last September, and also to me during my illness with the same disease prompts me to address a petition to you for his pardon and release.

He did not spare himself during the prevalence of the epidemic and absence of other medical aid, as was sometimes the case, especially during the illness of my husband and myself but was ready and anxious to render any assistance in his power to the sufferers. And to the last of my child's life, he was near him trying to relieve his dreadful suffering.

I shall ever remember his kindness in that trying time, and beg of you, if it is possible, to grant his pardon and allow him to return to his family in Maryland. He surely deserves some return for his services, and he has suffered enough in prison and hospital to atone for any wrong he may have done during the late war. Hoping this liberty may be pardoned, and the request granted,

I am,

Very Respectfully
    Your Obedient Servant

Lizzie C. Smith
    Widow of late Brvt. Major & Asst. Surgeon Jos. Sim Smith U.S. Army

April 13th, 1868
    159 Putnam Avenue
    Brooklyn N.Y.

01-29-1869: WILLIAM KEELER'S LETTER TO B.C. COOK

S ource: Samuel A. Mudd Pardon File B-596, RG 204, U.S. National Archives, College Park, Md

~

WILLIAM KEELER WAS the Navy Paymaster on the U.S.S. Florida when Dr. Mudd was taken to Fort Jefferson aboard that ship. In 1869, when Keeler read in the newspaper that Dr. Mudd was being considered for a pardon, he wrote the following letter to his Congressman:

La Salle, Ill.
 Jany 21, 1869
 Hon. B.C. Cook

Dear Sir

I learned by yesterday's Chicago Tribune that efforts are being made to procure the pardon of Dr. Mudd. The U.S. Steamer Florida, to which I was attached conveyed him and his associates from Hampton Roads to the Tortugas. In conversation with myself, & I think with others on our passage down he admitted what I believe the prosecution failed to prove at his trial - viz - that he knew who Booth was when he set his leg & of what crime he was guilty. I have thought it might be well to have these facts known if they are not.

Very truly yours

W.F. Keeler

02-08-1869: DR. SAMUEL A. MUDD'S PARDON

Source: Samuel A. Mudd Pardon File B-596, RG 204, U.S. National Archives, College Park, Md.

∾

THIS IS the full text of Dr. Mudd's pardon:

Andrew Johnson
 President of the United States of America.

To all to Whom these Presents shall come. Greeting:

Whereas, on the twenty-ninth day of June in the year 1865, Dr. Samuel A. Mudd was by the judgment of a Military Commission, convened and holden at the City of Washington, in part convicted, and in part acquitted, of the specification wherein he was inculpated in the charge for the trial of which said Military Commission was so convened and held, and which specification in its principal allegation against him, was and is in the words and figures following, to wit:

And in further prosecution of said conspiracy, the said Samuel A. Mudd did, at Washington City and within the Military Department and military lines aforesaid, on or before the sixth day of March, A. D. 1865 and on divers other days and times between that day and the twentieth day of April A. D. 1865, advise, encourage, receive, entertain, harbor and conceal, aid and assist, the said John Wilkes Booth, David E. Herold, Lewis Payne, John H. Surratt, Michael O'Laughlen, George A. Atzerodt, Mary E. Surratt and Samuel Arnold and their confederates, with knowledge of the murderous and traitorous conspiracy aforesaid, and with intent to aid, abet, and assist them in the execution thereof, and in escaping from justice after the murder of the said Abraham Lincoln, in pursuance of said conspiracy in manner aforesaid:

And whereas, upon a consideration and examination of the record of said trial and conviction and of the evidence given at said trial, I am satisfied that the guilt found by the said judgment against Samuel A. Mudd was of receiving, entertaining, harboring, and concealing John Wilkes Booth and David E. Herold, with the intent to aid, abet and assist them in escaping from justice after the assassination of the late President of the United States, and not of any other or greater participation or complicity in said abominable crime;

And whereas, it is represented to me by respectable and intelligent members of the medical profession, that the circumstances of the surgical aid to the escaping assassin and the imputed concealment of his flight are deserving of a lenient construction as within the obligations of professional duty, and thus inadequate evidence of a guilty sympathy with the crime or the criminal;

And whereas, in other respects the evidence, imputing such guilty sympathy or purpose of aid in defeat of justice, leaves room for uncertainty as to the true measure and nature of the complicity of the said Samuel A. Mudd in the attempted escape of said assassins;

And whereas, the sentence imposed by said Military Commission upon the said Samuel A. Mudd was that he be imprisoned at hard labor for life, and the confinement under such sentence was directed to be had in the military prison at Dry Tortugas, Florida, and the said prisoner has been hitherto, and now is, suffering the infliction of such sentence;

And whereas, upon occasion of the prevalence of the Yellow Fever at that military station, and the death by that pestilence of the medical officer of the Post, the said Samuel A. Mudd devoted himself to the care and cure of the sick, and interposed his courage and his skill to protect the garrison, otherwise without adequate medical aid, from peril and alarm, and thus, as the officers and men unite in testifying, saved many valuable lives and earned the admiration and the gratitude of all who observed or experienced his generous and faithful service to humanity;

And whereas, the surviving families and friends of the Surgeon and other officers who were the victims of the pestilence earnestly present their dying testimony to the conspicuous merit of Dr. Mudd's conduct, and their own sense of obligation to him and Lieut. Zabriskie and two hundred and ninety nine noncommissioned officers and privates stationed at the Dry Tortugas have united in presenting to my attention the praiseworthy action of the prisoner and in petitioning for his pardon;

And whereas the Medical Society of Hartford County, Maryland, of which he was an associate, have petitioned for his pardon, and thirty nine members of the Senate and House of Representatives of the Congress of the United States have also requested his pardon;

Now, therefore be it known that I, Andrew Johnson, President of the United States of America, in consideration of the premises, divers other good and sufficient reasons me thereunto moving, do hereby grant to the said Dr. Samuel A. Mudd a full and unconditional pardon.

In testimony thereof, I have hereunto signed my name and caused the Seal of the United States to be affixed.

Done at the City of Washington, this Eighth day of February, A. D. (Seal) 1869, and the Independence of the United States the ninety third.

ANDREW JOHNSON, By the President

04-19-1869: DR. MUDD'S LETTER TO DR. WHITEHURST

S ource: Weedon and Whitehurst Family Papers, Manuscripts Department, Southern Historical Collection, University of North Carolina, Microfilm call number I-4485.

∾

DR. MUDD WROTE the following letter to Dr. Whitehurst shortly after arriving back home from Fort Jefferson. St. Catherine was the name/address sometimes used for Dr. Mudd's farm.

St. Catherine, Charles Co. Md.

April 19th 1869

My Dear Friend,

I arrived at my home on the 20th March. Since then I have had scarcely an uninterrupted moment - being constantly besieged by friends & strangers. Several reporters have visited me & notwithstanding my resolution & endeavors to be reticent they have gleaned sufficient to pen a long letter to "the Herald" filled with misstatements & etc. I felt much grieved when I saw one remark relative to the treatment of Fever etc. I am made to claim an overdue success. Let me assure you my dear friend that I have on no occasion sought distinction for the small part performed by myself during the prevalence of Fever at the post - nor have I spoken of the subject with a view to detract from the noble & skillful services of yourself, or attaching credit to myself. The private soldiers through kind feeling made my conduct whilst in the hospital the basis of a petition for my release; and anything they could say that would tend to soften public opinion I had no objection, believing the object desired thereby would be effected. Whatever fame has been attached to my name belongs entirely to you. My duties were simply as nurse & dispensor of medicines, if as such, was worthy of mention, the greater praise is due you since I could not have occupied the position without your appointment.

I mailed the letter given me for your son from Baltimore, not being able to call. I wrote to him a day or two after and notified him of the letter & the health of yourself & kind family - also extended invitation to visit myself or Brother in Law in Baltimore, whenever his vacation or studies permitted.

I met on my arrival in Baltimore, our Governor and many of the prominent men of the city & state. I had no chance to speak relative to your request. I have since talked with many friends on the subject & they tell me the president is selecting all his appointments from the most Ultra Radical ranks & any advocacy of your claims by them they feared would result in your injury. I shall visit Baltimore in the course of a week or two & will try to get some of our Fraternity to visit the Secretary personally in your behalf. Remember me kindly to Mrs. Whitehurst & little ones, Father Allard & asst, Mr. Mallory, Mr. Mareno & others - & accept for yourself my highest regards & friendship.

Very truly etc.
     Samuel A. Mudd

06-24-1869: EDMAN SPANGLER NEWSPAPER ARTICLE

Source: *New York World* newspaper, June 24, 1869.

EDMAN SPANGLER and Samuel Arnold were pardoned on March 1, 1869, released from confinement at Fort Jefferson on March 21, 1869, and arrived back in Baltimore on the steamship Cuba on April 6th. Two and a half months later, the following article, written by Spangler, appeared in the *New York World* newspaper.

Washington, June 23.

Edman Spangler, who was tried and sentenced by a military commission in May 1865 on a charge of being engaged in the plot to assassinate President Lincoln, and pardoned by President Johnson, has prepared the following statement, asserting his innocence of all knowledge of the crime, and detailing the cruelties practiced on the prisoners before and after conviction. Spangler was a scene-shifter at Ford's Theatre, and was on the stage when John Wilkes Booth shot

Mr. Lincoln and jumped from the box. He also at times took care of Booth's horse.

The evidence against him was of the flimsiest character, not being even circumstantial, for it did not appear in that trial, or in the subsequent civil trial of Surratt, that Spangler had any connection whatever with any of the other so-called conspirators. Most everybody believed him innocent then, and the Military Commission doubted his guilt by sentencing him to six years at the Dry Tortugas, and giving the others a life term.

The Military Commission was organized to convict, and it convicted. Abundant testimony is now at hand to show the vast amount of perjury of that trial - perjury exacted by fear and dictated by malice. Spangler's allusion to the witness Weichmann being in the abduction plot is important. Weichmann's testimony, it will be remembered, hung Mrs. Surratt. The following is the statement sworn and subscribed to:

Statement of Edman Spangler

I have deemed it due to truth to prepare for publication the following statement - at a time when I hope the temper of the people will give me a patient hearing - of my arrest, trial, and imprisonment, for alleged complicity in the plot to assassinate the late President Lincoln. I have suffered much, but I solemnly assert now, as I always have since I was arraigned for trial at the Washington Arsenal, that I am entirely innocent of any fore or after knowledge of the crime which John Wilkes Booth committed - save what I knew in common with everybody after it took place.

I further solemnly assert that John Wilkes Booth, or any other person, never mentioned to me any plot, or intimation of a plot, for the abduction or assassination of President Lincoln; that I did not know when Booth leaped from the box to the stage at the theatre, that he had shot Mr. Lincoln; and that I did not, in any way, so help me God, assist in his escape; and I further declare that I am entirely innocent of any and all charges made against me in that connection. I never knew either Surratt, Payne, Atzerodt, Arnold, or Herold, or any of the so-called conspirators, nor did I ever see any of them until they appeared in custody. While imprisoned with Atzerodt, Payne, and Herold, and after their trial was over, I was allowed a few minutes exercise in the prison yard. I heard the three unite in asserting Mrs. Surratt's entire innocence, and acknowledge their own guilt, confining the crime, as they did, entirely to themselves, but implicating the witness, Weichmann, in knowledge of the original plot to abduct and with furnishing information from the Commissary of Prisoners Department, where Weichmann was a clerk.

I was arrested on the morning of the 16th of April, 1865, and with Ritterspaugh (also a scene shifter) taken to the police station on E street, between Ninth and Tenth. The sergeant, after questioning me closely, went with two policemen to search for Peanut John (the name of the boy who held Booth's horse the night before) and made to accompany us to the headquarters of the police on Tenth street, where John and I were locked up, and Ritterspaugh was released. After four hours confinement I was released, and brought before judges Olin and Bingham, and told them of Booth bringing his horse to the theatre on the afternoon of the 14th of April (1865). After this investigation I said: "What is to be done with me?" and they replied: "We know where to find you when you are wanted." and ordered my release.

I returned to the theatre, where I remained until Saturday, when the soldiers took possession of it; but as the officer of the guard gave an attache and myself a pass to sleep there, we retired at 10 P.M., and at 1 A.M. a guard was placed over me, who remained until 9 A.M. Sunday morning, when I was released. I did not leave the theatre until Sunday evening, and on our return this attache (Carland by name) and myself were arrested by Detective Larner. Instead of taking us to the guard-house he said he would accompany me home to sleep there, but we all went to Police Headquarters on Tenth street, and when Carland asked if we were wanted, an officer sharply said "No."

I returned to the theatre that night, and remained the next day till I went to dinner, corner Seventh and G streets. That over I remained a few minutes, when Ritterspaugh (who worked at the theatre with me) came, and meeting me, said: "I have given my evidence, and would like now to get some of the reward."

I walked out with Ritterspaugh for half an hour, and on returning to lie down left word that if anyone called for me to tell them that I was lying down. Two hours after I was called down stairs to see two gentlemen who had called for me. They said that I was wanted down street. On reaching the sidewalk they placed me in a hack and drove rapidly to Carroll Prison, where I was confined a week. Three days afterward, Detective, or Colonel, Baker came to my room, and questioned me about the sale of a horse and buggy (which belonged to Booth), and I told him all about it freely and readily. On the day following I was called into the office of the prison in order to be recognized by Sergeant Dye, who merely nodded his head as I entered and then he left. (Dye subsequently testified that he was sitting on the steps of the theatre just before Booth fired the shot, and to seeing mysterious persons about.)

I was allowed on the fourth day of my imprisonment to walk in the prison yard, but from that evening I was closely confined and guarded until the next Saturday at midnight when I was again taken to the office to see a detective, who said: "Come Spangler, I've some jewelry for you." He handcuffed me with my arms behind my back, and guarding me to a hack, I was placed in it and driven to the navy yard, where my legs were manacled and a pair of Lillie handcuffs placed on my wrists.

I was put in a boat and rowed to a monitor, where I was taken on board and thrown into a small, dirty, room, between two water closets, and on a bed of filthy life preservers and blankets, with two soldiers guarding the door. I was kept there for three days. I had been thus confined three days on the vessel when Captain Monroe came to me and said: "Spangler, I've something that must be told, but you must not be frightened. We have orders from the Secretary of War, who must be obeyed, to put a bag on your head."

Then two men came up and tied up my head so securely that I could not see daylight. I had plenty of food, but could not eat with my face so muffled up. True, there was a small hole in the bag near my mouth, but I could not reach that, as my hands were wedged down by the iron. At last, two kind-hearted soldiers took compassion on me, and while one watched the other fed me.

On Saturday night a man came to me and, after drawing the bag so tight as to nearly suffocate me, said to the guard, "Don't let him go to sleep, as we will carry him out to hang him directly." I heard them go up on the deck, where there was a great rattling of chains, and other noises; and while I was trying to imagine what was going on, and what they intended to do, I was dragged out by two men, who both pulled me at times in opposite directions. We, however, reached a boat, in which I was placed, and rowed a short distance, I could not say then where we stopped, for my face was still covered. After leaving the boat, I was forced to walk some distance, with the heavy irons still on my legs.

I was then suddenly stopped, and made to ascend three or four flights of stairs; and as I stood at the top waiting, some one struck me a severe blow on the top of the head, which stunned and half threw me over, when I was pushed into a small room, where I remained in an unconscious condition for several hours. The next morning someone came with bread and coffee. I remained there several days, suffering torture from the bag or padded hood over my face. It was on Sunday when it was removed and I was shaven. It was then replaced.

Some hours after General Hartranft came and read to me several charges; that I was engaged in a plot to assassinate the president, and the day following I was carried into a military court and still hooded before all of its members. I remained but a short time, when I was returned to my cell for another night and day and then again presented in this court. Mr. Bingham, Assistant Judge-Advocate, read the charges against me, and asked if I had any objection to the court, and I replied "No," and made my plea of "not guilty." They then wished to know if I desired counsel, and, when I answered affirmatively, General Hunter, the president of the court, insisted that I should not be allowed counsel.

He was, however, overruled, but it was several days before I was permitted legal aid, the court in the meantime taking evidence with closed doors. On every adjournment of the court, I was returned to my cell, and the closely-fitting hood placed over my head. This continued until June 10, 1865, when I was relieved from the torture of the bag, but my hands and limbs remained heavily manacled.

On one Sunday, while I was confined at this place (the Washington Arsenal), I was visited by a gentleman of middle stature, rather stout, with full beard, and gold-framed spectacles. He noticed my manacles and padded head. I afterwards learned that he was Mr. Stanton, the Secretary of War. It is proper to state that when the hood was placed on me, Captain Munroe said it was by order of the Secretary of War. My first thought was that I was to be hung without trial, and the hood was preparatory to that act.

The first time I ever saw Mrs. Surratt was in the Carroll Prison yard, on Capitol Hill. I did not see her again until we were taken into court the first day at the arsenal. My cell was on the same corridor with hers, and I had to pass it every time I was taken into court. I frequently looked into her cell, a small room about four feet wide by seven feet long. The only things in her cell were an old mattress laid on the bricks and an army blanket. I could see the irons on her feet, as she was generally lying on the mattress, and was the last one brought into court. She occupied a seat in court near the prison door. The seat was twelve inches high, and the chains between the irons on her feet were so short that she had to be assisted to her seat. She was so sick at one time that the court was compelled to adjourn.

On the 17th of July, about midnight, I was conveyed to a steamboat, and arrived the next day at Fortress Monroe, and was thence taken to the gunboat Florida. The irons on my arms were temporarily removed, but Captain Dutton, in charge of the guard, ordered heavy Lilly irons to be placed on me, when General Dodd, chief officer in charge, more humanely countermanded his order and had the irons again removed from my arms. I was placed for security in the lower hold of the vessel, and compelled to descend to it by a ladder. The rounds were far apart, and, as the irons on my feet were chained but a few inches apart, my legs were bruised and lacerated fearfully.

The hold where I was confined was close and dirty, but after two or three days I was allowed on deck in the daytime, but was closely guarded. I was allowed to speak to no one of the crew. We arrived at Fort Jefferson, on the Dry Tortugas, and were handed over to Colonel Hamilton, commanding, who placed me until the next day in a casemate. The next day I was brought before Colonel H., who informed me that he had no more stringent orders concerning me than other prisoners confined there.

I managed to get along comfortably for a while, though to some of the prisoners the officers were very cruel. One man by the name of Dunn, while helping in unloading a government transport, got hold of some liquor and imbibed too freely, for which he was taken to the guard-house and tied up to the window-frame by his thumbs for two hours. General Hill then ordered him to be taken down and be made to carry a thirty-two pound ball, but as the hanging had deprived him of the use of his thumbs, he was unable to obey. The officers, however, put two twenty-four pound balls in a knapsack, and compelled him to carry them until the sack gave way from the weight of the iron. He was then tied up by the wrists and gagged in the mouth by the bayonet from 8 P.M. until the next morning. He was then taken down and thrown into the guard-house, but was so exhausted that he had to be removed to the hospital. It was decided to amputate three of his fingers, but this was reconsidered. He lost however, the use of his thumb and two fingers. This punishment was inflicted by Major McConnell, officer of the day, and was carried out by Sergeant Edward Donnelly.

Another poor prisoner named Brown, was once excused by the doctor from work on the plea of illness, but the Provost Marshal insisted and finding him too ill and lacking strength made him carry a thirty-two pound ball. He staggered under the weight and was compelled from weakness to put it down. He was then taken to the wharf and with his legs tied together and his hands tied behind him, a rope was placed around him and he was thrown into the water and then dragged out. This was done three or four times, he begging for mercy most piteously. He was finally jerked out of the water and ordered to return to his ordinary work. The poor wretch crept off apparently thankful for any escape from such torments. Captain Jos. Rittenhouse was officer of the day, and his orders were carried out by Corporal Spear.

During the latter part of last October I was placed in irons and compelled to work with an armed sentinel over me. I did not know the reason for this, for I was unconscious of having given offense, and had conformed to every regulation. I was then closely confined and allowed to communicate with no one for four months. The pretense for this, I afterwards learned, sprang from an attempt of Dr. Mudd to escape.

Colonel St. George Leger Grenfel, aged 65 years, was taken sick and went to the Doctor to get excused from work. The Doctor declined to excuse him. He then applied to the Provost-Marshal, who said that he could not excuse him if the Doctor couldn't. Grenfel then tried to work and couldn't. They then took him to the guard-house, tied him up for half a day, and then took him to the wharf, tied his hands behind him, tied his legs together, and put a rope around his waist. There were three officers, heavily armed, who drove spectators from the wharf; I could see and hear from my window. The Colonel asked them if they were going to throw him into the water, and they answered "Yes."

He then jumped in, and because he could not sink, they drew him out and tied about fourth pounds of iron to his legs, and threw him into the water again, and after he had sunk twice they pulled him out again, and then compelled him to go to work. The officers who had him in hand were, Lieutenant Robinson, Lieutenant Pike, and Captain George W. Crabb, assisted by Sergeant Michael Glea-son, and assistant storekeeper G.T. Jackson, who tied the iron on his legs. Captain Samuel Peebles tied up Grenfel for saying that "he was capable of doing anything."

Colonel Grenfel was forced to scrub and do other menial work when he proved he was so ill as to have refused to eat his rations for a week. All of the officers hated Grenfel on account of a letter which appeared in a New York paper, which they said Grenfel wrote, about tying up the prisoner Dunn - which letter was truthful, as others and myself were witnesses to the details it related.

One very stormy night, Grenfel with four others, escaped in a small boat and was evidently drowned near the fort. His escape was discovered but the storm was so severe that it was deemed too dangerous to pursue them, although a steamer was at the wharf. Grenfel frequently declared his intention of running any risk to escape, rather than, to use his own words, "to be tortured to death at the fort." These are only two or three instances of the many acts of cruelty practiced at the fort. During my imprisonment at Fort Jefferson, I worked very hard at carpentering and wood ornamental work, making a great many fancy boxes, &c., out of the peculiar wood found on the adjacent islands; the greater portion of this work was made for officers. By my industry in that direction, I won some favor in their eyes. I was released in March of the present year by executive clemency.

(Signed) Edman Spangler

04-16-1883: TOWNSEND INTERVIEW OF DR. GEORGE MUDD

Source: Cincinnati Enquirer, April 16, 1883

~

JOURNALIST GEORGE ALFRED TOWNSEND interviewed Dr. Samuel Mudd's cousin, Dr. George Dyer Mudd, shortly after Samuel Mudd died in 1883. His article said:

New York, April 15. - Now I will note the talk that I had nearly on the eighteenth anniversary of Mr. Booth's visit for the last time to this region. At the plain old hotel at Bryantown - where we were eating shad fried in bread grease, cold fried chicken and some beef cut in little flat pieces and covered with a kind of pepper gravy - we ventured after a while to mention the name of Booth. A smart boy, who was celebrated all the time we were there for volunteering information loudly and possessing none whatever, said he knew there were a great many persons in the region who remembered Mr. Booth, but he could not name any of them. He thought the fact was enough, however, that there were some, and relapsed into a kind of ponderous silence.

Another person, probably from Baltimore, who was selling whisky by sample through this country, gave his entire conversation to the evils of the local option law, which, he said, was creating havoc and misery in the entire society, and driving all enterprise out of it. He said no vigorous community could exist without whisky, particularly of his brand. We endeavored to awaken him on the subject of Booth, and seeing that he had nothing to do with the local option law he merely grunted and looked at us to know whether we were quite right in our minds. We struck him on the question of jowl and greens, however, and then he awakened like a true Marylander, who is never so much at home as when he is either just going to eat something or has approved of something he has just eaten.

The landlord, hearing us mention the name of Mudd, however, suddenly burst in the door and said that the late Dr. Mudd's brother was on the porch. So we were taken out, on all fours as it were, to be introduced to him. There stood a man of the middle size, with a genteel, yet hardly cheerful countenance, and polite but somewhat reserved address. He had rather pale blue eyes, and prominent, rather Roman nose, and was dressed like a farmer. I fancied that the expression on his face, if any, was that of a man to whom times were somewhat hard, who did not see the future very bright before him, who paid no attention whatever to the past, and, perhaps regarded himself as drifting on to the decline of life with doubtful impressions of whether he could improve the condition of his family. I do not know that any of these things were in his mind, but that was my reading of him, considering the short conversation we had.

He was the older brother of Booth's surgeon, who, I understand, was the youngest brother in the family. My acquaintance had gone across the Potomac into the Confederate Army, and served, like many young men hereabout of slave-holding families, during a portion of the war. I told him I had seen his brother when he was being tried in Washington, and made such inquiries as would not provoke the suspicion of a people always a little doubtful about strangers. I found that this brother really did not grasp any facts about Dr. Mudd's work.

He went on to tell me a strange, disconnected story about Booth and his brother being in an operation together to buy large tracts of land in Charles County. I asked what the land was to be bought for, and he said that the Capital of the United States was to be extended across the eastern branch of the Potomac, and that would result in making a large city down towards Charles County, and Booth and Dr. Mudd and others were to control all the adjacent land and put it up in price. That, or something like it, was the short burden of this gentleman's remarks. He did not speak with much fluency or confidence, but rather like one to whom something had been told that he had not half grasped, and rather lost the little he knew in re-telling it.

I asked him if there was any trouble in that region with the negroes. "None, whatever," he said; and he was entirely right, for I observed next morning when I got up, about six o'clock, that the negroes had possession of Bryantown. They chattered and sauced each other, and exercised the immemorial rights of freedom as if they were a set of magpies up in the trees. Most of them were at work at something or other, but such work would break a Northern heart. One girl would come out to the front gate of the house and conduct a sort of horn-pipe courtship with a black boy in the street, who had been swearing for about fifteen minutes with such fiendish intensity that I thought he was going to disembowel the two other boys he was talking with, but discovered on close observation that he was merely practicing profanity, like something new that he had but recently picked up. In fact, the negroes in that region are left alone, and consequently they do nearly all the work, yet do it in pure negro fashion. They were the best-looking people I saw in Charles County. The malaria does not seem to affect them like the whites, and the corn and bacon agree with them. Some of the young men had a soldierly look, but the black women were not all fired up to the occasion.

Mr. Mudd, having expressed the view that the blacks gave nobody any concern, was then asked whether the country was not improving. "No sir," said he, "it is going back." He reiterated this without any expression of opinion or giving any reason, and, looking at his face again with some sympathy, I thought I discovered the penalties of a lost cause, of an independence almost entirely in slaves and now gone beyond recovery, and of an old and spent region thrown upon its own resources, when those resources were long ago exhausted, and only kept up the appearance of solvency upon the negro property.

After supper, which was the only meal we got in a ride of thirty miles - there being absolutely no hotels in all that region except in two or three new towns which have been made up by the railroads - I went over to the house of Dr. George D. Mudd. He is the most intelligent person in all this region, and was a Union man from the beginning of the war, and a Republican at the close of the war, and I think is so still. He is a man of both strength and sensibility, whose life I should guess was thrown away in such an unadvancing society as this. His age I can hardly guess at. I thought he wore a wig, and if he did not, he is probably fifty-five years old. If his hair is false, he may be sixty years old. He is a straight man, of rather the raw-boned type, yet well fed, and his cheekbones are somewhat high, his glance direct and candid, his skin smooth and sunburnt, red, with a mere tuft of beard.

You have little difficulty in advancing directly upon the matter in hand with him, though I was somewhat disappointed in the extent of his information. He is a man who does not indulge in theories, yet can form an opinion slowly, and express it very moderately. I had seen him for a few minutes about two years ago, and had been invited to call on him. His house is on that road or street which leads from Bryantown to the Catholic church, and is in Bryantown proper. It is a frame house, two stories high, with an office built at one end, and behind the office the kitchen addition, both of one story. He was eating his supper, but put us in the parlor and told us to continue smoking. A plain parlor, with an ingrain carpet and a picture on the wall of some saint, painted in oil, were all that struck me. On his return the doctor adjusted his long body and limbs in a chair opposite us, looking right into our eyes, and let us begin. I told him that I had some literary intentions as to Booth's conspiracy, and wanted to ask him a few questions. I then asked him about the interior arrangement of the Late Dr. Mudd's house. This answered, I asked him if he and Doctor Mudd had been friends.

"We were friendly," he said, "until two or three years before his death, when politics separated us. However, we met not long before his death at the house of a mutual friend, and again shook hands. The people in this community could not forgive me for a long time. I had been a Union man during the war, and seeing the situation for our people with decided convictions, I wanted to put them in accord with advancing times. A good many bitter things were said. I was a popular man here almost from my youth up, and in request at parties and gatherings for my anecdotes and sayings. It was rather hard for me to go through the experience I did."

"Is it all over now, Doctor?" I asked.

"Yes sir. I have no further privation on account of politics."

"What is your relationship to the late Samuel Mudd?"

"His father was my cousin, his mother was also my cousin, and he was my student, and studied medicine in my office. He attended lectures in Baltimore, and practiced in the infirmary awhile. Poor fellow, he is dead. The cause of all his troubles was an invincible, deep-set prejudice on the questions of politics and slavery. While he had nothing of the assassin in his nature - and I do not believe he would have gone into any scheme to kill Mr. Lincoln or Mr. Seward - yet there is no doubt of his having been connected with a previous intention of Booth to kidnap or abduct the president, and perhaps some other persons from the city of Washington, and bring them through this country. The nature of my cousin's mind was intense, rather narrow, and he had thought and talked himself into an obstinate condition, so that he became the prey for a strong, designing man like Booth. But his connection with that assassin never extended, I am very sure, beyond an agreement to help in the kidnapping scheme."

"Do you recollect, Dr. Mudd, when Booth first came to this region?"

"I have a general recollection. A man like that does not come in a plain society like ours, where an actor is never seen, without it being talked about. I knew very well that Booth was connected with my cousin, Sam Mudd, a good while before the president's murder, but my cousin Sam lived five miles from here, his house retired from the road, and I never dreamed that Booth was more than a casual acquaintance of his. When the facts were brought to my conviction that Booth had ridden to Sam's house straight from the theater where he killed the president, I was thunderstruck."

"I believe, Dr. Mudd, that you first brought to the notice of the military authorities the fact of Booth and Harold stopping at your cousin's?"

"Yes, I did. It happened in this way: The president being murdered on Friday night, the first information we had on the subject was a cavalry company coming into our town on Saturday afternoon. and instituting inquiries hereabouts. They did not bring intelligence that Booth was the murderer. The impression existed in our society that the president's murderer was a man by the name of Johnny Boyle, a horse-thief and desperado, who had figured in the early part of the war as a spy, blockade runner, &c., through these lower counties. He assassinated at his residence the commander of the Federal forces in these counties, Colonel Watkins. He went to Watkin's house, in Anne Arundel County, one evening when Watkins had sent for a doctor, and he opened it, and Boyle presented a pistol at his heart and shot him dead. That event was the principal thing talked about in our counties during the war, and an idea got abroad that Boyle had gone into Washington and murdered somebody, and that therefore the troops were in our vicinity hunting him. On that Saturday afternoon my cousin, Sam Mudd, rode into town from his house, went to the store and stayed about half an hour or so, and then rode back again. I little knew that he was accompanied to within sight of the town on that visit by Harold, Booth's companion, yet I afterward found it to be true."

"What was the first communication made to you on that subject?"

"Why, on Sunday morning I went up to Reeves' church, a mile or so from Dr. Sam Mudd's house. It was nearer Washington there, and I thought there might be more information about the murderer. After the service was over I was riding home, when my old pupil, Sam Mudd, rode sharply after me and overtook me. During the war I had been uniformly a Union man, while he had been a Southern sympathizer. It may have been for that reason he came to me, like one on the weaker side in need of a friend. He then said to the effect that this was a most annoying tragedy, because said he, it will bring suspicion on many innocent persons. He said that the country was full of go-betweens and strange, suspicious characters. Then he said that two such persons had come to his house in the gray of the morning the day before. He continued in that rather agitated way to speak of innocent parties being suspected. I asked him about those two men. He told me one of them had a broken bone in his leg, and that he had dressed it. He said the man then asked for a razor, and shaved himself so as to disguise himself, or that after shaving he was disguised. Now, you must remember I knew all this time that Booth and Sam Mudd were acquaintances. But he never said to me that Booth had been at his house. He said the men were strangers and suspicious characters. He said he did not know who they were.

After he left me, going toward his own house, I rode along the road, being profoundly moved at poor Lincoln's death, and I said to myself, What is the matter with Sam Mudd? He is more agitated on this matter than on any thing I have seen. What did he mean, I continued, by a man shaving himself, and therefore disguising his face? I thought about that some time, and then said: 'If these men were strangers to Sam Mudd, why did the man disguise himself? Sam must have seen him before, and the man looked disguised after shaving.' In short, I could make nothing out of it except that there were two men who had come to his house that ought to be looked after. The next morning, I think it was, I told the military officer in this village that there had been two men at Dr. Samuel Mudd's house at a very early hour after the president's assassination. They wanted me to go there with them. They had two or three interviews with Sam Mudd, and he mixed himself up to that extent that he was finally arrested, and, as you know, Booth's boot with Booth's name on it was brought down, that he had kept all the time."

"Now, Dr. Mudd, what is your explanation of your cousin's behavior at that time?"

"I think there is no question that Sam Mudd immediately knew Booth, and that Booth told him that he had murdered the president. If he had possessed the moral courage to have said at once: 'I will have nothing to do with assassination; I will give this man up to his government,' he would have stood very differently toward himself, his family and his fame. But you see those rebel views he had held, that obstinacy of character, his prejudices, his false sense of honor, made him secrete his information till he had actually made himself an accessory after the fact."

"You do not think, then, that he had any knowledge of Booth going to kill the president?"

"No, that design was entertained by Booth but a very little while before he did the deed. That Sam Mudd was privy to his scheme to kidnap the president I am confident; but when this man rode to his house he must have told Sam Mudd how he broke his leg and all the particulars. Their acquaintance had been considerable, far more than I had any suspicion of. Indeed, sir," Dr. Mudd remarked, "if all the evidence had got before that Commission, Sam Mudd would have been hanged on the same gallows with the others - not for being privy to any assassination scheme, but he was in the abduction scheme."

"Now," said I, "Dr. Mudd, what about the setting of Booth's leg?"

The doctor then demonstrated on my own leg, much better than I can memorize, the extent of Booth's wound. He said:

"There was no wound in Booth's leg sufficient to have diverted him far enough out of his course to go to Sam Mudd's house except from his knowledge that he had a friend there. The ride that Booth wanted to take to the Potomac River does not go by Sam Mudd's, and he had to make a detour of several miles, both to go to Sam Mudd's house, and to get away from it and go to the Potomac River. But those men had been in conference on the abduction scheme since the previous fall or winter. Booth could have gone through to the Potomac with such a wound as he had without experiencing any great inconvenience. There are two bones in your leg, the tibia and the fibula; it is very seldom that the fibula is broken alone. The larger bone receives the shock or fracture, and while it often breaks the other bone with it, the smaller bone is generally broken by a very peculiar kind of twist. The strange kind of leap that Booth made from that box probably threw his weight toward his heel somehow, so that the rear bone broke. Now, that wound required no setting. You do not put the leg in splints for a fracture of the fibula. That bone is held in its place by very powerful muscles, and it would soon set of itself, with rest; but you see that man had been riding hard for three or four hours after his crime, and, of course, he felt uncomfortable, the ends of the bone perhaps prodding the tendons and muscles.

All that Sam Mudd did with the leg, I suppose, was to wrap it around with something, and tell the man to rest it, and then he had him a crutch made by some one on the premises. Booth went to my cousin's house, turning out of his road, because of his acquaintance with him, and that we all knew through this district of country. Any body could have told you that Sam Mudd and Booth had been very thick."

"Then you attribute his misfortune to a want of good moral sense?"

"Yes, it was a want of the moral courage to resent being the confidant of an assassin; the want of the moral courage to defend his own fame and his family. He let that man impose such a bloody secret upon him, and make use of him, and he suffered the consequences - poor fellow!"

"What have you to say on Sam Mudd coming into Bryantown that Saturday afternoon?"

"Why, you see, he did not even give me his full confidence. The trouble with Sam's conduct at that juncture was that he put his life in danger by his constant evasions. We got to work here to save his life. We saw that he was in great danger from having harbored Booth and then concealed the fact. After he was arrested there was a unified effort on the part of his family to protect him, and General Thomas Ewing was employed as his counsel. Thirteen hundred dollars were raised for Mr. Ewing, but he had no idea when he commenced that defense that it was going to give him the amount of work it did. He made a first-rate defense of a most difficult case. Now, I will show you how difficult it was to defend Sam Mudd. The servants around the house saw these two men, Booth and Harold, there, and two of them testified that the unwounded man, during the afternoon, mounted his horse, and with Dr. Mudd rode towards Bryantown; that, when coming to the bridge within sight of Bryantown, they observed the soldiery, and that the stranger then rode into the swamp or brush, while Dr. Mudd came on, went to the store, asked some questions and returned. When he met Harold again, and they had consulted, the two men separated; Sam Mudd rode back to his house by a circuitous route, while Harold took the road and went to Booth as fast as possible to convey the news that the soldiers were after them. Now, these poor negroes who gave that testimony told the truth; but it became necessary for us to raise witnesses down here who would take the edge off these facts. We sent up to Washington two men Hardy and Farrall. Mr. Ewing gave them a private examination before they came on the platform, and he came out to us and said: 'Send these men home. I don't want them in town here.' He said what they knew was still more fatal to Sam Mudd than anything that had come out. Instead of telling the men to go right home and keep out of the way, the person entrusted with it merely said Mr. Ewing didn't want them. So when somebody asked Hardy and Farrall what they came there for, they replied: 'We don't know. All we know is that Dr. Sam Mudd told us on Saturday afternoon that Booth had killed the President of the United States.' That leaked out, and before those men could get far on the road the government had messengers out for them and brought them back and put them on the stand, and they testified that Sam Mudd had told them on Saturday that Booth had killed the president. Now, you must remember that nobody in our region knew on Saturday that Booth was the murderer. He therefore learned that fact from Booth himself, and through his doubts and fears let it out in gossip, and those men remembered it. Now, although more labor was spent on my cousin's case than on that of any of the prisoners, more witnesses summoned in his behalf, because he was the most intelligent person to be tried, yet it was very fortunate for him that the evidence was somewhat muddled, because if that Court had seen as clearly as I did how badly Sam had been engaged, they would not have spared his life. That is why I thought it was unkind of him, only two years before he died, to engage in a newspaper battle with me on political matters. I would have put him in the honorable course of making a clean breast from the beginning, and although he did not do so, I assisted in saving his life. The unqualified Union character I had during the whole conflict gave me a status as a witness before that Commission, and as a cousin of that man, and they imprisoned him instead of hanging him."

"Dr. Mudd, was your cousin a large land-holder?"

"I don't think he paid taxes on much, if any, property. His father had both land and slaves, and let him be a free tenant of his. In the early part of the war our society was thrown into a convulsion on the question of slavery, and Sam Mudd and several of his family took the Southern side strongly, and some of them went into the Confederate service. That made him ripe for Booth's wild scheme. Booth visited our country unquestionably to get ready for abducting Mr. Lincoln, and the different men he picked up were all adjuncts to that plan. The parties in the operation expected not only to do a service to the Southern cause, but to be rewarded."

"Why was it that your cousin, after he came back from the Dry Tortugas, never left on record any statement about his connection with Booth? As an intelligent and educated man, he should have done so."

"The reason Sam Mudd never spoke on that question," said Dr. Mudd, "was that he had prevaricated to his own neighbors, friends, and kin to such an extent that he was ashamed of himself. The people around here who had intelligently followed the matter knew that he was acquainted with Booth; that he had come to Bryantown with Harold, and that he gave Booth's name as the murderer the day following the crime, and yet all three things he had denied. Of course when he came back to this vicinity he saw that his best policy was silence, and he hardly ever talked on the question at all. I think the extent of his conversation was to describe professional and other occurrences while in his captivity. He made one effort to escape, if you remember, and, being missed, the vessel on which he had secreted himself was examined and he was brought back. But I understand he was treated with consideration and acquitted himself very well."

"Were you acquainted with John Surratt?"

"Yes, I knew him very well. He made my house, where you are, his stopping-place whenever he visited his sister, who was at the neighboring seminary. The seminary is now burned down. John has stopped with me many times. In those days, before the war, he was as modest and nice a young fellow as one could meet, but after the war began his tavern was made the stopping-place of spies and go-betweens, and he finally mustered up courage to cross the Potomac River. After that he was a changed man. He had become self-important. He wanted to distinguish himself, to have money, to be talked about. Therefore Booth made an easy prey of him; and he ran away from the danger, and let his mother be the sacrifice."

"What kind of woman was Mrs. Surratt?"

"Mrs. Surratt was a respectable, plain wife and widow, whose course of life would have been happy enough but for her intemperate thought and speech on questions of politics and the war. She worked herself up into a passion, hardened her nature, and so she too was ripe for Booth to come along and make prey of her, as he did of the others."

"Did you know Harold?"

"Yes, a little. Dave Harold was a kind of little dandy, who used to come down here from the city with a gun. He had some female relatives not far from here, who were known by some of our folks, and I used to see Dave there. He was a very poor sprig of a boy. Booth picked out all his instruments from rather low material, so they could look up to him. Of course, he could not get men of the first class into any such foolish scheme as his."

The conversation took a variety of turns, but the above are the principal points that were covered. Dr. Mudd always spoke of his cousin as "Poor Sam!" but evidently entertained the idea that what he had done wrong - had begun wrong, and had finally got so wrong that his life was saved almost by accident.

GATH

06-17-1883: TOWNSEND INTERVIEW OF FREDERICK STONE

S ource: New York Tribune, June 17, 1883

GEORGE ALFRED TOWNSEND was a popular American journalist during the 1800s, often writing under the pen name GATH. His articles appeared in various *U.S. newspapers, including the New York Tribune, for which he wrote a column entitled "*Broadway Note Book." In his Broadway Note Book article published on June 17, 1883, Townsend recounts a conversation he had earlier that month with "a lawyer in the South who defended one of the conspirators against President Lincoln's life." The lawyer was Frederick Stone, who had been co-counsel with General Thomas Ewing for Dr. Mudd. An entry in Townsend's diary for June 1, 1883 says:

> *Went today at 10:00 a.m. to see Frederick Stone at Idaho, his seat, two miles from Port Tobacco, Maryland. Met him on the train at Annapolis Junction and met his family at his house where I slept, talking with him over Mrs. Surratt, Herold and Dr. Mudd, for whom he was counsel.*

Dr. Mudd died on January 10, 1883, five month's before Townsend's article was published, so we don't know what his reaction to it would have been. Here is Townsend's article:

A lawyer in the South who defended one of the conspirators against President Lincoln's life recently said to me: "I recollect one little instance of the gentility of Governor Hartranft, of Pennsylvania, which I often mention. After Mrs. Surratt had been some time on trial and found the evidence deepening against her and her own contradictions painfully apparent, she became alarmed for her life; and, indeed, she had been, from the beginning. She sent me word that she wished to see me. The rule of the court-martial was that the prisoners should see their counsel in the presence of a guard but not necessarily in the hearing thereof. As it was a military court, of course every order it issued had to be obeyed strictly. Mrs. Surratt occupied one of the cells in the old penitentiary.

They were arched cells, hardly high enough for one to stand in upright, and with barred doors, and between each pair of cells stood a sentinel in the corridor to keep the occupants from exchanging conversation. Mrs. Surratt was brought out. She was ironed, but not heavily, like the others. There was a soldier in the room, and General Hartranft, as he was at that time, for he was in command of the prison, seeing the counsel come into the room shook his head at the guard, intimating for him to go out. Hartranft, without saying a word or nodding his head to the prisoner and counsel, then retired to the distant end of the room and looked out of the window, thus keeping the letter of the severe law but relaxing its spirit."

Said my informant above: "Reviewing the trial of the conspirators against President Lincoln's life, I have to say that, considering it was a military court, it was a fair court and one of ability. Judge Holt, the Advocate-General, was a very able man. The Court was courteous toward the defence. This was shown by the fact that an orderly sergeant was sent away down through lower Maryland to deliver at the house of Mr. Stone Herold's request that he come up and be his counsel. It was manifest to me from the start that this court meant to find guilty any person connected with the murder or the intended murders, but that they only mean to imprison or to give lighter punishments to accessories and those playing the spy or in the abduction plot.

The court therefore set itself seriously to work to ascertain who had consented to take arms and kill, whether they succeeded in killing anybody or not. Taking into consideration the feeling of the time and the enormity of the offence, I do not know but that they drew the lines of justice pretty well in their intention. Consequently they found Atzerodt guilty, because he had accepted a knife to kill Vice-President Johnson. They found Herold guilty, because he knew of the murder about to be committed and accompanied the assassin to the last and assisted him to escape. As to Powell, generally called Payne, he thoroughly admitted the justice of his sentence and regarded the whole trial in the light of a reminiscence, bending his mind upon death, which he knew he had obtained and would get. He was the only person in that bar who had any philosophy or composure whatever, because his mind was made up that he could not escape.

The court very nearly hanged Dr. Mudd. His prevarications were painful; he had given his whole case away by not trusting even his counsel or neighbors or kinfolks. It was a terrible thing to extricate him from the toils he had woven around himself. He had denied knowing Booth when he knew him well. He was undoubtedly accessory to the abduction plot, though he may have supposed it would never come to anything. He denied knowing Booth when he came to his house when that was preposterous. He had been even intimate with Booth. The proclamation of the government was straightforward, that death should be the penalty of any man who could give information about the convicts and would not do it. Yet Dr. Mudd was saved, and it is understood that the vote stood five to four. One more vote would have hanged him, as two-thirds of a court martial is necessary to allot the death penalty."

"I think," said my legal friend, "that Mrs. Surratt could have been saved with proper counsel." "What was the character of her counsel?" "She had two men named Aiken and Clampett, neither fit to defend a case of that importance. It is a remarkable fact that the bar in Washington City was ransacked for a lawyer to defend her and none would come forward. The effect of Lincoln's death, the immediate recognition of his justice and generosity and of the causeless assassination, paralyzed the bar. Reverdy Johnson was finally employed. He came forward and made an argument against the jurisdiction of the military court, to be read and applauded by the people, and then abandoned the woman. What did those soldiers care about the legal argument on the jurisdiction of the court? They were set there by their superiors to ascertain who took part in the murder of their loved commander. It was from her own sense, plain as that was, that Mrs. Surratt felt that she was being sacrificed by the incapacity of her counsel. She then made the appeal for help, but the man to whom she made it had double work already, and was trying to save the life of Dr. Mudd and barely did it."

"Was the combined character of those prisoners at all consequential?" I asked. "No. Cheaper, smaller materials never were engaged in a foolish scheme. The scheme to run Mr. Lincoln out of Washington was absurd from the start. Booth perhaps had a transmitted crack in his head, and we can understand how he thought the design was all right, but what can be thought of the common sense of persons like John Surratt and Dr. Samuel Mudd, an educated physician, who harbored the same idea? Dr. Mudd was an ill-balanced man, of very slight force of character, but little moral courage, a petulant temper, and it is hard to denote his ability anywhere.

There are a few young men in Maryland who believe that Surratt was the sharpest fellow in the conspiracy. He at least saved his life. I knew from the very beginning that he was not in Washington at the time of the assassination, and yet the government, with strange fatuity, went on to insist that he was there. But I can hardly wonder at this because there was a tailor who positively swore that he saw Surratt the evening Lincoln was killed and knew him well because he had made a suit of clothes for him. In exciting times men lose their memory and consecutiveness, and thus the government, particularly in the civil trial of John Surratt, was led astray by its own witnesses."

"As to Spangler, the scene-shifter, it was pitiful to see that poor fellow in dread of the gallows. He said one day piteously to me: 'Do you think they will hang me?' After the court that day I broke my silence and said to two of the members, Judge Bingham one of them: 'Gentlemen, it is no personal concern of mine, but I really do not see what you can hang poor old Spangler for, except finding a rope in his bag which it is plain he used to catch crabs with and stole it from the theatre for that purpose.' They smiled and took it in good prat. Spangler finally became poor and seedy and broken down with liquor, and he went to live with Dr. Sam Mudd, who allowed him to stay at his house, and I think he is buried at the Catholic cemetery at Reeves' Church, near Mudd's house, or possibly at the Bryantown Church. He died about two years before Dr. Mudd."

08-07-1893: DR. MUDD AND SAMUEL COX, JR

S ource: *J. Wilkes Booth, An Account of His Sojourn in Southern Maryland after the Assassination of Abraham Lincoln, His Passage Across the Potomac, and His Death in Virginia,* including handwritten personal notes by Samuel Cox, Jr. Maryland Historical Society, Baltimore, Maryland.

FOLLOWING IS the text of the notes written by Samuel Cox, Jr. on August 7, 1893, recording a conversation between himself and Dr. Mudd in 1877, eight years after Dr. Mudd was released from prison at Fort Jefferson.

The conversation took place while Cox and Dr. Mudd were campaigning together for election to separate seats in the Maryland Legislature. Cox won, but Dr. Mudd lost. Samuel Cox, Jr. was the adopted son of Samuel Cox, the farmer who arranged for Thomas A. Jones to help Booth and Herold get across the Potomac River. Here is the text of Samuel Cox's notes:

In 1877, after Samuel A. Mudd's return from Dry Tortugas and when he & myself were canvassing this County as the Democratic candidates for the Legislature, he told me he knew Booth but casually, that Booth had at one time sought an introduction to him through John H. Surratt on Penn. Ave, Washington. This was some time prior to the assassination, but he had refused and that Booth had forced himself on him shortly afterward and that subsequently Booth attended church at Bryantown where he spoke to him but he was particular in not inviting him to his house, but that Booth came that evening uninvited.

He told me he was not favorably impressed with Booth, and that when Booth and Herold came to his house the night after the assassination, they told him they were just from Virginia & that Booth's horse had fallen soon after leaving the river & had broken his leg, that he had rendered him medical assistance while in utter ignorance of the assassination.

That after he had set the broken leg, he, Dr. Mudd, took letters he had but a short time gotten through the contraband mail for distribution, and that in going to Bryantown to mail them he was surprised to find the village surrounded by soldiers, and upon being stopped by a sentry he was horrified when told the president had been shot the night before, and, upon asking who had shot him the fellow had answered Booth.

He then told me his first impulse was to surrender Booth, that he had imposed upon him, twice forced himself upon him, and now the third time, had come with a lie upon his tongue and received medical assistance which would be certain to have him serious trouble. But he determined to go back and upbraid him for his treachery, which he did. And that Booth had appealed to him in the name of his mother whom he professed to love so devotedly and that he acted and spoke so tragically that he told them they must leave his house which they then did and after getting in with Oswald Swan they were piloted to Rich Hill.

~

02-11-1909: MRS. SAMUEL MUDD'S LAST INTERVIEW

S ource: *Baltimore News,* February 11, 1909

 ~

THE *BALTIMORE NEWS* newspaper of February 11, 1909 carried an interview of Mrs. Samuel Mudd, which she said would be her last, and it was. She died on November 29, 1911. Here is the interview:

> One woman who was made to suffer, without fault of her own, because of the assassination of President Lincoln is still living and is now in Baltimore. She is Mrs. Sarah Frances Mudd, widow of Dr. Samuel A. Mudd, who was sentenced by the Military Commission that tried the alleged conspirators to imprisonment for life in Fort Jefferson, Dry Tortugas, but was pardoned by President Johnson near the close of the latter's term of office.
>
> Mrs. Mudd is hale, hearty and vivacious, vigorous in body and mind, and shows no indication in her well-preserved appearance of having passed through the harrowing ordeals occasioned by the arrest, trial and conviction of her husband more than forty years ago.

Mrs. Mudd claims her residence at the old Mudd homestead in Charles County, where she resided at the time her husband was arrested. She spends much or her time, however, in visiting her children and grandchildren in different sections of Maryland and in the District of Columbia. At present she is visiting her daughter, Mrs. D. Eldridge Monroe, once Miss Nettie Mudd, who recently edited and had published "*The Life of Dr. Samuel A. Mudd.*"

In Mrs. Monroe's home, 529 West Hoffman Street, Baltimore, may be found a number of interesting articles incidentally connected with the events immediately growing out of the assassination of President Lincoln. Among these articles are the antique davenport on which Booth was laid when his broken leg was set by Dr. Mudd; an inlaid center table, made by Dr. Mudd while he was a prisoner at Fort Jefferson; a ladies' work box, made by him at the same place; a number of shells gathered by him while he was a prisoner and arranged in the form of wreaths of flowers, and much other of his handiwork, all highly finished and giving evidence of his patient toil in his hours of loneliness as a prisoner.

Mrs. Mudd has for many years uniformly refused to be interviewed. When requested to tell her recollections of the events connected with the arrest and conviction of her husband she hesitated about doing so, but finally consented to make a statement.

The Whole Subject Unpleasant

I have already given an account of the visit of Booth and Herold to our home early on the morning of the 15th of April, 1865, which account has been published in my daughter's book. I will not repeat anything I therein stated. Indeed, the whole subject is unpleasant to me. I had much rather let the past rest. I had to go through so many trying circumstances and ordeals and have been so frequently and unwillingly brought before the public that I shrink from again giving an interview. I reluctantly do so only because there have been so many erroneous, indeed, absurd, statements made by irresponsible parties, which have gained currency, that I am constrained to speak in order that, if possible, the truth and only the truth should be made known.

I remember very distinctly what took place at our home on the 15th day of April, 1865. Booth and Herold came on horseback about four o'clock on the morning that date. We were aroused from our sleep. The Doctor went to the door to see who had called at that early hour, supposing that someone in the neighborhood needed his professional services.

Horses Tied in Front of House

The horses on which these two men, Booth and Herold, who gave their names as Tyler and Tyson, had ridden were tied to the horserack in front of the house. The men were then brought into the house, and the Doctor came to my room, stating that one of the men had a broken leg. I did not see either of these men until later the day, as I have stated in my daughter's book. There was no one in our home that night except the Doctor, myself, the children and the children's nurse, a white girl named Nancy Tilly. The children and the nurse were not awakened by the arrival of these visitors.

Frank Washington, a slave belonging to my husband, was the first person to come to the house after the arrival of the strangers. He (Frank Washington) lived in a tenant house not far from our residence. He is still living. He came on that morning at his usual hour, about daybreak, to attend to his duties as hostler. He took the horses of the strangers, led them to the stable and fed them.

Washington's wife (Betty), our cook, arrived with her husband. She is now dead. No other person came to our house that morning until the arrival of our old gardener, John Best, an Englishman, who came from his cottage on our farm at his usual hour, about seven o'clock. The Doctor alone received Tyler and Tyson, who afterward proved to be Booth and Herold; there was no one else present. As I have heretofore stated, neither the Doctor nor myself knew who these visitors were until long after they had gone. In fact, it was several days afterward before we really knew.

Very Dark Days

Those were dark, very dark, days when my husband was taken from me, tortured through the semblance of a trial and convicted and sentenced to life imprisonment at Dry Tortugas. Darker still were the days oftentimes while he endured the miseries of that desolate place. It will interest nobody, perhaps, to tell how hard was the struggle I had to make against the most adverse conditions. Yet through all I tried to keep a brave heart, support our children and encourage my husband to hope for his early deliverance from an unjust imprisonment.

I fear I could not have borne up under my trials had there not been the kind friends who gave me sympathy and encouragement that in the darkest moments awakened a more hopeful outlook toward the future. I could not in a limited space name all these friends. A few of them, however, who stand out conspicuously for the noble, Christian friendship they extended me, I cannot well omit to mention.

General Ewing a Good Friend

Foremost among them was General Thomas Ewing (I know he is in Heaven), who defended my husband before the Military Commission, and who was a brave Union soldier. Through all our long period of trial and distress General Ewing was not only my husband's counsel, but his and my sincere friend. I paid him all the fee asked, not an inconsiderable one, yet I truly believe that the least he thought of in his heroic and masterly defense of my husband was the matter of fee for his services. In all the dark days of the trial before the Commission, he tried to cheer my husband and myself with the hope of a successful issue, and he was tireless in his efforts to realize that hope. After the conviction and sentence he was indefatigable in his efforts to secure my husband's release, and wrote me many cheering and hopeful letters.

Another friend, scarcely second to General Ewing, was the late Richard T. Merrick, the eminent lawyer of Washington. Because of Mr. Merrick's well-known sympathy with the South, he was not brought into active participation in the trial before the Commission; but he was consulting counsel and daily conferred with General Ewing in reference to the defense of my husband.

Made Good Defense

I have always believed that so great was the bitterness and excitement at the time, and so intense the desire for victims to avenge the president's death, if it had not been for the unusual but masterly course pursued by General Ewing, aided by Mr. Merrick, my husband, innocent as he was, might have suffered the unfortunate fate of Mrs. Surratt.

General Ewing, as is shown in my daughter's book, in his argument against the jurisdiction of the Military Commission to try the accused, had warned the members of the Commission that the time would come when their acts would be judged impartially by posterity, and that it might then be determined that their jurisdiction was an assumption, and any sentence they might impose, only their own unauthorized acts.

General Ewing and Mr. Merrick came to the conclusion that unless the whole of the defense of my husband, including the argument to the jurisdiction and the argument on the testimony, as well as the testimony itself, was preserved in some permanent form and presented to the members of the Commission, that tribunal would likely exercise an unbridled license to condemn and inflict the greatest penalty, without regard to the law or the facts.

Had Record Printed

On the suggestion therefore of Messers. Ewing and Merrick I paid $2,000 to have hurriedly printed and bound 700 volumes, containing the arguments of General Ewing and all the evidence offered in the case against my husband. This work was finished early on the day before the Commission was to announce its decision. On the morning of this day General Ewing walked into the courtroom with his arms filled with a number of these volumes and handed one to each member of the Commission and one to the each party, Judge

Advocate General Holt and others, who had been officially connected with the trial.

I was not present on this occasion, but have been told that the incident was dramatic in the extreme. Neither the members of the Commission nor Judge Holt had anticipated it, and received the volumes almost with consternation. They realized that the record had been preserved as to this case in a compact form and by this record future generations would probably judge their acts.

Judge Stone Assisted

Another gentleman to whom I was indebted in my trouble, and whom I shall always remember with gratitude, was the late Frederick Stone of Charles county, afterward a judge of the Court of Appeals of Maryland. He was not employed in the defense of my husband, but took great interest in his case, both before and after his conviction, and gave all the aid in his power. I am indebted to a great many other people for kindness and sympathy, but cannot now name them all.

I passed through many trying, sometimes exciting, experiences, and met with many people whose names are now well known to history. I saw Judge Holt, in the interest of my husband, four or five times. I do not wish to speak harshly of the dead, and shall dismiss Judge Holt by saying of him only that he impressed me as a harsh, unfeeling, insincere specimen of humanity. This, I am sorry to say, is the highest tribute I can pay him.

I saw Secretary Stanton only twice in behalf for my husband. My reception by him was, on his part, so cold, unfeeling and, indeed, brutal, that I looked at him in both instances with as much of hauteur as I could command, and deliberately left his presence without any formal leave taking.

Called on President Johnson

I called on President Johnson the great many times. He always treated me courteously, but impressed me always as one shrinking from some impending disaster. He conveyed to me always the idea that he wanted to release my husband, but said more than once "the pressure on me is too great." On one occasion I took a petition to him asking their release of my husband; he told me that if Holt would sign it he would grant the petition. This Judge Holt refused.

Many persons have given statements in regard to the setting of Booth's leg by my husband, few, indeed, none that I have seen, being correct. I read recently of an interview with a person who claims to have held Booth's horse on the morning my husband set Booth's leg. I am sure this party never saw Booth at all, and never saw my husband until after his return from the Dry Tortugas. For myself, I with wish nothing more in relation to these matters than to commit them to the impartial historian of the future. I never again will be interviewed on the subject.

This was indeed Mrs. Sarah Frances Mudd's last interview. She died on November 29, 1911, surviving her husband by almost three decades.

~

UNDATED: REMINISCENCES OF GENERAL AUGUST KAUTZ

S ource: *Reminiscences of the Civil War*, August V. Kautz Papers, Manuscript Division, Library of Congress, Washington, D.C.

MAJOR-GENERAL AUGUST V. Kautz was one of the nine members of the Military Commission that conducted the Lincoln assassination trial. In his unpublished *Reminiscences of the Civil War*, Kautz included his recollection of the Lincoln assassination trial:

> I left on the 4th of May and reached Washington on the morning of the 6th and, having reported to Genl. Grant, was directed to report my name and address in the city to the Adj. Genl. and await orders. I learned indirectly that I was destined as a member of the Military Commission to try the assassins of the president. It did not transpire fully until the 9th when the first meeting of the Commission took place in a room fitted up adjoining the prison near the Arsenal grounds.
>
> We met, but we did not transact any business. The prisoners to the number of eight were brought in behind a railing. They were

masked and chained, and clad in black dominos so that we could not identify the prisoners. The Commission decided that they must be brought in, so that we could recognize the different prisoners, and be able to identify them. The mystery and apparent severity with which they were brought into the court room partook so much of what my imagination pictured the Inquisition to have been, that I was quite impressed with its impropriety in this age. The prisoners were never again brought into court in this costume.

On the 10th the Commission got so far as to swear the members, and have the charges read, and the pleadings of the prisoners entered. Gen. Hunter was the presiding officer. I was the third member in rank and sat on the left of the president. Gen. Lew Wallace sat on his right and Gen. Foster of Indiana sat on my left. There were three Judge Advocates: Genl. Holt, Genl. Burnett and Maj. Bingham. There were some changes; Genl. Comstock met on the first day with the Commission and did not appear again. We had Mr. Pittman and the Murphy brothers as shorthand reporters, and I was surprised at the facility, rapidity and correctness with which the work was done. They were able to read the record as rapidly as any other writing and we were able to make rapid progress. The 11th we met but the prisoners had not yet provided counsel, and we did not do much, but on the 12th we got fairly started and worked all day accomplishing so much that it took two hours of the morning of the 13th to read the proceedings of the previous day.

The leading incident of the 13th was the objection of Genl. Harris, one of the members, to the introduction of the Hon. Reverdy Johnson as Counsel for Mrs. Surratt. The objections were that he had sympathized with the action of the Rebel element in Maryland. Mr. Johnson, when the opportunity was given him to say a few words, his indignation was very manifest by his flushed face, but his remarks were quiet and dignified, and full of irony, and showed the ill-advised nature of the objection in such a light that Genl. Harris must have regretted that he made the objection. If he had any sense of the absurdity of a Court or Commission such as ours, raising an objection to a member of the U.S. Senate, appearing before it as a counsel on the ground of disloyalty. Mr. Johnson did not do us the honor to appear before us again after this insult to his dignity. He did the other members great injustice if he supposed they united with Genl. Harris in his ill advised objection.

The court met as a rule at ten in the morning, and sat until after six p.m. usually, taking a recess about noon for lunch which the Secretary of War had served for us in adjoining room to save time and the necessity of our having to go back to the city. Ambulances were supplied by the Q. M. Dept. to take us to and from the court room to our rooms. This was the daily programme. The weather soon became very warm and the confinement was very trying on account of the number of visitors that were permitted by pass to visit the court room, preventing the free circulation of the air.

On the 16th the court met informally, at the theater where Mr. Lincoln was shot, before going to the court room, in order to acquaint ourselves with the scene of the assassination. This was the only change from the daily routine. We worked very faithfully and there was little leisure, often sitting until seven o'clock in the evening, and rarely adjourning before six, except when no work could be done for want of witnesses which happened occasionally.

The prosecution was continued until the 26th of May when the defense began. The evidence was very clear as to the conspiracy and that all the parties arraigned were connected with it in various ways. The original and avowed object was a conspiracy to kidnap the president, and it was so understood by nearly all concerned. The testimony showed J. Wilkes Booth and John Surratt to be the heads of the conspiracy. The order to kill did not go forth until about eight o'clock p.m. on the 14th of April. There was evidence produced that tended to show that the heads of the Confederate government knew of the conspiracy and also that the agents of the same in Canada were cognizant of it. It was shown that a proposition to kill Mr. Lincoln was made to Jefferson Davis and, over his signature, the paper was forwarded for the consideration of other officials without any adverse comment.

The defense lasted through until about the 19th of June when we began to hear the arguments in behalf of the prisoners. An attempt was made at the close to prove insanity on the part of Payne, who finally defeated the attempt of his counsel by maintaining his sanity, that he knew what he was doing when he tried to kill Mr. Seward. The interest of the case centered mostly about Mrs. Surratt and Payne.

Dr. Mudd attracted much interest and his guilt as an active conspirator was not clearly made out. His main guilt was the fact that he failed to deliver them, that is, Booth and Harold, to their pursuers.

Mrs. Surratt was shown to have been active in the conspiracy to kidnap, prior to the capture of Richmond. That she was a willing participant in his death was not clearly made out. My own impression was that she was involved in the final result against her will by her previous connection with the conspiracy. Booth was a fanatic in the matter and craved a notoriety that would appear heroic if he survived the act, and prove martyrdom if he perished. He, no doubt, held most of his confederates in the conspiracy under the impression that it was organized for the purpose of kidnapping, who would have been deterred if they had known that they might be required to kill.

During the many weeks that the court was in session I never saw the face of Mrs. Surratt. She sat behind the railing furthest away, and her face was constantly screened by a large palm leaf fan. I could not even recognize her picture for she was entirely unknown to me. I presume this is the case with every member of the court. All the other members of the court were indelibly impressed on my mind. Harold was a simpering foolish young man, so short of stature that he appeared like a boy and never seemed impressed with the gravity of his position. He must of been simply a plastic tool in Booth's hands.

Payne was a sullen character whose expression rarely changed. He seemed to be fully aware that he had taken a desperate chance and lost, and had the nerve to abide the result manfully. He was manly and strong in every respect, but how much moral character there was in his make up was not apparent on the surface.

Atzoroth looked the hired assassin and the testimony went to show that he failed to perform his part of the compact, which was to kill Genl. Grant, either from want of courage or want of sufficient intelligence. He excited no sympathy from anyone.

Dr. Mudd was the most intelligent looking and attracted most attention of all the prisoners. There was more work done in his defense. His subsequent career showed him to be a man of more character and intelligence that anyone of the prisoners.

Spangler does not seem to have been a conspirator knowingly. He was simply a tool of Booth's and held his horse for him, and cut the stick with which Booth held the door to the box, in which Mr. Lincoln was in at the theater. His greatest crime was his ignorance, and that he did not see the ends to which he was being used.

Arnold was shown to have been associated with the conspirators, but what part he performed and to what extent he was implicated was not shown to the Commission. He was a good looking, amiable young man, who seemed to have gotten into bad company. The same degree and character of guilt applied to McLaughlin.

All of the prisoners had counsel but the greatest effort was made in behalf of Mrs. Surratt and Dr. Mudd. The Hon. Thom. Ewing made an elaborate defense of Mudd and Mr. Johnson, by proxy, defended Mrs. Surratt, through Mr. Aiken.

The members were not released until the 30th of June when the Commission adjourned sine die. The deliberations were not protracted, the last ten days were taken up with time allotted to the counsel and Judge Advocates to make their arguments in the case. The Judge Advocates, under the influence of the Secretary of War, evidently, were very persevering and wanted evidently to have the seven prisoners all hung, and they were very much put out when a paper was signed by a majority of the Commission recommending Mrs. Surratt to executive clemency on account of her sex. We, who signed it, did not deem it wise or expedient to hang her. This paper afterwards became a matter of much controversy. When public sympathy, as we who signed the paper foresaw, had reacted to such a height as to make it desirable for Mr. Johnson to shift the responsibility, he endeavored to do so, by claiming that this paper was withheld from the proceedings, and that he never saw it. This did not seem to be very sincere, in view of the fact that within a day or two after the adjournment of the Commission, the recommendation with the names of those who signed it, and there were five of the nine members, was published in the daily papers.

It was apparent that if John Surratt had been one of the prisoners tried, his mother's life would have been saved. In those early days after the assassination the country seemed to require victims to pay for the great crime. It was apparent to me however, that there would be a reaction and that those who were instrumental in causing her execution would regret that they had permitted Mrs. Surratt to be hung.

The reaction came even before the close of Mr. Johnson's administration and he alleged that the recommendation of the court was not attached to the proceedings when he acted on them. Judge Holt and Bingham, however, denied that any mutilation of the proceeding had taken place and that the papers were intact when submitted to the president.

There has been much controversy over the course pursued by the Administration to punish the conspirators, mostly originating with the adverse political element. Some of my Democratic friends were fond of telling me that when the party got into power again, I would hang for my part in the proceedings. There might be abuse of the slight statutory authority for Military Commissions, but the one organized for the trial of the assassins will never, I think, be styled such by posterity. It was the only way for speedy result which the loyal spirit of the country seemed to demand at the time. The result of the trial of John Surratt by the Civil Courts a few years later, go to show that the civil courts could not have been depended upon for a speedy result in this remarkable case.

BIBLIOGRAPHY

The Life of Dr. Samuel A. Mudd, 1906, by Nettie Mudd

The Mudd Family of the United States, 1971, by Dr. Richard D. Mudd

American Brutus: John Wilkes Booth and the Lincoln Conspiracies, 2004, by Michael W. Kauffman

In The Footsteps of an Assassin, 2012, by Michael W. Kauffman

Memoirs of a Lincoln Conspirator: Samuel B. Arnold, 2009, edited by Michael W. Kauffman

Thomas A. Jones: Chief Agent of the Confederate Secret Service, 2009, by John M. and Roberta J. Wearmouth

Lincoln's Assassins: A Complete Account of Their Capture, Trial, and Punishment, 1990, by Roy Z. Chamlee, Jr.

The Assassination of President Lincoln and the Trial of the Conspirators, 1865, by Benn Pitman

Trial of the Assassins and Conspirators at Washington, D.C., 1865, by T.B. Peterson and Brothers

The Conspiracy Trial for the Murder of the President and the Attempt to Overthrow the Government by the Assassination of its Principal Officers, Benjamin Perley Poore. J.E. Tilton & Company. Boston. 1865.

Trial of the Assassins and Conspirators for the Murder of Abraham Lincoln, Barclay & Company. Philadelphia. 1865.

Jesuit Slaveholding in Maryland, 1717–1838, by Thomas Murphy, S.J.

Slave Narratives from the Federal Writers' Project, 1936 - 1938, Maryland. Library of Congress. Applewood Books, Bedford, Massachusetts.

One Million Men: The Civil War Draft in the North, 1980, by Eugene C. Murdock

Patriotism Limited - 1862 - 1865 - The Civil War and the Bounty System, 1967, by Eugene C. Murdock

Doctors in Blue, 1996, by George Worthington Adams

The Mighty Revolution – Negro Emancipation in Maryland 1862 – 1864, by Charles L. Wagandt

Reconstruction, 1863-1877, 2011, by Eric Foner

A True History of the Assassination of Abraham Lincoln, by Louis J. Weichmann, edited by Floyd E. Risvold, 1975.

The Bicentennial History of Georgetown University, 1789-1889, 2010, by Robert Emmett Curran, S.J.

Colonel Grenfell's Wars: The Life of a Soldier of Fortune, 1995, by Stephen Z. Starr

The Assassination of Abraham Lincoln, 1901, by Osborn H. Oldroyd

Fort Jefferson and the Dry Tortugas National Park, 2003, by L. Wayne Landrum

Pages from the Past – A Pictorial History of Fort Jefferson, 1999, by Albert C. Manucy

Fort Jefferson Research Memorandum No. 6, by Albert C. Manucy, 1938

Lincoln Collector: The Story of Oliver R. Barrett's Great Private Collection, 1949, by Carl Sandburg

Bleeding Blue and Gray, 2005, by Ira Rutkow

American Ocean Steamships 1850 - 1870, 1986, by the Steamship Historical Society of America, Princeton, Rhode Island

Early American Steamships, 1953, by Erik Heyl

The Army's Navy Series - Dictionary of Transports and Combatant Vessels, Steam and Sail, Employed by the Union Army, 1861-1868, 1995, compiled by Charles Dana Gibson and E. Kay Gibson

Hospital Transports, 1863, by Frederick Law Olmsted

Civil War Medicine, 2002, by Alfred Jay Bollett

The Army Medical Department, 1818-1865, 2002, by Mary C. Gillett

The Travels, Arrest, and Trial of John H. Surratt, 2003, by Alfred Isaacson

Maryland Voices of the Civil War, 2007, Charles W. Mitchell

AFTERWORD

Dr. Mudd knew John Wilkes Booth well. Booth had stayed overnight at Dr. Mudd's home in the fall of 1864, and the two men met again a few weeks later in Washington, D.C. for drinks and conversation with John Surratt and Louis Weichmann. The assassination took place just four months later.

Although Dr. Mudd was innocent of having anything to do with the assassination of Lincoln, the government's position was that any person assisting the escape of the assassin, even if not an active participant in the assassination, was guilty of being an accomplice in the murder of the president. Although he knew Booth well, Dr. Mudd told those hunting Booth he didn't recognize the man whose leg he treated.

Dr. Mudd's lead attorney General Thomas Ewing, his co-counsel Frederick Stone, and Dr. Mudd's cousin Dr. George Mudd were the three person's most intimately involved in preparing Dr. Mudd's defense at the trial.

General Ewing left no comments about Dr. Mudd, but in an 1883 interview shortly after Dr. Mudd died, attorney Frederick Stone said of Dr. Mudd:

He had denied knowing Booth when he knew him well. He was undoubtedly accessory to the abduction plot, though he may have supposed it would never come to anything. He denied knowing Booth when he came to his house when that was preposterous. He had been even intimate with Booth. The proclamation of the government was straightforward, that death should be the penalty of any man who could give information about the convicts and would not do it. Yet Dr. Mudd was saved...

In another 1883 interview after Dr. Mudd passed away, Dr. George Mudd said of his cousin:

While he had nothing of the assassin in his nature - and I do not believe he would have gone into any scheme to kill Mr. Lincoln or Mr. Seward - yet there is no doubt of his having been connected with a previous intention of Booth to kidnap or abduct the president...

Although he had nothing to do with the assassination, Dr. Mudd may have been afraid that if captured, Booth would tie him to the original plot to kidnap the president. Whatever his motive, Dr. Mudd's fate was sealed when Secretary of War Stanton learned about Dr. Mudd's undisclosed meeting with Booth in Washington, D.C. Dr. Mudd's claim to not have recognized the man with the broken leg now seemed like a deliberate attempt to mislead those hunting Booth.

President Johnson's pardon summed it up well:

I am satisfied that the guilt found by the said judgment against Samuel A. Mudd was of receiving, entertaining, harboring, and concealing John Wilkes Booth and David E. Herold, with the intent to aid, abet and assist them in escaping from justice after the assassination of the late President of the United States, and not of any other or greater participation or complicity in said abominable crime.

Whatever his mistakes, Dr. Mudd's selfless and heroic work

during the terrible 1867 yellow fever epidemic at Fort Jefferson saved the lives of many people who would otherwise have perished. This will always be remembered as a redeeming part of his life's story.

ABOUT THE AUTHOR

Robert Summers has published two books. In addition to this book, *The Assassin's Doctor*, Robert has also published *Maryland's Black Civil War Soldiers*, the story of Maryland's 19th Regiment, U.S. Colored Troops. The book contains a history of the 19th Regiment's actions during the Civil War, but primarily consists of short biographies of each of the thousand soldiers in the regiment. Anyone conducting genealogical research on these soldiers will find this information invaluable.

Maryland's Black Civil War Soldiers is a large book - a ten year project - requiring the personal review of the soldiers' military and pension files at the U.S. National Archives in Washington, D.C. The regiment was organized and trained at Camp Stanton, only ten miles from Dr. Mudd's farm. Most of the soldiers were former slaves from farms in southern Maryland and the eastern shore of Maryland. Some had been slaves on Mudd family farms.

~

Made in United States
Troutdale, OR
04/08/2024

19048522R00206